The Literature of Cinema

THE LITERATURE OF CINEMA presents
a comprehensive selection from the multitude
of writings about cinema, rediscovering materials on its origins, history, theoretical principles and techniques, aesthetics, economics,
and effects on societies and individuals. Included are works of inherent, lasting merit
and others of primarily historical significance.
These provide essential resources for serious
study and critical enjoyment of the "magic
shadows" that became one of the decisive cultural forces of modern times.

The Art

of the

Motion Picture

Jean Benoit-Levy

ARNO PRESS & THE NEW YORK TIMES

New York • 1970

Reprint Edition 1970 by Arno Press Inc.
Reprinted by permission of Coward-McCann, Inc.
Reprinted from a copy in The New York Public Library
Library of Congress Catalog Card Number: 70-112568
ISBN 0-405-01603-4
ISBN for complete set: 0-405-01600-X
Manufactured in the United States of America

THE ART OF THE MOTION PICTURE

THE ART OF
THE MOTION
PICTURE

JEAN BENOIT-LEVY

Translated by Theodore R. Jaeckel

NEW YORK

COWARD-McCANN, INC

TO HENRI FOCILLON, *in memoriam,*
JACQUES HADAMARD,
DR. ALVIN JOHNSON,
JACQUES MARITAIN,
JOHN MARSHALL,

whose thoughts and acts have always been directed toward an improvement of human relations by raising the spiritual, cultural, and social level of mankind, I dedicate this work.

To the Rockefeller Foundation, whose moral and material support enabled me to live in the great country where I wrote this book, my heartfelt gratitude.

PREFACE

BY ALVIN JOHNSON

THE MOTION PICTURE, as Dr. Benoit-Levy somewhere remarks, represents potentially the greatest advance in human intercommunication since the invention of printing. In a sense, it parallels the early service of printing in promoting transnational culture. The early printers were largely occupied in setting to type Latin treatises and distributing them throughout the lands where Latin was the accepted scholarly medium of intercourse. The motion picture made its appearance when the best thought was already directed toward a world society, world culture. Through the motion picture a world-wide dissemination of human interests and ideas becomes possible. The American and European can communicate with the Chinese without having to surmount the rugged barrier of ten thousand characters.

The educational potentialities of the motion picture are incalculable. All educators are aware of this fact, but in America the creative energies of the artists and artisans, the managers and promoters have been heavily committed to the motion picture as a form of popular entertainment. An American book on the motion picture would be largely engrossed by accounts of the brilliant successes of particular productions, the fame of particular artists. This fact gives special pertinence to the publication of Dr. Benoit-Levy's book. More than any other publication in the field it is oriented toward the educational functions of the motion picture.

Primarily Dr. Benoit-Levy is an educator. His work does indeed range over the whole field of the motion picture, and his insistence

vii

upon the necessity of distinguishing clearly the several genres and keeping each performance within its own genre will be useful to the student and the critic. But his heart is in the educational role of the motion picture.

To a large extent Dr. Benoit-Levy's attitude is conditioned by his national experience. The French have been the great pioneers of the motion picture. They have made most important contributions to the technique and more than other people have known how to develop the art of the cinema. From the outset they have been deeply interested in the motion picture as a means of instruction and a tool of research.

We Americans have also come to realize the immense potentialities for education of the motion picture. The war, destroyer of so much else worth while in life, has played the part of a constructive force in education, particularly in the application of the motion picture. The field is so immense, however, that one can only say that a beginning has been established. In the future development we shall need the co-operation of many minds, many techniques.

More than any other educational medium the motion picture is international, and developments in one nation are of immediate use to the rest of the world. Benoit-Levy's book offers to the American educator an approach to the French contribution to the educational film. We need not assume that here, as in so many fields, they do better work in France. They do unique work, that can be of the greatest significance to us.

CONTENTS

ILLUSTRATIONS

INTRODUCTION

THE MOTION PICTURE is certainly the most powerful medium for the diffusion of human thought that man has discovered since the invention of printing in the fifteenth century. I consider it advisable, therefore, in lieu of introduction, to sketch an outline showing the various steps in research and invention that culminated in the present form of camera and motion picture projector.

Since prehistoric times, men have sought to reproduce the movement and life about them. The Idea was thus germinating and urged the more inquisitive minds along paths of research. Successively, often simultaneously, researchers in countries far apart gradually overcame the obstacles confronting them. The primary characteristic of the researcher is of course his scientific ability, but in addition to this, and perhaps most important, he must be prepared to anticipate the consequences of a phenomenon which occurs fortuitously.

Because the inventor's genius partakes of the imaginative and intuitive, he may be compared with the poet and the painter. I take pleasure in bringing out this relationship while I review the history of an invention that was to give the artist a new medium of expression, the significance of which may be greater than that of any other.

I. Preliminary Observations on the Value of Motion

Even as far back as ancient Greece, Aristotle had observed that a ray of sunlight, coming into a dark room through a shutter hole, cast a luminous circle on the wall. This observation became the point of departure for the discovery of the three elements of projection:

a source of light (the sun);

a dark room;

a screen (the wall).

In 1640 Kirchner exhibited his magic lantern, which resembled the still projector of modern times, naturally without electricity. He also invented a winding drum which enabled the operator to change pictures at will. He used to color various scenes such as the sun, the head of a lion, a donkey, and so forth. Kirchner was the precursor of visual education.

II. Early Animated Projections

In 1824, a country doctor by the name of Roget was studying the phenomenon of motion. One day, while looking through the slats of a Vention blind at an approaching baker's cart, he noticed that he could see the cart advancing in a series of jerks. He was thus able to perceive the different phases of the movement.

In that very year, Roget presented the London Royal Society with a study entitled "The Persistence of Vision in Relation to Motion."

It was during this period that Sir John Hershell noticed while idly spinning a shilling that he could see both sides of the coin at the same time. The incident was related to Fulton, who staged a demonstration with a cardboard disk hung between two pieces of string. On one side of the disk he had drawn a bird and on the other a cage. When the disk was rapidly spun between the strings, the bird appeared to be in the cage.

In Paris, Dr. John Ayrton invented the thaumatrope, while in Gand, Dr. Plateau, and in Vienna, Simon von Stampfer were studying the same phenomenon. By a stroke of coincidence all these researchers came to the identical conclusion: they discovered a way to see images representing the different phases of a single movement.

Thus movement was analyzed, but it was not until the invention of photography that its synthesis could be studied.

III. The Invention of Photography

Nicéphore Niepce invented photography at Chalon-sur-Saône, France, in the year 1829. His collaborator was Daguerre, a well-known painter and the manager of a diorama. The invention was perfected by the latter, Niepce having died prematurely.

Toward 1865, celluloid was invented in the United States and came into use, replacing glass photographic plates. And, in 1889, Eastman invented a photographic film that would register images in fractions of a second.

About this time, Leland Stanford, the governor of California and a noted lover of race horses, had an argument with some friends as to whether all four hoofs of a galloping horse left the ground at the same time. Stanford bet $25,000 they did and called on Edward Muybridge to furnish photographic proof. Muybridge went to work with the help of an engineer named Isaac and succeeded in taking twenty-four pictures of the movement by using a battery of twenty-four cameras.

Meissonier, the great French painter, became interested in these photographs and asked Stanford to send Muybridge to France.

Meissonier at once grasped the significance these pictures might have in the study of motion for art education. He exhibited them in Reynaud's Praxinoscope before some painters and authors, among whom were Edouard Detaille and Alexandre Dumas. There was a heated discussion, but with Muybridge's snapshots Meissonier was able to prove that the natural postures of animals in motion were not what tradition had made them. This discovery had a considerable influence on graphic and pictorial art.

IV. Toward the Synthesis of Motion

It was Dr. Marey who first introduced the graphic method, that is, photography, in the field of biological science.

I cannot lay too much stress on the importance of this stage in the development of the invention, for it constitutes the point of departure for the role which the motion picture will later play in scientific research.

Indeed, at this time Dr. Marey wrote: "The phenomena of motion are at times of such short duration that they no longer correspond with the time lapses necessary to the perception of visual sensations."

In 1880, Dr. Marey, with the help of Demeny, invented a camera which he named the Chronophotograph. With this camera he was able to take high-speed pictures of a moving object. He could study the beating of the heart and arteries, and with his photographic gun he could record the flight of birds.

In 1886, Edison, assisted by Dickson, decided to improve his phonograph by the addition of animated pictures.

Three years later, Eastman, the Kodak manufacturer, discovered a new film formula which gave Edison the answer to the problem he had been working on for so long. While Edison was attending the World Exhibition in Paris, Dickson improved the process, and, when his employer returned, was able to show him the first animated projection, in which Dickson himself appeared, smiling and raising his hat, while uttering these words of welcome: "Good morning, Mr. Edison; glad to see you back. I hope you are satisfied with the Kineto-Phonograph."

This device was christened the Kinetoscope and may be regarded as the ancestor of the motion picture projector. It consisted of a strip of film several yards long bearing images which were passed one by one before a window furnished with an eyepiece. Yet this was nothing more than a box of animated pictures into which only one person at a time could look. The device was put on the market and had a great success when it first made its appearance on April 14, 1894, in a hall located at 1155 Broadway. But Edison, who was already thinking about other inventions, had neglected to take out a patent; and so, during the same year, a quantity of similar devices blossomed forth, such as the Pantoptekon, which actually differed from the Kinetoscope only in the size of the film used.

There were a great many obstacles to be overcome before the motion picture as we know it today could be developed. It was necessary to obtain a sensitive and homogenous film, one with high tensile strength, inflammability and resistance to distortion; its jerky movement had to be made more even; the shooting as well as the projection had to be perfectly synchronized; and there were many other problems.

In 1893, Demeny took out a patent on a projector based on the following principle: "The film is unwound by means of an electric cam placed within the circuit of the film, while the intermittent movement is obtained by means of gears which rotate continuously."

Demeny was unable to exploit his own patent; he sold it to the Gaumont company, which a little later made use of this principle to manufacture its projector.

V. The Cinematograph

There appears to be no doubt that Messrs. Louis and Auguste Lumière were the first to work out projectors which did away with all the problems encountered and to project publicly a film under technical conditions which closely resemble those present in our modern projectors.

There has been a tendency to build up the myth of a competition between the inventions of Marey and the Lumière brothers.

Actually, Marey never got beyond the field of chronophotography. He hoped one day to come across a device that would recompose movement and project it, but on his own admission he never succeeded.

Marey himself declared in 1897: "Messrs. Auguste and Louis Lumière were the first to succeed with this type of projection, using the device they called the cinematograph."

In fact, Louis and Auguste Lumière patented their "Cinematograph" on February 13, 1895, and in December of that year they gave a public exhibition with it in the hall of the Grand Café, Boulevard des Capucines, in Paris.

On that day the synthesis of motion was achieved for the first time by means of a practical and original device which permitted a "moving picture" to be projected upon a screen for the benefit of marveling crowds.

Since that date, the basic principle of motion picture photography and projection has remained unchanged. Only the invention of synchronized sound and image was to modify their use.

To conclude this historical sketch of the invention, I would like to recall that the honor of having first exhibited a talking picture goes to M. Léon Gaumont.

Indeed, on December 12, 1909, he exhibited a synchronized talking picture before the French Society of Photography.

On December 27, 1910, Professor d'Arsonval gave a lecture before the Academy of Sciences, illustrated by a talking motion picture in which he himself appeared. The Gaumont chronophone was the first to contribute the final solution of the problem: sound recording at a distance by means of a microphone, amplification of the sound, perfect synchronization between image and sound.

It is rather interesting to note that neither Edison nor the Lumière brothers had foreseen the importance of their invention and the future that lay before it, at least in the economic field. We have already seen how Edison refused to take out a patent, regarding this discovery to be practically useless or at most capable of playing only a very minor part among all the inventions he contemplated.

The day after the exhibition at the Grand Café, Louis Lumière received a visit from Georges Méliès. When the latter asked the inventor to sell him a projector so that he might undertake a production right away, Louis Lumière replied: "Young man, our invention is not for sale, and besides it would ruin you. It may be exploited for a while as a scientific curiosity, but apart from that it has no commercial future."

Nevertheless, Louis Lumière was not slow to see that his invention had a tremendous educational mission. He has often told me about his faith in the destinies of the motion picture, his regret at not having spent more time nursing his child in order to direct it more carefully toward its principal mission, and shield it from purely mercenary compromises. True, he realized that the motion picture would have a great part to play in the field of entertainment, of recreation, that it might become an important branch of the show business. But only on condition that its aim be one of educating, in the broadest sense of the word. It is Louis Lumière whom some of us can thank for that sense of responsibility incumbent on all those who serve the motion picture.

I owe it to my uncle, Edmond Benoit-Lévy, for having taught me to see the greatness of its artistic mission and its power as a medium of information. He was the first to proclaim the artistic and literary qualities of the film as he had done for the phonograph record, thereby pointing out to the motion picture the true path it was to follow.

And lastly we owe it to the first great patrons of the motion picture, Charles Pathé and Léon Gaumont, for having set an example in their own firms by always nourishing this sacred garden, dedicated to the culture of the mind.

I would like the reader to accompany me into this sacred garden and let me try to show him the varieties of flowering life it contains and the ways there are to cultivate them.

Indeed, the motion picture is not one but many. Like all the arts, it is made up of several genres. It is therefore important to know these, to study them in order to understand them as well as to appreciate them. On this visit to a garden so rich in blooms, I will endeavor to play the part of the old gardener, proud of his fine trade, about which he has a little knowledge, thanks to his teachers and to his experience.

PART I

THE MOTION PICTURE IN EDUCATION

1

FUNDAMENTAL LAWS

THE PIONEERS who undertook to implement this new and powerful vehicle of human thought did not at once take cognizance of its advantages and inconveniences. Not until the motion picture had attained its adolescence could the discovery be made that it was really a medium of expression, that it mirrored humanity itself, never altogether good nor altogether bad. Owing to the fact that an animated image leaves an immediate and lasting impression on the human mind, the motion picture became a two-edged weapon which could do a great deal of harm or a great deal of good, depending on how it was used.

In the beginning, the motion picture was not an art. It was merely a question of using sensitized film to record scenes of life or little sketches, such as, for instance, the very first films made by the Lumière brothers: *"Arrival of the Train at La Ciotat"; "Workers Entering the Lumière Factory";* or the first film made by Pathé: *"Arrival of the Train at Vincennes";* or else the first comic film Gaumont produced: *"The Calf's Head."* These films possessed no individual creativeness: they were merely photography. There was no attempt at composition, and nothing like the expression of an idea or a feeling.

It was Méliès, the predecessor of all film authors, who really applied to it a personal conception, an effort to provide a setting, and to whom we should pay tribute in passing. Indeed, Méliès laid the foundations for a filmic technique, on which our technique today is still partly based. But Méliès' films had at the same time also created a new genre, which brought the motion

3

picture close to being a mature art, and this was the fairy or dream genre, which was not without a certain influence on the later poetic film.

Gradually, as men's minds began to assimilate this new method of expression, various film genres were created, became intermingled, and a confusion arose from which the motion picture has not yet been able to extricate itself. This confounding of genres resulted in large part from the fact that the intellectual creators had not yet waked up to the fact that they had at their disposal a novel means of translating their thoughts into visual terms. In its infancy the motion picture was only a curiosity, and for a long time was regarded as a sort of rustic entertainment.

Despite the far-sightednesss of its precursors, it was not perceived until later that this new art was fundamentally similar to all other arts. The motion picture permits the author, following his bent, to write scholarly books, scientific treatises, poetry, comedies, or dramas. Each of these literary genres has its corresponding genre in filmic art, to which must be added all the potentialities of visual representation and the power of suggestion that are in the motion picture.

The basic principle of all art lies in the selection of ideas and the form in which they are presented.

For a writer, the selection of the original idea consists in being able to filter through his own sensibility the profusion of thought vibrations rising out. of his subconscious, in order to extract and retain the essential idea which he will bring to life under abstract or concrete forms. Having done this, he will express himself through the command of his art or craft. In some genres, there is also an express intention, an aim to be achieved, which must be carefully determined before the idea is sought. In this latter instance, the artist must observe a very strict mental discipline so that he may concentrate his imagination and talent on how to state his idea most convincingly. This would apply to those genres which involve teaching at every level of education and to which the artist's collaboration, as master of his specialized technique, is no less important than it is to works of the imagination. For that matter, we shall see later how indispensable this discipline is to all film authors.

The natural—let me say congenital—discipline of the scientist had foreshadowed this separation of genres even before the invention of the motion picture had passed from the laboratory to the field of practical application. When, in 1880, Dr. Marey made use of his picture gun to record the flight of birds, he was impelled by motives of scientific research, which, quite naturally, prevented his thoughts from taking another direction. But much later, after the invention of high-speed photography, the improvement in technique enabled the artist interpreting life to study the same phenomenon for purposes that were confined strictly to an education in art.

Ignorance of these fundamental laws concerning the aim to be achieved, the selection of the idea through previous determination of the genre, resulted in the motion picture being kept for a long time in that chaotic and elementary state which has had such disastrous consequences. The genres concerned with teaching and education were lost to sight, and, as a result, this first, great aim of the motion picture could not be achieved. Since the motives were regarded primarily as a freak show, for the entertainment of rubbernecks, film producers lost all sense of their artistic and social responsibility toward an art whose great aim, as in fact that of all arts, was to elevate the thoughts of men, to delight them in the knowledge of things and of the world.

However, there is some excuse for these early film producers, since technique was then in its preliminary, fumbling stages. Gradually, the motion picture developed its own means of expression, became capable of translating all thoughts into images. The moment D. W. Griffith really discovered visual writing, rhythm, filmic punctuation, the art of expression, that moment marked the birth of a living art, and it was only proper that it should be given the same fundamental principles concerning the selection of genres on which its elders were based. It was of particular importance that each of these genres should be assured the opportunity to fulfill its aim. It is the sum total of these genres that gives the motion picture its greatness, for actually they derive their inspiration from man's multiple intellectual, social, and economic activities.

It follows that all who, in some capacity or other, serve this living art must be conscious of its aims and of the responsibility incumbent on them to ensure its true destiny.

In ascertaining that the destinies of the motion picture have not been assured and that its varied aims have not been fully achieved, I believe we may find the reason for this to lie in the fact that its fundamental principles have not been adequately stated or followed.

The motion picture is an art in itself, having its own laws, its own technique, its own manner of expression. Since Griffith's day, it has been an art of expression, and it participates in the life of the other arts through laws that are common to all of them. It derives inspiration from them, breathing the same air they breathe. It calls on their collaboration, altering the form to suit its own laws but preserving the spirit. Poetry, the dance, music are its sisters whom it welcomes, borrowing their complementary coloring. But always it preserves its own form, its own character. What it borrows from the other arts it assimilates, it transposes, but it must never copy them. The motion picture is truly that seventh art mentioned by the good Canudo, that visionary writer to whom we owe our first gospel, just as we owe a large part of our film esthetics to Louis Delluc.

I would like to quote briefly from a book entitled *L'usine aux Images,* which Canudo wrote in 1927 and in which he defined what he had christened the "Seventh Art."

"I have been asked whether this is not an arbitrary definition. All we need do is to reflect that there are two arts which truly encompass all others. They represent the two foci of the sphere in motion, that sacred ellipse of the art of man, who has always thrown the best of his emotion, the profoundest meaning of his inner life, the most vivid signs of his struggle against the ephemeral aspect of things, into Architecture and Music. Painting and Sculpture are but complements of Architecture, they are merely the sentimental representation of man or of nature;

while Poetry is merely the effort of Speech and of Dance, the effort of the flesh, to become music.

"That is why the motion picture, which summarizes these arts, which is plastic art in motion, which comprises elements of the static as well as the dynamic arts or, to use Schopenhauer's terms, of the spatial arts, or, in another sense, of the plastic and the rhythmic arts—may be called the seventh art."

The motion picture takes for its own the laws common to all arts. It needs them even more than the others do, and it must follow them even more strictly, for its power to magnify makes basic faults appear to be irreparable. Logic, intellectual and visual clarity, become indispensable to an art wherein thoughts are expressed by means of a mechanical device which unreels animated pictures at a fixed speed of twenty-four images a second. The spectator seated before a screen does not have the opportunity, as he would with a book, of going back to meditate on a thought or to gain a better understanding of the writer's intention. It follows, then, that the essential idea of the film must be presented clearly and logically, which does not mean that imagination or feeling cannot be there in abundance.

The first general law to be observed is that which concerns the selection of an idea and the discovery of the best form in which to present it.

The second is the law of the multiplicity of genres, which must be kept in mind, either *when searching for the idea once the aim of the film has been determined* (education) or *when classifying an original idea in one of the genres.* This determining process is necessary for the reason that each of the genres involves a different conception, technique, or style of creation. Observation of these two fundamental laws will have a considerable bearing, not only on the achievement of the work but also on its appreciation by the public. The latter will eventually learn to judge a film as a product of the genre to which it belongs and not according to the dictates of its mood or taste at the time. This will at least result, let us hope, in motion picture theaters becoming specialized, as is the case with theaters devoted to drama, comedy, music hall, circus, and so on. This rather optimistic outlook would nonetheless, if borne out, have considerable effect on film production, as creative artists would be compelled to observe the great natural law of selection.

The law of genres creates certain specifications for each of them, which I shall endeavor to define in the following chapters.

2

THE FILM IN THE CLASSROOM

FOR A LONG TIME, the school and the motion picture were enemies. But no matter how much the school condemned, the local movie house kept on ringing its bell and attracting young people, eager to see the animated pictures. These two apparently contradictory forces stubbornly maintained their ground because neither one nor the other could find a meeting point.

Finally, some educators realized that it was useless to ignore or to combat the powerful attraction of the screen and that they would do better to turn it to their own use. The school began to take stock of the motion picture.

Actually, we believe that the principal aim of all motion pictures is to educate. Whether this education be consciously or unconsciously assimilated by the recipient, it must constitute that marvelous flowering of the sacred garden whose species we are trying to describe. In return, the school must promote the growth and development of the tree from whose fruits it derives so much benefit.

The motion picture, thus considered as a whole, is able to teach us how to live our own life, in accordance with an ideal set by example. According to each individual's interpretation of it, the motion picture establishes our relations toward the world for our physical and mental well-being. The teaching film studies this outer world in order to cultivate our mind from its earliest stages through scientific methods. Each film is deliberately designed to teach a particular point of discipline. Thus, the first step is to *set a goal,* and then to *find the idea* that will permit this goal to be attained. That is why teaching films belong to the first group. More than any other, this type of film must not be confused, for its theme and its aim give it a very special mission to fulfill.

It may truly be said that since prehistoric times man has felt the need to translate his thoughts into pictures. The cave man reproduced the object of his desire either by modeling clay or by drawing graphite pictures on rocks. Much later he found expression in the dance or in pantomime. Still closer to our time, shadow plays tried to animate images which were projected transparently from behind a screen. Man needs to think in terms of animated pictures.

If we study the psychology of a child, we perceive that he thinks intensely; he would like to discover the universe in a flash; he still lacks the experience which gives each human being a truer appreciation of the notion of time and assimilation of knowledge, as well as an awareness of the limitations on the latter in terms of his life span. But the child, with his irresistible need to be in motion, thinks in terms of action.

Textbooks mean nothing to him without the help of visual interpretation. He starts right in illustrating by means of the drawings, cave paintings we might call them, with which he decorates the margins of his book.

But he wants this illustration to come to life.

That is why, instinctively, he adds something to the picture accompanying the text: a pipe, or perhaps a mustache, to a portrait, a touch of smoke to a chimney, a bird in the sky. He puts life into the text and takes delight in animating what he reads or what he sees, thus going beyond his teacher's explanations.

He would like nothing better than to make the animals walk, the cars move forward, and satisfies this wish with a few strokes of his pencil.

One day, a very small girl showed her father a picture of a

hippopotamus standing on the edge of a lake and cried out:
"Look, Daddy, I want him to go into the water!"

The child is disconcerted by a picture that does not move
and shows this feeling for movement in the awkwardness of
his drawings, just as the primitive cave dwellers sought to express
it in their rock pictures.

A little girl wants her dolls to come to life, while a boy de-
lights in animated puppets. On observing a crowd of children
watching a Punch-and-Judy show (the ancestor of the motion
picture), one notices at once their delight in everything that
moves, everything that is animated. For them, movement is the
primary language of things. They see what is related to them
and they excel in relating what they have seen. But the child
must also interpret what he sees in accordance with a true
understanding of things! That is precisely what teaching aims
to do.

Kant summed up this principle perfectly when he wrote:
"Vision without understanding is meaningless; understanding
without vision is blindness."

We may translate this into ordinary terms in the following
manner:

The teacher's great aim is to utilize motion pictures in order
to make his pupils "understand" his explanations by "showing"
them animated pictures and to make them understand the
pictures (vision) by his comments (understanding). Such is the
problem, the whole problem, and it applies to every level of
teaching, but more especially to elementary teaching.

Teaching films, planned and made within the limits of the
scholastic program, may be used by teachers in a classroom with
the aid of a screen placed beside the blackboard.

This definition underlines once more the principle that a film
must be planned and made for its subject so that it may surely
achieve its aim. More so than any other, the teaching film demands respect for this principle.

The planning and making of teaching films require the collaboration of two specialists: the teacher and the film author.
Each should preserve his own particular technique, but their

high-mindedness should permit them to collaborate closely in mutual understanding of each other's professional talents. The teacher, whether in elementary school or in college, should have a profound understanding of film pedagogy, that is, the art of using motion pictures in order to teach better.

A course in visual instruction should be created in normal school to train teachers how to teach with pictures, particularly with animated pictures. Unbelievable as this may seem, we have never been able to get such a course accepted in France, in spite of the efforts made by Edouard Herriot when he was Minister of National Education. Most of the time, the embryo teachers are taught a smattering of motion picture technique, which makes poor amateurs out of them, whereas the teaching film requires a mastery of technique.

In the United States, great advances have been made along these lines, which I described some years ago in a book.* Courses are given to teach them how to use films in the classroom and instruct them in all the possibilities of this new and potent factor in teaching. Teachers thus informed about the resources placed at their disposal will be able to bring to the motion picture the fruit of their everyday experience.

THE AUTHOR OF TEACHING FILMS

Whatever genre he devotes himself to, the film author must have full command of his technique. But the teaching film calls for specialized and extremely elastic technique. Not only must the author adapt it to general principles of teaching but he must also invent new techniques to render the idea or demonstrate it more clearly. The preparatory stage is of great importance. It is then that intellectual collaboration between teacher and film author occurs. The finished product will derive 90 per cent from this stage. This means that during the shooting stage film technique must be adapted to the written outline, which is to say that the director must be able to resolve

* *Visual Education in the U.S.*, J.B.-L., Editions du Cineopse (Paris), and in the Film Library of the Modern Museum of Art in New York.

all the problems that come up during his collaboration with the teacher.

The author of teaching films should be primarily an artist so that he may delight the eye with his works. He should be gifted with an inquisitive and sufficiently encyclopedic mind to assimilate the most diverse subjects in such fashion as to express them by his pictures in simple, clear, and attractive terms. All these qualities spring from natural gifts that cannot be acquired in any school. So that he may learn this specialized technique enabling him to overcome all obstacles, another school is needed, one whose conception is very clear to us but which exists nowhere.

Indeed, this school can be none other than the school of experience and can have no value unless accompanied by an institute for pedagogic and scientific research through films.

The aim of this ideal institute would be to seek the solution of all teaching problems relating to the motion picture, from elementary education up to and including higher education. Each study would culminate in a film prototype that would serve as a model for educators and independent producers. Another function of the institute would be to promote scientific research by means of films, which in this field have a splendid mission to perform. Thus, the young motion picture student, specializing in teaching and research, would have an opportunity to acquire motion picture technique and would devote himself to disinterested research. Praiseworthy attempts have been made in this direction, but nothing great and permanent has ever been achieved, so that we may truthfully say there has never been any scientific training given to teachers and authors of specialized films, as we understand them.

The teaching film forms part of a group called *Visual Instruction*. This group consists chiefly of the following: 1) Pictures and Photographs; 2) Objects projected by means of episcopes; 3) Dioramas and charts; 4) Slides; 5) Films.

It follows, therefore, that the motion picture is merely a part of this group and should not be used for teaching except in cases where it really answers the purpose and possesses the highest artistic and technical qualities. The use of motion pictures should not be considered obligatory. A good slide is better than a bad film.

If we call upon the motion picture as an instrument of teaching, we must be especially careful not to demand more than it can give. The motion picture does not replace the teacher: it is merely a magnificent instrument placed in his hands. No matter how perfect, how well made this instrument may be, its efficiency will depend on the ability of the user.

A lesson which makes use of a film must remain a lesson, that is, an active exercise of the mind, in the course of which the children are constantly being forced to observe, to judge, and to reason.

The use of a classroom film cannot be considered as a means of making the pupil digest a lesson and thus suppressing in him every effort to think and act.

At this point, I would like to specify once more that I am now dealing with strictly pedagogical films, that is, films adapted to an academic curriculum; these should not be confused with the other film genres, which find other uses in the school and which I shall take up later on.

The teaching film thus defined must be planned and made in such a way as to allow the teacher, in visualizing his teaching assignment, to stimulate the intellectual reactions of his students, to excite—if I may use the term—their brain, and to guide them in their work toward the conclusions he had planned to reach.

For this result to be achieved, there are certain general principles applicable to teaching films that are conceived in the aim of emphasizing or illustrating a lesson, whether in elementary, scientific, or technical instruction.

For every topic, every subject, every field, the film must draw on what is most suggestive in a picture.

A teaching film can and must consist of clear and attractive images, capable of bringing satisfaction that is both intellectual and æsthetic. I have heard children burst spontaneously into applause at a vivid shot of a test tube in which a splendid chemical reaction between two elements was taking place; intellectual clarity and visual satisfaction had combined to produce a thrill of joy. They shivered before so vivid a manifestation of life.

These, briefly described, are the general principles which should be followed in planning and making classroom films. In my opinion, these principles are immutable and constitute the very keystone of the motion picture applied to teaching at every level.

The next thing to determine is how motion pictures are to be used in school, if we consider separately every course in each of the echelons which go to make up the academic hierarchy.

Broadly speaking, we may still say that a different conception will apply to every subject, to every grade. But we cannot formulate such rigid principles so far as each particular case is concerned. In fact, although we say that every film should correspond to a specific level of teaching, there are cases in which the same film can be used in both primary and secondary instruction.

In such instances, it is not the construction of the film that changes but the pedagogy, that is, the manner of teaching.

Actually, a great deal of serious research has been done and many problems have been solved. Nonetheless, it is true that there are still numerous gaps which can only be filled by the creation of a research institute such as the one I mentioned above.

I have already drawn a number of conclusions from the experiments I carried out in many different types of schools. I have acquired a very clear picture of the problem. I have been able to clear up some of the questions, but most of all I have gained a notion of the scope of the problem, which actually comprises nothing more nor less than the art of teaching the sum total of human knowledge. This is equivalent to saying that such a task will never be completed, if we admit that civilization will continue to flourish. Teaching through the motion picture is a science that requires much research and many researchers. No research is possible without organization, without system, without laboratories. We are forced back to that conclusion every time.

One much-argued question is whether teaching films should be silent or not. This is a highly important point and deserves to be treated in all seriousness. By that I mean we should avoid making generalities and above all that we should set forth the problem as it is. To start with, there are other kinds besides silent film and the sound film. There are the silent film, the talking film with commentary, and the synchronized talking film, assuming that sound film applies to films which have sound effects only.

For one thing, the purpose of the film must be clearly determined before deciding whether it should be silent, talking, or sound.

If, for instance, a school wishes to make use of the motion picture to give very small children a glimpse of the world, they might be shown a very short film about the sea. In that case, it is obvious that the film should reproduce the sound of waves, which many of them would never have heard before, save perhaps through holding a sea shell glued to their tiny ears. Similarly, they might be shown a film about a forest, in which they would hear the wind rustling through the trees.

For the nursery school child, there is no question of teaching but of preparation to receive teaching. This is one of the most delicate tasks, involving on the part of the teacher concerned an intimate knowledge of child psychology and particularly a deep love for children.

This earliest stage of teaching, therefore, will demand films specially designed for that purpose and using only sound effects, thus leaving it up to the teacher to interpret the scenes in such a way that they may be understood by her tiny charges.

Let us now pass on to the next level: primary and secondary instruction. And let me specify once more that for the time being we are concerned only with films designed to illustrate the lessons dealing with courses in the curriculum, for instance, such as geography.

The experience I have had leads me to declare that, in the vast majority of cases, these films should be silent.

The classroom film should be no more than a marvelous means of enabling the teacher to show what he is teaching and of helping the pupils to understand better by seeing.

But let me say again that the film must never replace the teacher. Looked at from another standpoint, good teaching is based on the principle of making collective instruction as individual as possible. The teacher adapts his lesson to the mental powers of his pupils. While following the general outline of the lesson, he will use a different approach with each pupil in asking questions or illustrating a point. In short, the film is a means by which he can induce each of the pupils in his class to work; it should not replace his freedom of initiative.

In secondary instruction, where courses become less general and the help of a specialist is needed, the film may have a commentary. With such films, professional knowledge is indispensable.

Finally, all documentary films dealing with the outside world may have commentaries or even synchronized speech.

Those are some of the general principles which may be set forth.

As an illustration of the foregoing considerations, I shall take for an example my own film, *The Mountain,* which I made with Mlle Vergez-Tricom, at that time full professor of the staff of the *lycée* in Lille, who, I am certain, must now be "resisting" somewhere in France and to whom I send an affectionate greeting.

We made this film in my little research center in Paris, after two years of preparation.

The experiments we carried out in France and those I made myself in New York, in public schools and high schools, were conclusive.

Here is the outline of the experiment, which was always practiced on two different classes, one consisting of children between eight and ten years old, the other of children between eleven and fourteen.

1. Subject of the film;
2. Shooting;
3. Utilization;
4. Outline of the film;
5. Projection of the whole film.

Subject of the Film: The Mountain

Geographical observation is difficult because, in nature, geographical features never stand out by themselves but are merged into a oneness which is confusing and hard to interpret, especially for pupils. We therefore tried to *dissociate these features* by breaking the film up into five parts, each of which suggests a few precise observations to the *eye* and to the *mind*. By doing this, it was possible to prevent the audience's attention from wandering. The film as a whole, that is, the sum of the lessons, presents a review of the purely physical characteristics of the mountain, about which it gave a *general idea,* studying its relief, its *climate,* as well as the *wearing effects of its waters.* In addition, from the standpoint of vocabulary, the film pointed out the pertinent terms of geographic nomenclature.

SHOOTING THE FILM

To make this film, we chose characteristic views of different mountains, all of which, however, were in temperate countries.

The film technique, shooting and editing, has naturally been specifically laid down, in view of the teaching aim. It endeavors to meet the requirements of a lesson on the physical characteristics of a mountain.

The subtitles, reduced to a minimum, are there merely for the purpose of pointing out one or two precise and simple facts. In no case do they try to explain. They allow the teacher complete freedom of initiative and the pupils an opportunity to reflect and to work.

The images are kept on the screen long enough for every detail to be seen and assimilated. The teacher has an opportunity to point out features which the pupils might have missed at first. The technique in making a teaching film inevitably calls for a judicious use of animated drawings. In order to simplify a scene and retain only the important features, we superimposed animated sketches, which appeared on top of the landscape, then partly faded out to show the essential lines, and finally blended back into it. This method not only forcefully presents a fact but at the same time shows how the essential features of a landscape may be taken out and put down on paper.

At the end of each part, we introduced a blank strip with the title STOP. At this point the teacher should stop the projector and question the pupils to make sure they have understood. When necessary, he should turn the film back. The conclusion of each part does not come until after the STOP in order to sum up the work already accomplished.

For convenience' sake, the separate parts of the film have been assembled together, so that the whole film can be shown as a single unit for purposes of review. But it must be clearly understood that the film consists of several different lessons to be used as the teacher sees fit, depending on the age of his pupils and the requirements of his lecture.

Use of the Film

The Mountain may be used for elementary and junior high school teaching. In the first instance, it corresponds to one of the lessons devoted to the mountain (8, 9, and 10 years). In the other, it corresponds to the course in general geography given to 6th and 10th graders (11 and 15 years), as well as to the course in natural science given to 8th graders (13 years).

Depending on the age of the pupils, they might be asked:

a. to make drawings of what they have seen (*a task eminently suited to geography*);

b. to explain these drawings (*practice in narrative*);

c. to account for what they have seen.

Thus the film will have accomplished its threefold purpose:

1. To compensate to some extent for the travel and direct observation which are not possible, by giving a clear idea of what a mountain is;

2. To stimulate and direct powers of observation;

3. To awaken curiosity and provoke requests for explanation or to make the pupils give their own explanations.

OUTLINE OF THE FILM

First part: *Idea of the Mountain.*

Points to be observed: 1. The idea of altitude, great differences between the foot and the top; 2. Various zones differing greatly from each other.

Example of review: A mountain is a raised mass of earth. There are great contrasts between the foot and the summit.

Second part: *Zones and Slopes of the Mountain.*

Points to be observed: 1. The various zones seen in greater detail with their peculiar characteristics; 2. Valleys and the important centers of life they represent: cultures, dwellings, passes; 3. Slopes steeper than those found in the valleys, sometimes insurmountable.

Example of review: A mountain has five different zones. The slopes of a mountain are steep, sometimes inaccessible. Valleys shelter cultures and dwelling places, and afford a means of passage; these are the mountain zones of life.

Third part: *Mountain Peaks.*

Points to be observed: 1. The mountain group and the chain; 2. Shape of the peaks: rounded, jagged, sharp, crested; 3. Observations on image and on drawing; 4. Why the various shapes?

Example of review: Mountains are found in groups or chains. Their peaks take different shapes; rounded in the case of older mountains, jagged in the case of younger mountains.

Fourth part: *Waters and Valleys of the Mountain.*

Points to be observed: 1. How the torrent is formed; 2. Shape of the torrent's bed, its banks; 3. Variations in the flow of the torrent; 4. The work of the torrent: erosion, deposits; 5. Advantages and disadvantages of the torrent.

Example of review: Mountain waters flow in torrents. The torrent's bed is narrow, with steep banks. Its flow is extremely variable, depending on the season. It may at times cause a great deal of damage, but it may be harnessed and used in the production of electricity.

Fifth part: *Climate of the Mountain.*

Points to be observed: 1. Why do mountain zones rise one above the other? 2. Observations on the heavy rainfall and the drop in temperature at higher altitudes; 3. Observations on the length of the winter; 4. What the mountain looks like in winter; 5. Occupations.

Example of review: The zones of the mountain may be explained by the abundance of rainfall and the lowering in temperatures as the altitude increases. Nature of the climate and length of the winters. The mountaineer has only a short time in which to work; his life is a rugged one.

I have endeavored to give some idea of the motion picture's role as an instrument placed in the teacher's hands to lend added strength to his teaching. These few remarks are inadequate to give a complete picture of the multiple ways in which it may be applied. In other words, a subject of this magnitude deserves to be treated in a separate book which I intend some day to write. Nevertheless, I would like to go a little beyond the strictly academic use of the motion picture. In this function, it is a magnificent instrument, but one confined within the limits of the teaching curriculum. It has an even greater task to perform in the school: that of introducing all the life of the outside world, all human activities, into the classroom. In this role it becomes what I like to call: *The Classroom Window Opened on Life.*

The motion picture has the privilege of being able to *transport life;* it constitutes the sole means of conveying, through that classroom window opening wide upon the world, a current of fresh air that will sweep away all prejudice, all outdated methods. The motion picture will play the most prominent part in that progressive movement which is trying to satisfy the young in their thirst for knowledge and furnish them with illustrations from life.

A simple documentary film about asbestos and the way that stone is transformed into fabric will correct the impression left in the pupil's mind by the arbitrary division that has been made between the mineral and vegetable kingdoms, and thus give him a large-scale view of the kingdom of life, in which there are no chapter divisions but only differences of degree.

Films dealing with universal knowledge are not guided by the same principles of conception and production as those I have attempted to describe in the preceding sections. As opposed to pedagogic films keyed to the academic curriculum, the ones which now concern us may be used in many different ways; their purpose is far more to stimulate the mind and appeal to the eye than to teach scientific principles or laws. From this, it is clear that a new genre is in question, and the role of the film author changes. Although he continues to specialize in teaching from the psychological standpoint, he is allowed more artistic freedom. The idea, though remaining linked with the predetermined objective, may be expressed somewhat more freely or come closer to the Film of Life, which I shall take up later on.

With this film genre, the chief consideration is the use to which it will be put. The children's minds must be gradually awakened to the wonders of the world, must have time to assimilate each separate bit of information shown to them; for this, enthusiastic teachers are needed, trained in the mental gymnastics required to put life into a class or an assembly of pupils.

I can recall vividly those classes I used to attend in the community schools of Paris as well as in the public schools of New York, at which the teacher's questions would bring forth answers or more questions from every corner of the room, blending together in a symphony of sound. True, such teachers must be temperamentally suited to their task and thoroughly trained. But what satisfaction they must get out of molding all those young minds and determining their reactions and enthusiasms at will, without giving it a second thought! Having played this intellectual game myself, I can truthfully say there is nothing to compare with the satisfaction one derives from it. That is why I return once more to this essential idea: incipient teachers must be taught at normal school the motion picture's potentialities in school. In that way, they will be provided not only with a wonderful instrument for teaching but also with a source of professional delight that will keep up their enthusiasm and give them renewed faith in their noble task. Such teachers will be able to utilize a good film for several purposes. For instance, they will understand that a film about Bernard de Palissy may be used by the art teacher to illustrate a lesson on ceramics but that such a theme may also furnish fine material for a lesson on courage and perseverance in work.

And what a splendid lesson may be learned from the study of a piece of work, not just contemplated in its finished state but taken at its source, at the very moment of inspiration, and followed through all the phases of its execution! This is what was done in the film: *A Great Artist and Craftsman, the Master Glass Blower, Maurice Marino.*

Maurice Marino was one of the last artist-craftsmen to flourish in France. I decided that only the motion picture could preserve for posterity the work of those artists who stand out in their period as Bernard de Palissy did in his. That is why, together with René Chavance, I conceived the idea of dedicating a series of films to their memory, the first two of which were devoted to our two greatest artist-craftsmen: Auguste Delaherche, the great ceramist, since disappeared, and Maurice Marino. The war interrupted this project.

Marino found in his professional ideal the faith and the high talents of the medieval craftsmen. He gives birth to his masterpieces alone in the provincial attic which a kind friend lets him use several hours a day.

In making this film, what was the problem lying before us? To show the miracle of art in sensitive, clear, and intelligible terms, to unveil the mystery of this magical creation, to portray its grandeurs and its agonies.

To achieve this aim, I settled down near the artist, together with my dear collaborator and friend, Edmond Floury, as discreetly as my apparatus and projectors would permit. I watched his struggle with the raw materials, surprised him in his research and his marvelous hand-to-hand clash with the ideal which enabled him to wrest the secret from nature's hidden harmonies.

He draws his inspiration from that same nature. First, in order to stylize them, he captures on paper the shape of a plant, the rhythm of a wave, or the vitality of a flame.

"There is one particularly thrilling moment, when one sees that shapeless paste at the end of the blowing iron gradually become clear, rich in reflections, and finally catch the light through a thousand facets. A splendid triumph of will power over matter. Magic of man and fire. With breathless emotion, the watcher beholds this difficult conquest of beauty over brute matter, and, while the glass blower breathes life into this fragment of light which is alive, which trembles, which hangs defenseless, we see the sweat roll down his forehead, the veins in his face thicken, while with the same gentleness his hand revolves the blower at the end of which is being born this shape, plucked out of nothingness, atom by atom.

"In the burning radiance of the open fire, the spark of life within the molten glass begins to fade away. The artist barely has the time, before this living light is frozen, to emprison within its core what is most precious in this fading fairyland: the artist's thought. Before the scintillating soul of the glass has a chance to escape the crystal substance, it must be locked in so it may survive forever." *

This film can furnish the teacher with much material for lessons, for instance, the striking analogy with the life of man, who,

* Emile Vuillermoz, film critic for *Le Temps*.

before he vanishes, must hurriedly mold his heart and mind in order to leave some trace of his stay on this earth. Or perhaps a few lessons on being proud of one's trade; on the artist's education through the emotion he derives from creating something, from studying the beauty of forms; or on the joy to be found in doing work and the development of a sense of beauty. A moral lesson, furnished by the example of a life made happy by work. A lesson in appreciation of the value of human labor.

A great many educators have recognized this magnificent function assumed by the motion picture, and I can remember most vividly the numerous experiments I was able to carry out in France, thanks to my public school friends there. I remember in particular the principal of a girls' school on the rue Picpus, in one of the most populous quarters of Paris. This splendid woman regarded the hundred girls in her care as her own children and lived only for her school: it was her whole life. Whenever I had finished a new film, Mme Bizet would quickly gather all her pupils in the assembly hall, from the youngest to the oldest, and would ask me to explain my ideas to them. And in doing so I would experience a thrill of delight to find myself before an audience so eager to learn and at the same time feel a tremendous sense of responsibility in the knowledge that every word I uttered would be engraved on these young and sensitive minds. When the teacher feels those hundreds of eyes trained on him like so many cameras, he becomes conscious of the magnitude and difficulty of the trust laid upon him, which obliges him to assume the enormously heavy burden of revealing the world to them. But also what a feeling of strength and security he derives from that reel of film lying next to him, ready for use, from which in a little while a thousand rays will flicker, bearing to each of the little beings making up the audience the gift of being able to think for herself and have her own reflexes, of becoming aware of her budding personality.

When I had finished my talk, Mme Bizet would say to her pupils: "My children, you are going to see the film, and I want you to watch it closely. Afterward, you will take a sheet of paper and put down the ideas which the film gives you. And, so that you may be free to think, I will make an exception this time and shut my eyes to mistakes in spelling."

To give some examples, here are a few of the astonishing reflections that were jotted down by children between seven and twelve years old:

A little girl wrote: "One must love what one makes." Another declared: "To be happy in life, one must love one's work." Already we have two thoughts which alone are worth more than all the moral lessons in the world. Merely by showing this artist-craftsman at work, we were able to give these two children an inkling of the whole philosophy of life, which Jean Jaurés so well expressed in his credo:

"Stay clear of everything that might lower your professional merit; for, in a life well filled with work, this will be the foundation of your merit as a man.

"Have a care for and a pride in work well done."

Let me also choose the following two among the many thoughts written down by children: "This film teaches one to respect a vase." "Whenever we put flowers in a vase, we shall think of the person who made it." In other words, these children were moved by the artistic and manual labor they saw; they learned to respect man's handiwork. May we not regard this as another great lesson aimed at strengthening that splendid and powerful bond which should unite all men: the respect due to every form of work, the love felt for one's trade? This feeling of appreciation for the work of others will be applied to everything in life. Carefully cultivated by an understanding teacher, it will lead children to respect not only works of art but all human work down to the humblest occupation. The result is that, althought the unique product of Marino's brain will meet with exceptionally fervent appreciation, the child will have learned to show the same kind of respect for an inexpensive factory-made vase which reveals the artist's inspiration in the beauty and purity of its lines.

How are we to obtain this result? By developing, in very simple terms, the idea that art and industry should co-operate in order to popularize, to spread abroad the beautiful things of life. *Industry needs artists to create the patterns, which have always been reserved for a privileged class. Art needs industry to popularize,* distribute through the humblest homes, the pure forms conceived and executed by the artist-craftsman. And this applies not only to objects that are purely decorative but also to things in everyday use. The teacher will have only to emphasize the role of the tradesman or worker to make his charges understand that all work, on whatever scale it is done, has its beauty, its greatness, and its social usefulness. The child's recollection of the creative artist will be no less vivid, as indicated by the writer of this final quotation: "The vase, once finished, makes me think of a waterfall cascading down a mountain." We may indeed marvel that this young child should have understood how the artist rendered into glass an impression received from one of nature's displays. And we may take comfort in seeing these youngsters lead us back to refreshing sources of inspiration, putting us in touch with those whose divinely appointed mission is to spread beauty through the world.

The motion picture, in addition to opening the classroom window on the world, has a similar role to play in every sphere of life. It may be used not only to increase man's stock of knowledge but also to create and keep alive a philosophy emphasizing the joys of right living. To live right in society, that is, to know, appreciate, and love one's neighbor. The very principle on which the immortal Bible is based, since all advances made by civilization have been merely the evolution of the fundamental principles laid down by the prophets. Spirituality cannot be separated from reality as easily as some people seem to think.

If the motion picture is to expose men to loftier concepts and demonstrate the universal quality of certain sentiments, it must also give them an understanding of their mental processes and their reactions toward certain dramatic circumstances or environment. This brings up the question of human relations. "Human relations," a splendid title which gives a precise definition of the goal pursued: to study human relations in order to improve relations among men.

In attaining this goal, we must make use of great dramatic

films based on universal concepts, to promote organized discussions directed by the teacher. Choosing these films is an extremely delicate process; very few of them can withstand the searching scrutiny of the adolescent mind. Some well-meaning teachers extract certain portions of these films in order to show the governing idea or a few of the incidents. Such a procedure has seemed to me in practice to be extremely dangerous, for an extract almost always distorts an idea when there is no time to follow its exposition, its psychological development.

Actually, we would do better to leave the motion picture free to open the classroom window in its own way, so that it may show life in all its truth and beauty. And in doing so the motion picture will accomplish its principal aim: to inspire those who will soon be setting out into the world with a love for life that will make their journey seem more pleasant.

THE CALL OF LIFE

The teacher's role at times extends beyond the limits of the classroom, and in such cases merely opening the window is not enough! There are a number of delicate tasks for which the teacher will need the co-operation of the parents and in which he will have to educate them. I am referring to a kind of lesson that neither academic curriculum nor textbook can provide— that deals with *sex education*. This is an extremely delicate matter, before which people are far too often inclined to remain silent.

Very well, let's not say anything, let's be silent, let's turn out all the lights and allow the screen to illuminate the darkness. There are luminous pictures which alone are capable of expressing what we dare not put into words. "Only movies can tell."

The motion picture should help man to live. It is the best means of preparing youth to answer *the call of life,* that powerful compulsion coming from nature herself, who desires that every living creature, between birth and death, should propagate itself. It is one of the most powerful instruments of sex education, for it can prevent the morbid approach.

It should be inspired by two distinct aims: educating the parents and educating the children. The first of these is by far the more important, for it bears on the second.

Many parents make the grave mistake of trying to stifle this call of life. They may as well try to stop up their children's senses—their noses, ears, and mouths—make them deaf, dumb, and blind, condemn them to eternal solitude and silence. Even in such a crippled being, deprived of all contact with the outer world, that great voice will make itself heard, picked up by some unknown, mysterious antenna, a voice bidding all life to the universal banquet.

Whatever precautions may be taken to conceal the facts of life from Peter, the day will come when he will no longer believe that his little sister was bought in the department store and will ask one of those questions that leave parents speechless.

And at that point the time will have come to give him a serious answer. There are parents who tell their children to hush up: "One doesn't talk about such things." Are they so foolish as to think that the call of life may be stilled? Peter will go and ask his questions elsewhere: in the servant's quarters, in the court-yard, in the street. What sort of answers will he get there?

If parents want their child to have a healthy mental outlook and not be led astray into furtive conversations, they must gain his confidence to such an extent that he will come straight to them with his questions, which they must be able to answer at once.

These answers are a complete art and a science. That science must be learned, and it will be up to the teachers to organize meetings of their pupils' parents, at which the latter will be given instruction in that art, that science, which cannot be invented but which comes from experience and from daily contact with children.

Adults have a habit of evading these childish queries by telling what they conceive to be cunning lies, while a knowing look passes between them, well above that little head which is so eager for the truth. They think they are being clever, but they are only being petty, ridiculous, and guilty of a grave error.

Obviously, the phrase "Tell me, Mummy," which so often comes from the lips of children, can sometimes be quite embarrassing. Interestingly enough it is the two extremes of life—birth and death—which fascinate children most of all and which are most carefully concealed from them.

Needless to say, parents must be taught that they can and always should tell the truth but that they can do it in such a loving way that no harm will come to their children.

These fresh young minds, when confronted with nature, have their own delightful and comforting interpretations, which are drawn from nature itself and which the finest poet would be proud to call his own. For instance, a little girl who had been given to understand that "to die" did not mean "to go on a long voyage from which there is no return" but—at least physically—meant to return to the earth, and who had learned elsewhere that this same nourishing earth produced flowers and fruits, was ready with her own condolences on the occasion of a death in the family: "Let's not cry for Cousin Jack, because he's going to be a rose."

It may readily be seen that the most tremendous tact must be shown in making disclosures of this nature. The character of each individual child must be taken into consideration, and only a loving mother can be entrusted with the task, provided she is careful not to invite questions but will wait until they come naturally at the proper time, and will never evade them.

Under the circumstances, it is obvious that sex education, properly speaking, in childhood cannot be given in a classroom at a fixed time, in front of forty different pupils. Whatever the teacher would say, though perhaps excellent for one child, might be harmful to another. Only the father or mother is in a position to watch over the child with tender care and hearken to life's first call.

On the other hand, adolescents should be given sex education by their teachers, along the lines laid down by the academic authorities. This should include instruction both in the physiology of the human body and in prophylaxis against venereal diseases.

For instance, it is unthinkable that a course in physiology should stop at the pelvis. Whatever is ignored, purposely passed over in silence, the true facts concealed, quickly becomes monstrous to the imagination. The professor of natural science, expanding his course to include all the organs of the human body, will be led to talk about their hygiene and to warn the students of the risks they can run.

Even at this stage, the parents will have a part to play. At this stage too, and even more so, there are "calls to life" which will be confessed only to them. "Tell me, Mummy," may be heard less frequently from adolescents than from children but with far more vehemence. With boys, it will often be replaced by "Tell me, Father."

Although we may clearly differentiate between the sex education given to children and that given to adolescents, each requires just as much love on the part of the parents and, as time goes on, more and more knowledge. Knowledge of life in general and of the learner in particular. Knowledge of his body and knowledge of his soul.

The motion picture can give them that knowledge and help them pass it on to their children. Its role as an educator is primordial.

It will teach parents elementary principles of physiology and concepts of child psychology, drawing their attention to specific cases and showing them examples of what they must avoid.

The Russians have produced an educational film designed to show parents how the practice of corporal punishment can result in harming their children. It would be equally useful to make a film showing that there are words which can harm children even more than blows.

But the chief importance of the motion picture, in the hands of parents and teachers, lies in its use as a means of sex education for the children themselves.

We have said that sex education proper of children comes largely from the parents; but it is the school's duty to reveal the origin of life. Only the screen can help the child in his anxious quest for a solution to the mystery of birth, by providing him with the fresh and comforting picture of a chick hatching in its shell, a silk worm curled up in its cocoon.

It is unthinkable that an act which is the basis of all life should be concealed from our children as though it were a crime. In any case, concealment is futile. We have seen how, very early in life, a child develops an amazing awareness of all those things which are kept from him. Every parent has had the startling experience of being asked some question which revealed unsuspected knowledge on the part of the child. "Where in Heaven's name did he learn that?" He learned it everywhere: from a whispered conversation, a word read in a book, a picture glimpsed, from everything about him, and especially from himself. The parents must not express surprise or indignation; they must give the child a serious answer, taking great care not to lie, not to hide the truth as though it were ugly or mean, but to give it in all its simplicity and greatness.

Yet, despite the beauty of this truth, we still find it hard to tell, precisely because we are not great and simple enough ourselves.

This truth, which goes beyond us and encompasses all nature, can be revealed to very small children *only by the motion picture*, without hurting them, but in the gentle, pure, and tender language of the screen, so much more effective than any maternal words.

By using the method of acceleration, the screen can combine all the phases of a flower's fecundity, the germination and dispersal of seeds, into one single graceful act, the sublime act of Life.

We are not obliged to conceal this act from our children. They may watch it in perfect innocence, for a flower will never suggest anything obscene to them. This fairy-like flower, made by acceleration to move and stir on the screen like an animal, can do no harm. In its motions, all becomes gentle, sweet, and pure.

Then, but only then, may the teacher's motherly voice be heard saying that this act of the lily is the grandest act of nature and forms the basis of all other life in the universe. And so the child, no longer believing in cabbages and storks and understanding that it is his mother who will give birth to the expected little one, will in his heart associate this generous mother with all the flowers of the earth, subject to the same law of life, and will not look upon her as a grotesque creature, deformed and unclean.

For adolescents, a scientific film can provide an excellent lesson in physiology and teach them the structure of the human body. It can also furnish the basis for a model lesson, which the academic authorities will have prepared in advance, with the help of psychiatrists, to guard against a too enthusiastic teacher overstepping the bounds.

Without going in for childish sentimentality, we can and must use sufficient tact in revealing the facts, even to boys and girls of 17, so that no one will be hurt. In short, motion pictures can provide the truest and finest moral lesson to illustrate "the call of life" throughout the entire universe, and, in their images, can associate the origin of all human life with the origin of all vegetable and animal life. In this way, the propagation of life no longer appears as a monstrous phenomenon to be dissembled but as a universal phenomenon, grand and beautiful, rising far above and beyond all the limitations of convention.

The adolescent who hearkens to the call of life within him should not think of himself as a guilty exception but rather as a part of a whole, subject to the same compulsion and the same harmony. This knowledge should banish all concern and produce a feeling of peace, which alone can make us fully understand one of Jean Cocteau's most beautiful poems:

> *If you love, my poor child,*
> *DON'T BE AFRAID ...*
> *It's the universal law.*

DON'T BE AFRAID ... The educational film that shows us the germination of a seed, the hatching of a chick, the birth of all living creatures, can and must teach our children not to be afraid of life. But also, by warning them of the risks they can run, it must help them to live right. So that the *call to life*

may be a call to a grander, healthier, and finer life, and not a
call to death.

SCIENTIFIC RESEARCH AND TEACHING

The scientific, medicosurgical motion picture came into existence through the initiative of Dr. Doyen, who had himself
filmed while performing an operation, with a camera he had
built for his own personal guidance and that of his pupils.

In the *Revue Critique de Médecin et de Chirurgie* for August
15, 1899, Dr. Doyen wrote: "When for the first time I saw one
of my operations on the screen, I realized how little I knew
about myself. . . . Much of my technique, which I had always
believed satisfactory, now seemed defective to me. I corrected,
improved, and simplified where necessary, so that the motion
picture enabled me to perfect my technique to a considerable
degree."

It would be hard to find a better definition of the motion
picture's role in scientific research and teaching. For even at
this early stage Dr. Doyen had understood its dual function. He
used it for "his own guidance and that of his pupils" and also to
"correct defective methods, to perfect his technique." He goes
on to express his thoughts, writing: "The use of cinematography
in the teaching of operational technique may be considered one
of the most splendid conquests of surgery, for this marvelous
invention will spread through all the world knowledge of the
best procedures, the surest methods to rescue a portion of
mankind from suffering and death."

Dr. Doyen's testimony, confirmed by usage, and the testimony
of several American universities are precious to us for their
affirmation of the motion picture's role as an auxiliary to science.

"Every time," wrote the eminent doctor, "there is an interest
in following the successive movements of a particular case,
everything must be recorded by motion picture camera.

"Thus, it would be impossible to preserve the confused
bearing and movements of certain patients with nervous diseases
on photographic documents were it not for the motion picture."

Dr. Doyen's courses had already been made more interesting,

and more practical, through the use of motion picture slides. They were a continuation of those begun by Charcot at the Salpêtrière, which caused such a sensation in their day. Charcot, who had no motion picture to help him, exhibited the patients themselves and was sharply criticized for his living exhibitions.

In another field, that of biology and microbiology, October 26, 1909, was a memorable date. On that date, Dr. Commandon first exhibited before the Academy of Sciences films showing live microbes, ready to be studied. Up till then microbes had never been photographed. Through the generosity of M. Charles Pathé, Dr. Commandon was able to carry on with this remarkable and universally appreciated work for a number of years. From then on, it was possible to watch these infinitesimal creatures in action, instead of examining their corpses, as had formerly been the case. The motion picture enables us to study the evolution of all kinds of microbes. Ultramicroscopic cinematography not only makes possible the study of microbes living in the human system and the pathological consequences of their action but also the discovery of unknown microbes and even of certain filtrable viruses. And so we see that scientific research may be carried on through the medium of the motion picture, which now and then carries us to such dizzy heights that our brain can scarcely keep up with it. I remember having once recorded the different stages in the life of a chicken cell over a period of one year. That cell was constantly alive. We are led to metaphysical speculations that go beyond the powers of the human mind.

Micro-cinematography enables us to see each microbe, each cell, living its own, distinct life, and thereby make use of it for study and research. We can uncover a whole world, merely by staying in our own laboratory.

Many years ago, a biologist told one of his students who was planning a trip to Africa to study the habits of wild animals: "Instead of going so far to seek the unknown, my friend, why don't you try to penetrate the thousand dramas or scenes whose only stage is a drop of your blood?" The caprice of yesterday's scientist has today become a reality, thanks to the motion picture.

Since that time, so close to us in years but so far away within the comparatively recent existence of the motion picture, numerous scientists in every country, especially in France and the United States, have made use of films. Technique has slowly improved, and, in particular, the introduction of sound has increased the educational value of instruction in science through films. The invention of panchromatic film has made it possible to obtain all the half-tints which, in a surgical film for instance, enables every anatomical detail to be brought out. Thanks to color, tissues and organs may now be shown as they really are.

Another point to be considered in connection with this film genre is that it must be thoroughly reorganized to avoid waste of time and money.

Ever since the motion picture has been allowed to share in scientific research and teaching, it has been consistently used in the most disorganized fashion. One need only attend a medical and surgical conference to see how many of the hundred or so films shown really fulfill their aim, from the standpoint of conception and technical realization. A central institute of research is needed, similar to the one I have mentioned in connection with academic teaching films.

In Paris, we had set up a Committee of Medical and Surgical Studies. This Committee was honored by the patronage of the Ministers of National Education and Foreign Affairs. The latter Ministry had an interest in the matter due to the fact that French schools abroad came under its authority. The Committee was presided over by Professor G. Roussy, rector of the University, Member of the Academy of Medicine. The executive board consisted of Professors A. Gosset and Ch. Laubry, vice-presidents; Professor Roger Leroux, secretary; and myself. Professor Léon Bernard was vice-president at the time of his death.

The Committee had the following aims:

1. To advance methods of scientific research and teaching, particularly in the field of medicine and surgery, by the application of motion picture technique.

2. To perfect motion picture technique, as applied to these researches.

3. To organize collaboration and intellectual exchanges of such nature as to favor the use of the motion picture in teaching and research: to perfect the methods, technical procedures, and types of apparatus relating to these researches.

4. To produce films of interest to research in biology, medicine, and surgery or to the teaching of these sciences.

5. To make known to all interested parties the results obtained, as much from the standpoint of advances in motion picture technique as from that of scientific achievement.

This research center was established in 1930. It comprised two technical laboratories, one for research in biology and pathological anatomy at Villejuif, the other, under Professor Gosset at the Salpêtrière Hospital, for surgery.

I do not want to take this time to relate the full story of our labors, but I would like to give some idea of the infinite pains we took. For instance, we spent four years developing our technique to the point where we were able to reproduce on the screen the precise movements of a surgeon operating at his normal rhythm. This apparently simple task actually involved a great many problems which I do not intend to describe except to say that the principal one was this: Given an operation to perform, reproduce this operation through the motion picture camera as the eye of the surgeon sees it, using exactly the same rhythm as that of the various stages in the operation, without obliging the surgeon to make one unaccustomed movement in order to facilitate the shots or interrupting the normal succession of steps in the operation.

All these technical problems were solved, and we were able to make a number of film prototypes which met with appreciation, notably from the Academy of Medicine in New York.

In other fields covered by the aims of our Committee, we obtained some very fine results, especially in the field of pathological anatomy, with the *Technique of Autopsies*, which was in production for six months.

Instruction in autopsies is an essential part of the medical student's curriculum. He learns his normal anatomy at the dissecting table. But he must go to the autopsy table to acquire the foundations on which his knowledge of general and special pathology will rest.

Although there are a great many excellent treatises on normal anatomy and dissection, very few manuals have been written on autopsy and pathological anatomy. An autopsy, required to verify or correct a clinical diagnosis, is always apt to teach something to the person who performs it correctly; yet only too often it has little effect because in many instances it is performed incompletely and unmethodically.

In the film *Technique of Autopsies* we started off with the first part of the operative act. It describes, down to the smallest detail, the various moves to be made so that the organs will be extracted in logical order, with the minimum chance of damaging or forgetting something.

A second part of the film deals with the systematic dismembering of the organs or viscera after they have been removed. The preferred cuts are pictured in detail; they show how very important it is to adhere strictly to method so that nothing will be forgotten.

The film is about 6,900 feet long, and divided into five lessons. Taken thus, it presents a composite whole, eminently technical in nature; it is also a precious guide for the teaching of topographical anatomy and observations in pathology.

In 1939, when war was declared, the Committee was in full swing. Our laboratories contained the necessary apparatus, some of which had been specially constructed in accordance with the results of our experiments. At the Hospital of the Salpêtrière, an operating theater had been specially equipped. Scientists came from all over to benefit by our experience and our equipment. Surgeons took note of a new operational technique or the effects of a new instrumentation. Some beds were reserved for patients whom these surgeons brought from other hospitals or even from the provinces.

Our Committee became a real center of research, a workroom, a pole of attraction. Many surgeons and scientists, who had wasted their time and their money on amateurs with negligible results, took advantage of our researches and found that in our laboratories results were assured and precious moments saved.

I am anticipating a perfectly natural objection: such centers cannot be established everywhere, while the scientists and surgeons of a large country like the United States could not move from San Francisco to New York, for instance, in order to take advantage of such an institution. I would answer first by saying that similar centers can be set up in all important areas, for they are far more economical than the experiments of individual amateurs; but that is not the point. These centers, once they have been set up in the more important geographical areas, should not only be research laboratories but should also become training centers for specialized technicians who will swarm all over the world.

There are, nonetheless, special cases where the doctor will have only himself to rely upon. Not a day passes but that psychiatrists and orthopedists see patients in their offices or clinics whose reactions or attitudes they have the greatest interest in recording. In such cases, they must act right away and on the spot. The doctor should have a minimum of technical knowledge. By spending some time at the research center, he will acquire that minimum of technical knowledge. But this is merely a question of notes and records, of documentation in support of scholarly treatises. It has nothing to do with teaching and research films as such.

And so we see once more that the teaching film, indeed like all films, is a serious matter which must be handled by professional experts. The scientific film assures the motion picture its true greatness, reveals it in its primary role, for in this genre it is acting in the service of the scientist, whose true function is to contribute to the good of mankind.

That was how our own great Pasteur conceived it, when he wrote these lines, the significance of which has never been so great:

"Two opposite laws today seem to be in conflict: a law of blood and death, which, by inventing every day some new

method of combat, forces people to remain in a perpetual state
of readiness for the battlefield, and a law of peace, of work, of
health, which has for its sole aim the deliverance of man from the
evils which assail him.

"The first seeks only violent conquest, the other only the solace
of mankind. The latter places the life of a human being above
all victories, the former would sacrifice hundreds of thousands
of lives to the ambition of one."

The teaching film spreads its mission throughout all degrees,
all branches of learning. It applies as much to high school and
elementary school as it does to the university. It has performed
tremendous services in the specialized fields, notably in agriculture, both in school and in direct practical instruction of farmers.

In the military sphere, after the First World War, it was used
to demonstrate strategy and, historically, to reconstitute the
important battles, as seen by the Commander in Chief. At
present, it is being used for the accelerated training of soldiers,
and the American Army derives much benefit from the splendid
technique of Walt Disney, who has also adapted himself to war.

This hasty survey brings out the fact that the motion picture's
first and greatest aim is to teach more thoroughly and more
permanently, and at the same time to bring to the classroom a
foretaste of the life which lies outside.

3
THE EDUCATIONAL FILM

EDUCATIONAL FILMS, though having their roots in teaching films, are nevertheless vastly different.

We may say that in theory teaching requires the consent of the mind whereas education requires the consent of the heart, that is, of the individual sensibility. Naturally, this is only a postulate, for in reality mind and heart are not so easily separated.

As a matter of fact, the educational film, distinguished from the teaching, or classroom, film, is intended for all ages at the same time. Its ultimate aim is the education of the masses, and that is its whole function.

For the very reason that it covers so much territory, this film genre must of necessity be divided into two distinct categories: 1. Films meant to be preceded or followed by a lecture; 2. films having a clearly educational purpose, capable of being self-sufficient.

I. Films Accompanied by a Lecture

These films tend, in short, to continue in the adolescent and adult the teaching they received in school. Consequently, they should retain most of the qualities possessed by teaching films. But there will be a difference in technique. The film maker will have to assimilate his subject by learning it from a specialist, that is, through pedagogic means, but his art should consist in converting the instruction he has received into a form acceptable to the public, which, though willing to be educated and desirous of being enlightened, is incapable of following a lesson.

He will have to exercise his ingenuity to capture the public's attention through the interest and diversity of his scenes, without ever losing track of the educational aim set forth. He will find happy inspiration in the words of Lamothe, who wrote in the seventeenth century: "Boredom one day was born of uniformity." Therefore, it is important to educate by pleasing the eye and mind with the diversity achieved through movement, changes in procedure, beauty of scenes; in other words, by making a filmic work of art. To render agreeably palatable to the public, to facilitate its understanding of the great scientific or social truths—such is the aim of this film genre, whose primary function is to popularize.

Popularization is both an art and a trade; it may be achieved in any form, using any means of expression—a book, treatise, or lecture; but again it must be admitted that none of these means is as powerful as the "picture mill," whose function is precisely that of grinding out ideas and projecting their reflected light onto the sensitive plate of the human mind.

We shall, therefore, endeavor to consider a few of the forms in which the postgraduate educational film fufills its aim, with the help of some concrete examples.

THE EXAMPLE OF GREAT MEN

One evening, I had two friends visiting me, one the manager of a circus and the other a businessman. The former announced gleefully that he had hit a new box office high that week with Marcel Thill (the great prize fighter). I timidly expressed the opinion that if the 1500 people in his circus had been asked who M. d'Arsonval was, very few of them would have been able to answer. Whereupon my businessman friend proceeded to ask: "I suppose M. d'Arsonval is another champion prize fighter?" This anecdote is by no means unusual: it is a tragic sign of the almost complete failure of education. My two friends, whom I take as typical of millions of similar people, were well-taught but they were not *educated*. Teaching has been widely diffused, and rightly so, but in my opinion not enough attention has been given to the fact that education should accompany teaching. Education may be compared to the body glands that secrete a liquid designed to assimilate foods. Without education, teaching is of no advantage to a human being and, poorly assimilated, often becomes dangerous to the intellectual stability and social existence of the individual. The motion picture should bring to this assimilative function its precious and unequaled support.

I am not underestimating the utility of sports and the physical and mental value derived from their practice. I admire a champion prize fighter, tennis player, or football player, just as I admire anything that is the completely successful product of long labor, of will power concentrated on achieving perfection of form and increasing man's power. But are we to believe that great men like Pasteur, Edison, Lincoln, who gave so much toward improving the physical, material, and moral existence of their fellow men, do not deserve at least as much publicity as that accorded to athletic champions? A publicity, in the finest sense of the term—the art of making known—that will popularize the work of these great men and also increase the store of acquired knowledge. At the same time, it will put before the public fine examples of life, thereby educating it to consider existence and its aims in quite a different light.

I was fortunate enough to be one of M. d'Arsonval's intimate friends. Quite often, my family and I used to visit him in his laboratory at Nogent-sur-Marne, an annex of the Collège de France. He would tell us stories about his past, of which he had an inexhaustible fund. He had known all the great scientists of his age: Claude Bernard, Pasteur, Thellier, "the father of cold." I listened to this fascinating storyteller, who took such care to make himself understood by my very small daughters. He popularized the work of the century's great scientists, and threw light on their careers, while I dreamed about all the wonderful films that could be made! One Sunday, this oldster of 82 took my daughters to see the equipment he had used sixty years before in making his discoveries on the use of high-frequency currents for medical therapy, called "Arsonvalization" after him. This time, I was unable to resist the impulse to have everyone share in the joy, the privilege of such a lesson. I took my camera and filmed the demonstration along with the master's commentary. He took his Serpollet machine out of the garage, the one he had used while making his first experiments in the provinces, and drove it around himself before my camera. Then he drove his modern car over to the hospital, where I was able to make a filmic record of his visit to the department he had established. In this department, thousands of sick people have been nursed, given relief, or cured, thanks to the discoveries of this great scientist, who had related his marvelous story to two little girls.

The purpose of this film was not to teach science: it was designed to popularize the principles of a discovery, to describe the ways in which it can be used, and especially to give an example of a life devoted to disinterested research.

What a fine lesson, for instance, might be drawn from this thought expressed by M. d'Arsonval, which I have in his hand-writing, dated January 1936: "Because it shows us the lacunae in our knowledge, we should look upon science as a school of modesty and not of pride."

The completed film was accompanied by a commentary written by my friend Dr. Louis Chauvois, the master's friend and faithful collaborator, who painted a fuller picture of M. d'Arsonval's tremendous work. Nor did we neglect the life of the man himself, a very simple one, made up of curiosity and love. D'Arsonval liked to tell how he had played truant from school until he was twelve. But he had taken advantage of this unlimited freedom to educate himself on the outside world, to learn how to do things with his hands. "I learned how to learn from contact with life," he used to say. Thanks to this appren-ticeship, he was able, like Louis Lumière later on, to use his hands until the last day of his life to do the work his active brain directed. Abstract scientific research did not satisfy him unless it led to concrete results. He constitutes a splendid link with our great artist-craftsmen. They, too, could find no release from their dreams until they themselves materialized the dreams. We may thus find in all creative work a relationship with art and poetry because it concerns man's great dream in which he is ever in search of some new chimera, which he sometimes succeeds in capturing.

Here is another example, one among numerous others: How many people have ever heard of Dr. Banting? And yet his discoveries have saved hundreds of thousands of lives. Diabetes was an incurable disease before Dr. Banting, haunted by visions of the dead lying in hospitals, devoted his life to seeking a means of curing diabetics or at least of letting them live. He triumphed in the discovery of insulin.

A very fine American film shows the scientist's dramatic struggle against the disease. The story alternates between hope and disappointment. At last the day comes when the first experiment on man is to be made. The element of conscience is present. Like Pasteur, when he first tried his treatment for hydrophobia on the little Meister boy, Banting hesitates for a moment, then, confident, inspired by the noblest kind of courage, he makes his first human experiment with insulin.

An agony of fear ensues, until finally victory comes, the greatest victory of which man can boast: the victory of Life over Death. The patient is miraculously snatched back to life, and from that day on, children, adults, human beings by the thousands, are saved. Zinneman's film brings all this to life with an intensity of feeling that reveals the author's talent. One might be tempted to class this film in the dramatic genre. In my opinion, this would be a mistake because it must be accompanied by a lecture to provide the complementary information needed for a fuller explanation of the problem of scientific research involved. The film, as it stands, constitutes a vivid and sympathetic illustration from the human standpoint: it could not at the same time move its audience and enumerate a series of facts in time and space.

It should be the function of the lecture to relate faithfully the logical succession of steps in the discovery. In this case, the two determining factors: the discovery made by the pathologist Lancereaux, and by the French histologist Laguesse.

THE FIGHT FOR HYGIENE AND SOCIAL HYGIENE
AGAINST SOCIAL SCOURGES

Without abandoning this classification of films accompanied by lectures or commentaries, I would like to lay particular emphasis on the motion picture's function in hygiene, social hygiene, and prophylaxis.

In doing this work of public interest, the motion picture becomes part of the equipment of the social worker or the visiting nurse. In most cases, they will use and explain such films in order to educate and convince. They have the same great mission as those magnificent social workers who are the indispensable collaborators of the doctor. The film author who must see to the making of these films should go at it in the same spirit as the doctor and the visiting nurse. By that I mean he should, like them, be conscious of the greatness and manifold nature of his task. I am convinced that these films can only be made by a social worker or at least by someone who has lived in those surroundings and been deeply affected by them.

The visiting nurse must have the vocation to as great an extent as the doctor, whose work she complements; it is not a profession alone, but far more a trust, and the noblest of all.

I remember those splendid doctors of the Moroccan bled, all imbued with Lyautey's civilizing passion, transmitted to them by one of his most precious collaborators, Dr. Colombani.

Lyautey wrote to Clemenceau one day: "I will trade you four battalions for three doctors." Nor was this a fantasy but a true representation of fact. Lyautey's conquest of Morocco was due partly to the efforts of his doctors, who symbolized the whole theory of French colonization. I have kept a vivid recollection of all those French doctors, isolated in their distant posts, with their wives acting as nurses. They were surrounded by the gratitude and respect of the natives. The native tribes would come to submit to these great chiefs, whose only weapons were their lancets and syringes.

A perfect blending of functions performed by the doctor and

his visiting nurse, represented far, very far in the south by a courageous French couple.

Many similar examples could be found in the big cities of the home country. A famous doctor, ordinarily cold and almost inaccessible, would become human, show himself to be kind as well as efficient, the moment he stepped across the threshold of his own department at the hospital. There, too, beside the doctor, would be his indispensable auxiliary, the social worker. The latter would concern herself with the social situation of the patients, provide for the most immediate necessities with regard to their families, so as to assure them a maximum peace of mind during their treatment or convalescence.

Having lived in this stimulating environment which affords a truer criterion of human values, the film author will be competent to create films that will help the doctors and nurses accomplish their daily tasks.

First of all, the splendid work of the visiting nurse must be made known to the people who will benefit by it. This idea was very well brought out by a young American film author in his film *Day after Day*. Fred Stewart might have contented himself with showing dispensaries and card files. Instead, he preferred to bring these cards to life, each of them representing a human being, and to show the human side of social service. Those splendid lay saints, the visiting nurses, go their way nursing their patients, both physically and morally, combatting prejudice and bad habits. From dawn to dusk, and often at night, the visiting nurse fulfills her noble office. Her simplicity, her smiling kindness, light up her surroundings, inspiring confidence and hope.

In the same vein, my own film *The Sacred Veil* showed the even more extended field of the visiting nurse in the country. In one symbolic shot the nurse's veil was shown superimposed on the landscape of the small territory she covered, like a kind of reassuring protection against the enemy she fought: Disease.

My late regretted friend, Louis Forest, that king of common sense, who presided over the general committee of propaganda against tuberculosis, one day expressed his instructions in this manner: "Although there are many diseases for the doctor, there is only one health for the patient. Therefore, the struggle *against* disease should be resolved into a struggle *for health.*" One of the most important functions which should be performed by the educational film is precisely that of preventive education. It should, therefore, popularize elementary concepts of hygiene and will often give information to adults while seeming to address children.

But let me repeat once more that every aim must have a particular conception. If, for example, the film is designed to popularize the knowledge necessary to the proper functioning and preservation of the body, then it must be treated with greater precision than a film dealing with a more general topic. The choice of technical means will become far more important. Animated drawings, for instance, will make it possible to show what photography cannot.

One day I was led to make *The Human Engine Taught by the Automobile Engine,* based on the work of Dr. Louis Chauvois. Starting from the idea that all young people are interested in machinery and particularly in the automobile, my friend Dr. Chauvois and I drew up a complete parallel between the organs of the human engine and those of the automobile engine, naturally keeping it on a purely mechanical level. With this method, we were able to obtain some astonishing results concerning knowledge of the human mechanism. By showing the causes of engine trouble, such as the effects of alcohol on the human carburetor—the liver—we were able at the same time to teach the care and preservation of man's organs.

Many preventive films have been made and have had the most beneficial effects whenever they were planned and made with a definite aim in view and put to good use. Given these conditions, the screen has always accomplished its aim to preserve, by educating the public in favor of cleanliness, lung hygiene, household hygiene, etc.

The Struggle against Disease

Nevertheless, disease exists, the social scourges can devastate the world when man's folly alone does not help the Grim Reaper. Therefore, disease must be overcome, the social scourges limited, by bringing prophylaxis to the stricken quarters, while the sick must be brought to the doctor or to examining centers. This, too, is the task of the visiting nurse, just as it is also one of the motion picture's aims. The latter may accomplish its purpose by two different methods: one through fear, the other through confidence. It may give either the dark or the bright side of the picture.

So far as the social hygiene film is particularly concerned, some of them have gone in for deliberately instilling horror of a disease which they illustrate in its most repugnant details. But the film will be far more certain of achieving its aim if it awakens the desire for health, the desire for an integrated life, a confidence in the doctor, a faith in preventive and curative precautions.

One day I was asked to make a film on cancer. As always, I studied the question with specialists, in this case Professor Gustave Roussy and Professor Roger Leroux. I lived among the unfortunate patients suffering from this frightful scourge; but I acquired confidence in an institution where the disease was prevented, where the patients were nursed and often cured. I deliberately left out everything capable of inspiring fear and horror, retaining only the preventive and curative elements. For instance, I compared the patient at the start of his illness to a train headed along a bad track straight for disaster but halted in time by a friendly signal which sends it off in another direction, corresponding to the treatment given the patient before it is too late.

This experiment was remarkable in that it avoided all morbid aspects of the subject and emphasized the only really efficacious method, that of the early diagnosis.

Apart from this schematic arrangement, the film "lived" in the very human atmosphere of the daily consultation. Of the numerous people who came for consultations, many were given a negative diagnosis. The facts, realistically presented, highlighted the idea that a person does not automatically get cancer merely because he goes to be examined at a specialized center having the most competent medicines and most modern apparatus. In this way, the film accomplished two things: it popularized the need for a early diagnosis to ensure that every chance for a cure is taken; and it imbued the public with confidence, justified by the facts, in the doctor's skill and the excellence of the equipment placed at his disposal.

We obtained the following results. Previously, cancer centers had been avoided for the reason that the word cancer had become synonymous with incurable disease. Only as a last resort and in utter despair would people be driven to enter them. But after this film had made the rounds, the cancer hospitals became instead a symbol of hope and received an unprecedented influx of patients.

Naturally, I took advantage of this to give an example of the heroic lives of scientists who were exposing themselves to the dangers of X rays in order to save human lives. It was under these circumstances that I had the sad privilege of filming the ceremony at which the ribbon of the Legion of Honor was given to the great scientist Bergonié, who was to die a week later after having undergone a series of amputations.

Syphilis is another great enemy of public health, and here again the motion picture is called upon to perform the same function of popularizing and spreading confidence. This time, the task is both more delicate and easier. More delicate, because of the existing prejudices regarding venereal diseases, which must be overcome. Easier because this disease is curable. The same two methods are available here, one utilizing fear, the other based on confidence. I believe that the only effect of the former has been in the increased number of suicides, whereas the latter has always resulted in a lowering of the mortality rate. It should be stated here that films used to fight against syphilis ought to vary with the age and type of audience they are aimed at. They must therefore be planned and made in accordance with their use. We always come back to this fundamental law governing the motion picture.

For instance, the section in the Ministry of Public Health concerned with prophylaxis for venereal diseases and headed by Dr. Cavaillon put out a film designed solely for North African natives. It was a kind of animated picture book of cutouts in which the principal characters were a tiger and a native, the latter a victim of the disease. The tiger symbolized strength and virility, the man sickness and humiliating weakness. Then came the treatment at the dispensary, and the man, like the tiger, regained his strength, his agility, his pride.

The makers of this film had kept in mind, as should always be done, the psychology of the people at whom it was directed. The film exploited the proud and noble character of these native peoples for their own good. The Schleus can drape their tattered djeballas around them to such effect that they give the appearance of being great aristocrats. Their mental outlook is similarly constituted, for they respond to every appeal directed at their pride, at their dignity as strong men. The whole art of motion pictures should be founded on a psychological study of its audience, and that is why it is so important to distinguish between the genres.

Another example will illustrate how the same idea may be interpreted differently when the audience is different. In this case, the film was intended for a group of men who had been abruptly snatched from their normal surroundings and habits, and exposed to real dangers of contamination. The sudden raising of great armies, miraculously assembled in a year by the United States, wrenched hundreds of thousands of citizens from their customary existence. These soldiers, far from the girls for whose sake they had an obligation to keep themselves mentally and physically healthy, far from their wives and families, were sent to the four corners of the world and thereby exposed to the most natural, as well as the most dangerous temptations. The Health Service of the United States Navy has put out a particularly successful film which should be very effective. The doctor first reminds the men that they should resist their physical needs by making an appeal to the moral ties binding them to those they have left at home and for whom they are in duty bound to stay healthy. After this, he describes in a suitable commentary the various prophylactic methods that may be taken in such cases—more frequent than others—where physical needs are stronger than moral restraint. The film points out the dangers and shows the development of venereal diseases, with their casualties and their consequences. But it also points out the means, though altogether relative, by which they can protect and, eventually, cure themselves, provided they obtain treatment soon enough.

At the same time, the film constantly communicates a feeling of confidence in the doctor, who appears far more as a friend, someone to be trusted, than as a superior officer. This is a good example of a film that has been planned and made with a specific aim in view. Obviously, the effectiveness of such a film depends on how it is used. It should be shown only to a military audience. Shown in a theater before a mixed audience, it would have disastrous effects. Another proof that the motion picture is a two-edged weapon which must be handled with caution. Let us also remember that we are still dealing with films which are either preceded or followed by a lecture. The latter not only enables additional information to be imparted but also provides a better adaptation to the mentality of the audience.

Finally, let me take as a last example a film designed to give all young people of school age a general idea about this disease and to be used in connection with sex education. The aim here was a particularly delicate one which involved opening the eyes of the very young to one of the dangers that all normally constituted beings must face, and at the same time being careful not to rob the sacred act of life of its poetic splendor. Together with Dr. Louis Devraigne, head of the maternity section of the Lariboisière Hospital in Paris, I made a film called *There Were Three Friends,* in which we were able to describe this disease without destroying the deep faith in love and splendid idealism of the young. The story was quite simple; the action took place in the country, which enabled us to draw on the beauties of nature for the necessary breathing spells and sweeten our rather gloomy subject with a breath of fresh air from the peaceful countryside of the Ile de France with its demitint coloring. It was precisely those demitints which made up the film author's palette and allowed him to clothe the delicate points at issue without concealing them.

The film was used in numerous educational institutions, public, private, and religious, for postgraduate courses. It was an extremely edifying experience to read the letters written by parents to the people who organized these showings. I remember the mother of a family who wrote to the principal of the school her daughter was attending: "My husband and I had always wondered how we would warn our children about this terrible disease. I am grateful to you for providing the means. Now we talk about venereal diseases the same way we do about grippe or measles."

That was precisely what we aimed to do: get people to discuss it at home as naturally as they would other diseases. We believe that only the motion picture can ensure the success of this aim.

TUBERCULOSIS

In 1916, with the war in full swing, a survey conducted by the General Staff of the Army Health Services revealed that 100,000 men had been given medical discharges for tuberculosis. For the first time, the attention of the public authorities was focused on the effects and ravages caused by Koch's bacillus.

In 1917, the Rockefeller Foundation, informed about health conditions in France and willing to lend its material and technical support for an all-out fight against the disease, with its customary generosity set up a committee in Paris, entitled the American Committee for Protection against Tuberculosis.

Under the eminent guidance of Professor Seleskar Gunn, the Committee prepared an offensive against this other enemy, which was also claiming so many victims.

Besides the suggestions it made for launching an anti-tuberculosis campaign, such as setting up dispensaries, preventoriums, and sanatoriums, the Committee concentrated particularly on propaganda, which it organized in a manner quite novel to France. Posters, handbills, educational lectures were of course largely employed. Mobile groups of lecturers were created. A principal item of their equipment was the motion picture, an offensive weapon which they were able to use with good effect.

In 1918, the Rockefeller mission transferred all its personnel, headed by Lucien Viborel, in charge of propaganda, to the National Committee for Defense against Tuberculosis, which had been founded by Léon Bourgeois and which later continued its career under the guidance of André Honnorat.

Educational propaganda was immediately recognized to be an essential factor, and the directors formed a general committee of propaganda under the man most qualified for the position, Louis Forest, the great publicist, the "King of Common Sense."

Contrary to usual practice, this Committee did not degenerate into a mutual admiration society, but instead launched into an intensive campaign, with which I had the privilege to be associated.

The Americans had already proved the effectiveness of using motion pictures, although the films available at that time were of a rather primitive nature.

We undertook a serious study of the problems involved in using motion pictures in the fight against tuberculosis. Thanks to this definition of aims to which the various film genres corresponded, by 1940 we already had the finest collection of educational films anywhere in the world.

For our campaign, we adopted the following principles: to popularize science, and spread a reasonable degree of optimism. On these basic principles, we erected the different genres called for by the diverse campaigns to be undertaken.

Three chief aims were assigned: prevent, cure, and ensure prophylaxis to contaminated areas.

PROPHYLAXIS

First of all, the preventive approach was tried with films about individual and collective hygiene. These were followed by films suggesting the idea of establishing open-air schools and vacation resorts and describing how this could be done. Others gave a picture of the daily life that went on in the model preventoriums springing up all over the country, thus inspiring parents with confidence and asking them to follow the doctor's advice and temporarily place their ailing children in these establishments where they would receive preventive treatment.

Sometimes a film would be hurriedly made in order to avert a tragedy. The Lubeck accident was a case in point.

It is well known that Calmette and Guérin, of the Pasteur Institute, discovered the anti-tuberculosis serum (the B.C.G.). After years of laboratory experiments and tests on animals, this serum was used on children in hospitals, notably by Dr. Weil-Halle, Director of the Institute for Child Care of the Paris Faculty of Medicine. Without going into the purely medical history of the serum, we may assert that it had very appreciable effects and in some cases saved the lives of hundreds of children. Largely owing to skillful propaganda and to the fine work done by visiting nurses, the use of the serum was spreading in a satisfactory manner, when suddenly, in 1930, the Lubeck tragedy occurred. A girl working in one of the laboratories in that town was guilty of a tragic error when she handed the doctor a solution of the mother culture containing virulent bacilli instead of taking the real B.C.G. serum from its proper place. A great many babies, thus infected with virulent Koch's bacilli, died, and the serum was accused by its detractors of having been the cause of this mass killing. It was necessary to take immediate steps to deny this accusation, which had put a complete halt to using the serum, and thereby once more exposed to contagion the children whose protection it was meant to ensure. Hastily, we made two films. The first was strictly scientific and set forth with minute precision the different phases in the preparation of the serum in the laboratory of the Pasteur Institute by Professors Calmette and Guérin themselves. This film was a visual lesson in science, accurate right down to the smallest detail. It was sent to every laboratory in the world which distributed the serum to doctors, and since then no more incidents have been recorded.

The other film was designed for the general public, particularly for the use of members of the National Committee for Defense against Tuberculosis. It popularized the scientific work carried out in the laboratory—preparation and testing—and showed the results obtained with the serum by means of animated graphs giving the decrease in infant mortality from tuberculosis since its use. It was not long before the public had regained confidence, and, thanks to the film, doctors and visiting nurses were able to resume their work.

The task of persuading the sick to enter institutions providing treatment was made easier by films which told the truth about them and inspired confidence in the treatment and eventual cure. A great many films of this type were made, describing the life of the patients in sanatoriums such as Odeilho and Berck for tuberculosis of the bone, Passy-Praz-Coutant for tuberculosis of the lungs.

From the prophylactic standpoint, the visiting nurse was helped in her task of convincing by films which went into details about the necessity for taking all needed precautions in contaminated areas.

One of the most delicate and painful duties performed by the visiting nurse involved saving the newborn child of a tubercular mother or father.

Professor Léon Bernard had founded an Infant Placement Service, which saw to it that babies were placed with wet nurses distributed through the interior or around villages having medical centers equipped for examination.

Whenever one of the parents was tubercular, they would have to be persuaded to part with their child for a while and send it to some place where the service operated. When the father was the one affected, it was easier to obtain a decision because the mother, if healthy, could accompany the child to a house chosen for that purpose, remaining there during the nursing period. But when this involved separating the child from the mother, it may readily be seen that such a decision entailed a real sacrifice.

One film showed how the babies were cared for, how lovingly they were treated by the wet nurses, and what results were obtained. This made the task of the visiting nurses easier, and also showed the humane side of this splendid service to those who, at first sight, were able to see only its pitiless aspect.

This, then, is the task performed by the motion picture, as an instrument placed in the hands of the great men who have devoted their lives to the fight against one of the most terrible enemies of man's health.

CHILD CARE

To prevent, to inspire confidence in the treatment of disease, to protect healthy people from infection—these are the primary duties of the doctor and visiting nurse which the motion picture can help them perform.

Another task of the utmost importance involves teaching mothers and prospective mothers how to raise their children.

It was with this aim in mind that, several years ago, I made a film on child care with Dr. Devraigne, which was called *The Prospective Mother*. This consisted of a course on child care in seven lessons, designed for use in primary schools. But the presence of a number of characters, including a little girl of twelve, her mother, a newborn child, and an old aunt, who stood for old-fashioned notions, provided a tie-up, a plot, which enabled the film to be shown as a unit before special gatherings of the public. The action took place in a rural setting.

In this connection, I would like to mention, for its symbolic value, the co-operation I received from the Ministry of Agriculture. This is not quite as surprising as it may seem, for the minister at that time was a doctor. Indeed, Dr. Queille was fully prepared to understand the importance of teaching child care to the farmers' wives so that they would come to know as much about taking care of their babies as they already did about caring for calves.

The Prospective Mother achieved tangible results, both in teaching children at school and in educating the general public.

I would like to go into some detail about one of the experiments we made with this film. In a way, this example sums up the motion picture's tremendous social mission.

One day I received a letter from a big manufacturer in the north of France. This is what he wrote:

"We have just shown your film, *The Prospective Mother*, to the employees in our factories. We employ 2,000 women. We decided to conduct a poll. Nineteen questions were made up, and the workers were asked to answer them. Out of the 2,000 present, 1800 gave accurate answers to the questions asked.

"The answers to the last question were particularly edifying. We are happy to assure you that a perusal of these answers revealed that your film had done a great deal of good. We found that many of the young women possessed very fine sentiments and a true desire for maternity."

Our curiosity aroused, we asked the writer to send us a list of the questions as well as the replies, whereupon we received a folder, together with the following comment:

"Most of the answers, as you will see, reveal some very fine sentiments. Special note should be taken of the social environment in which we are situated; furthermore, you will see by the spelling and style of the answers that the average schooling received by our female workers is unfortunately far below the requirements for an elementary school certificate.

"Nevertheless, the film taught them something they would never have learned in books. If any further proof were needed of the motion picture's educational value, this would be it."

The first eighteen questions were all related to some particular point in the film. For instance:

"Name all the items of the layette in which the child is dressed by his sister. What important precaution must be taken before putting the child into his bath? What are the weight and length of the average child at birth? Can the mother drink milk? Why? What is the best milk for a nursing child? Where are nursing babies examined in your community?" And so forth.

The nineteenth question was phrased as follows: "What are your personal impressions about the film? Would you like to see it again in a year or two?"

Here are some of the answers to this last question. Their touching sincerity was even more apparent in the awkward writing of the original text.

A stenographer: "This picture is interesting from three different viewpoints. It can render a great service by persuading mothers of families to abandon certain outdated notions that leave much to be desired from the standpoint of hygiene. It also fills in the gaps left by a very inadequate instruction in child care. It gives us certain examples of the part hygiene should play in the fragile life of a child, for whom no precaution should be neglected. Many mothers would not be grieving for the death of their children if they had been able to see this film and make practical use of this lesson in child care. I would like very much to see this film in another year in order to be reminded of the general outlines and especially to note certain details which might have escaped me."

A winder: "It's really a piece of good luck for us workers to have a chance to learn something, especially about a subject of such interest to young girls. I think it was a real privilege that I could see it and even more that I could take the examination because it shows what poor little creatures we can produce in our ignorance as girl mothers. With all my heart, I thank those who give us such good advice and devote themselves to us. I would gladly see this film again, not in two years, but as soon as possible."

A spinner: "Sir, I am very glad to have seen the film: *The Prospective Mother* and to have learned how to dress and take care of a baby; though I am twenty years old, no one till now has given me or shown me the slightest idea of how a baby should be cared for. Thanks to this instructive film, if I am ever lucky enough to become a mother, I will know how to take care of it, dress it, nurse it, what to eat myself, and especially whether the food I give my baby is doing it any good. The film, *The Prospective Mother*, should be seen and its lesson put to use by every woman. I would like to see this film again in a year, and also, if possible, a film showing how to recognize the early symptoms of some infant diseases."

A piecer: "The film, *The Prospective Mother*, is very interesting and I thought it fascinating. It's also an instructive film that will be of interest to all women and spare a great deal of trouble and worry to prospective mothers who see it and conscientiously use it to good advantage. As for me, I will not have to go through the grief of losing a child because of carelessness and if I'm lucky enough to have a baby, I will closely follow the good advice given to us by the film, *The Prospective Mother*."

Another piecer: "I am very interested in the film. It made a big impression on me because I'm a mother with a little boy. I see that it's real and very instructive for a good mother of a family. Also I would ask to see it again as soon as possible in one year."

This is just one example in a whole series of experiments carried out during the last twenty-five years, which I have carefully jotted down and classified as scientific observations. My faith in the destinies of the motion picture does not derive from purely imaginative or intellectual sources. It stems from known results which confirm my use of the experimental method. That is both my reason and my excuse for quoting myself so often in the course of this book.

2. Independent Educational Films

It might be said with perfect truth that all film genres are educational, including even those designed for the general public. I have said that the first category, the one I have just been examining, was especially designed to appeal to the mind. But the experiment with *The Prospective Mother* proves that it is very difficult to make such a clear distinction between mind and heart. The maternal feelings of my cotton spinners were affected quite as much as their intellectual comprehension.

The educational film intended to be shown in theaters to the general public in most cases uses a plot, a story, in order to get its meaning across. The general public is made up of "the man in the street." This man is selfish; like all men, he is in a hurry; his fellow creatures push him around, and he pushes back. He goes to a theater to be diverted, not to be educated or to learn something. But this same "man in the street" has a heart, the same heart that beats in all the other men he passes in the street: a human heart.

This heart must be touched in order to educate the man. In short, these films are designed to popularize, to spread ideas that are capable of both arousing emotion and instilling education. I might say that they are propaganda films, had this word not been perverted in recent times by so much misuse. Their aim is to exalt the decent instincts lying dormant within the mob. To achieve our purpose, all the film has to do is to make this instinct come out. To make an impression on humanity, the film must itself be filled with humanity.

And to produce its effect on human feelings, it need not always be built around a story: a mere glimpse of life is usually more potent than an imaginative creation. A great educative concept may be emphasized by the charm of the images shown and the emotion they convey. I am thinking, for example, of a delightful, amusing, and touching film produced by Joe Losey and directed by John Ferno: A Child Went Forth.

The film has intrinsic artistic merit in the beauty of its images and in its presentation of a segment from the life of very small children. The children, shown in a completely natural state, are going about their chosen occupations, apparently without any supervision. The audience is never aware either of the camera recording their every movement or of the vigilant teacher, who nevertheless is there with them, invisible to the eye but present in spirit, mind, and heart.

Because this film possesses artistic qualities and is charged with emotion, it could be shown in theaters and interest the general public in the educational idea behind it. This idea is concerned with progressive education for children, which is so important to the molding of the future citizen—a citizen enjoying freedom of will and possessing characteristics of sincerity and honesty developed through contact with nature and in freedom. But a freedom conforming to the basic laws of social existence, that is, limited by the rights of others, his own duties, and the natural obstacles to be overcome.

This little film might therefore constitute a kind of prelude to a series of others or to a great work dedicated to democracy.

For years I have thought of making an educational film that would show young citizens the greatness of the democratic idea and the normal functioning of our institutions, that would make them realize how lucky they are to be free and remind them of the debt of gratitude they owe to their ancestors, who won that freedom for them.

Indeed, over a long period of time that word "democracy" had come to lose its true value due to the fact that it had become separated from the great principles for which it stood. People had forgotten to cling to those great spiritual values and to the democratic ideal, turning instead to political verbiage and electoral platitudes. The masses had even forgotten how republican institutions operated. And yet there must be an apprenticeship to freedom, one must be worthy of it and capable of preserving it.

Are we to believe that a young man or girl, on the threshold of twenty-one, suddenly and miraculously becomes endowed with all the necessary qualities for using the sacred right to exercise his civic duties? Far from it! Prospective citizens must be trained to exercise their power, they must be given the most elementary notions of their responsibilities. They must be made fit to live in society, and this can be done only through the experience acquired in life!

This is called civic education, and the state has the duty to impose it. Any citizen may be manufactured to suit a given regime: the totalitarian regimes have given ample proof of this.

It is easier to develop the base instincts potentially present in the children of men than to combat them and mold a youth which is enamored of freedom. It is more difficult to arouse love than hate. But the task is also a nobler and a higher one; the state must of necessity concern itself with pointing out to the young the bright path they should follow.

The film I dreamed about would have attempted to revive the democratic ideal by restoring its true greatness. It would have reminded young citizens of the unwritten debt of gratitude they owe to their ancestors for having enabled them to live in freedom. They would have learned the true balance between duties and rights, without which there can be no lasting democracy.

Freedom is a natural good, as much a part of man as the fresh air he breathes. Good health is never appreciated as much as when there is sickness. In the same way, when life is all happiness, there comes a time when the reasons for that happiness are lost to sight and then it will not be long before the happiness itself is lost.

The film would have served both as a barometer, which never remains unalterably set to fair weather, and as a salutary warning of the danger threatening free governments.

As a matter of fact, I never imagined that such a theme could be treated in a single film but rather in several frescoes, each one being a tryptich whose panels would have shown England, the United States, and France.

Had my dream come to life, it would have taken the form of films with an educational theme, treated in such a way that they could have been shown on the usual theater program.

This film genre derives its power of attraction from its artistic and emotional qualities and can be accepted by the public only if it does not attempt to preach.

Indeed, great care must be taken not to deceive the public by confusing the genres, lest a very serious prejudice be created against the motion picture as a whole. When going to the movies, the public is perfectly willing to be given an opportunity for reflection, but it demands to be entertained; it is willing for the film to suggest ideas, but it refuses to be lectured. On the other hand, it is disposed to enrich its knowledge, provided it is called together for that express purpose. It does not want to be taken by surprise.

Referring to an article by Dr. Jamerson and Dr. Pinthus which appeared in *The American Scholar,* I find the following account:

"About two years ago, a Hollywood company planned in conjunction with the C.I.O. to present against the background of an entertaining story the growth of the worker from the status of a wage slave to that of a free individual and union member; but after a great deal of inquiry John L. Lewis was told something like this: 'The wives of our members want to see Shirley Temple. When they want to hear about labor questions, they go to meetings.' Consequently, the picture was never made."

These union men were perfectly justified; they were thus expressing their desire to be treated in all fairness, as free men. They had the right to demand special educational meetings and decline to accept an education thrust upon them without warning.

It must be said that this desire for knowledge, so often expressed by workers, has never been given serious consideration by the unions. There, as elsewhere, the fact has never been taken into account that instruction without education cannot be assimilated.

Films have been used to record a strike and describe its technique. This was merely a question of actualities, little more than a newsreel. But the strike itself is only the result of a social and economic conflict; it is sometimes a necessary weapon in defense of the right to live, but it does not provide a solution for the problem. Only the individual's moral and spiritual value and the consciousness he has of his duties can confer on him superiority and authority in the defense of his rights.

It is important to keep the workers posted, inform them about the larger issues of the day concerning political economy or the advances that are constantly modifying world conditions. It is important to develop education in unionism itself so that the great principles on which these groups are based do not gradually become lost to sight. Finally, it is important that this necessary education contribute to molding the rank and file.

The experience I went through with the C.G.T. in 1936 was conclusive. The mass of workers knew nothing about the problems which would often come up in dramatic fashion. Hence, it followed that in most cases the union ballot was taken in as much ignorance as the political ballot, with the artificial talents of "skillful" orators exerting a decided influence. The devotion and sincerity of the ranks could not take the place of the knowledge that is so indispensable to the leader, whatever position he may hold, and I am convinced this is the chief reason for the failure.

Trade unionism is a movement which has made a vast contribution to the material liberation of workers and which should constitute one of the finest foundations of future society. It will not accomplish its aim unless it becomes cognizant of the responsibility incumbent upon it in the great struggle that will have to be undertaken against ignorance. The motion picture is ready to lend its strength in this struggle, provided it is wisely and competently directed.

But, if the unions have sinned through defaulting on their obligations, industrial leaders have used the motion picture for tendentious ends and in a paternalistic spirit the danger of which has only recently been recognized.

If the men directing such groups are true leaders in the finest sense of the term, which justifies authority on the grounds of moral, intellectual, or technical superiority, then they should be willing to provide the people who elected them with mental as well as material benefits and give them an opportunity to enrich their store of knowledge about the world.

In short it is the duty of the state, as well as of the group movements, to guarantee culture to the members of the community.

Léon Bourgeois, our great statesman who, long before the founding of the League of Nations, drafted a covenant, stated a long time ago: "Democracy is not in the flower and the fruit, but it is inevitably at the roots, and the roots must draw their nourishment from a rich and ever newly fertilized soil."

This tree of democracy, today shaken by a storm yet still hardy and flexible as La Fontaine's reed, must be able to find the nourishing sap even in its most distant rootlets.

It is in this sense that the motion picture must carry out its mission, bringing to this frail human plant the nourishing sap that will ensure its permanent growth.

Although the motion picture in general does not expressly state such an intention, it does take on a specifically educational character in the genres we have just been discussing. Later on, we shall see that every genre has its own particular aim but that all of them must tend to promote man's spiritual growth.

4 DOCUMENTARIES

I. The Promotional Film

THE TERM "documentary film" has been used in so indiscriminate and confusing a manner that it has lost its true meaning. The finer sense of the word "documentary" has been distorted to embrace all kinds of productions, often of inferior grade, and has lumped together under a single heading teaching films, promotional films, films of documentation, and films of naturalistic art.

The films that usage has incorrectly grouped under the heading of "documentaries" actually comprise a number of quite distinct genres whose only common bond is the fundamental law of "selection" by which all films are governed.

Nevertheless, the various film genres fall into a natural and logical sequence which may easily be visualized so long as the observer has the proper perspective and abandons all preconceived notions. The motion picture's aims are all concerned with man himself and his spiritual or material activities. Therefore, it is most important to determine what makes man great and to show respect for the nobler side of his activities.

Love for one's occupation is an essential condition of happiness. This should be written down below the work charter, by virtue of the moral law which states that science did not invent machines for the abasement of some and the profit of others but in order to lighten man's burden.

Big industry should, both as a duty and in its own interest, allow man to keep his initiative and responsibility, so that he may preserve this love for his work upon which his life is based.

All work done lovingly and conscientiously gives joy to him who does it, is useful to others, and contains joy in itself. Under these conditions, all work is truly a human creation.

Man must create in order to live.

That is why love for his work is a basic element of man's nobility.

One day, I was visiting a school for salespeople run by the Chamber of Commerce in Paris. In one class, I heard a grocer talking to his pupils about his trade, his products. For this man, a grocery store was his nobility, the distinctive sign of his humanity. He was talking about the work he had done all his life with love.

Whenever human feelings are expressed with such sincerity, they are bound to affect our own emotions. Fascinated, I listened and immediately fell in love with grocery stores. In another class, I listened to a hardware merchant showing his pupils how to tie up a package of nails; it was like listening to a kind of poem. That day, I developed a real appreciation for hardware.

By performing very simple tasks, but performing them with love, the grocer and the hardware merchant were ennobling their trades. The same is true of an art that is all too often misunderstood but nonetheless possesses qualities of greatness, beauty, and aliveness: THE ART OF ADVERTISING.

Obviously, when an actress loses her necklace or lap dog in a taxi, the solid citizen who reads the account of this incident at breakfast will shrug his shoulders and comment cynically, "Just a publicity gag," using the term as a synonym for bluff.

But publicity, or advertising, is quite another thing: *it is the most vivid manifestation of man's activity.*

The chief accusation leveled at advertising is that it takes up too much space. I admit that I have often been annoyed, particularly while on a trip to Morocco, to see the entire slope of a hill decorated—if that is the proper term—with an advertisement for automobile tires, laid out on the ground in white stones. Similarly, in the vicinity of New York, I have been disagreeably surprised at the quantity of billboards concealing the superb landscape.

But, provided the beauties of nature are respected, I can appreciate the thrill of seeing man proclaim his deeds throughout the world, in the open country, on city walls—as on magnificent Broadway in New York, sparkling with animated lights —and even in the very sky.

What man has never felt a surge of emotion on reading the name of some product which an airplane spells out across the sky in letters of smoke? Although the letters disappear almost immediately, for a minute, way up there, they have proclaimed that hundreds of men on the ground below are occupied in manufacturing this product, are earning their living from it, are making themselves useful to others, are putting their best into it—in a word, are working.

Advertising, whether done with smoke, with printed words, or with pictures, is primarily *a sign of work.* It is something to gladden the eyes and the heart.

The general lack of knowledge about the art of advertising has usually been expressed by scorn directed against promotional films. For many æsthetes, this is the lowest form of the motion picture and should be forcibly divested of all artistic qualities. Before attempting to dispel this prejudice and all the better to do so, I shall have to go back to the origins of the promotional film, that is, to the picture poster.

The animated picture was born of the inanimate picture. Is it really inanimate? There are such vivid posters that a single glance in passing suffices to leave a lasting imprint on our mind.

Pictures are used intensively for advertising because their power of suggestion is stronger than that of mere words.

Children often provide us with the most striking examples of our psychological phenomena.

I know a little girl, a rebel against all book learning, who would certainly have had a hard time learning by heart a written definition of the mechanics of a solar eclipse, but who thoroughly understood a visual representation of it, which she illustrated in her sketchbook by a smiling, yellow moon partly covering a scowling sun, green with jealousy.

She certainly did not acquire this clear understanding of the majestic movements of astral bodies from her studies in astronomy, but rather from frequent contemplation of the advertisement for a well-known wax, prominently displayed all over the city.

The picture posters exhibited in that "people's gallery" which is the street are not just billboards. They are often works of art having their own rules, determined by what they are intended to do.

"To surprise" is the psychological aim of advertising. Therefore, a poster must be a surprise to our senses. It must capture our attention forcibly, in a single glance. To do this, it assaults us through its design, through its colors.

No matter how varied and fanciful the design of a fixed image may be, it cannot hold as much surprise for us as a moving image, for the latter's very motion gives it an advantage. This is amply proved by the crowds that always collect to see an advertising film being shown in the street, whereas there is never a crowd before a poster, no matter how original it may be. This lifelike quality of the moving image has been imitated by the fixed image.

But motion pictures have had an influence on the poster; we need only look around us to see the proof. We have all seen the wheels of an express shown on posters in railway stations and revolving at eighty miles an hour. We have seen a picture of the rubber heels on the shoes of a man viewed from below in perspective, from his feet to his head, which is just what the human eye would see if it were to imitate the vision of the camera eye, which revolves each object around in all directions so as to extract its full value. The poster shown in this book, which was done by the well-known artist Jean Carlu, expresses all the muscular dynamism of a powerful hand, seen in "close-up." The artist has caught and held a single instant of the movement in order to express the power of human labor.

But, if the poster often borrows its methods of attack from

the motion picture, it also has other weapons that are specifically suited to it.

Having only a brief moment to impress itself on us, the poster makes use of color. That is its chief triumph. It is curious to note how it contrives to capture us altogether, solely through our sense of sight. For instance, a poster which, during the hottest part of the year, urges us to drink some iced beverage or other, manages, merely by picturing the blue-green color of the drink, to convey a sensation of coolness that is full of suggestion.

We see, therefore, that the promotional film originates in the poster. Far from suppressing the latter, it has endowed it with life and movement. The motion picture and the poster are two different agents which complement each other. It is proper that we should acknowledge their relationship.

Summing up, we may say that advertising is the art of convincing. The art of convincing is related to the art of teaching and educating; this tie-up brings us to the highest function of the promotional film, which, originating in the poster, reaches its purest form when allied to the teaching and educational film and even, at times, to the dramatic film.

In general, purely promotional films have a psychological aim in trying to attract attention to an advertisement by using humor. This type is really more of an animated poster than a motion picture. However, in recent years we have had animated cartoons and puppetoons in color which were of real artistic interest. Some of these would transport their audience into fairyland, such as the film *The Sleeping Beauty*. These films are naturally quite short; so, if they are to yield any returns, they cannot hope to keep up the illusion for very long. The Sleeping Beauty could not afford to sleep too long, on account of the wine, which after all she was supposed to be selling. I repeat that this is nothing more than animated advertising, but often not without artistic value.

Industrial, or more generally subsidized, promotional films are put out by manufacturers or organizations who want their customers to see their equipment, how their products are made and their machinery operated, or their organizations.

Such films are related to the educational films and have the same aim: to convince. This similarity of aims should be accompanied by a similarity in technique, characterized by clarity of thought and beauty of form. The film should afford real entertainment.

But there is more to it than that! In order to educate, one must first learn; in order to make known, one must know oneself; in order to convince, one must be convinced.

Unfortunately, the making of this type of film has all too often been left in the hands of incompetents, even of amateurs. But it is not enough merely to have a cameraman take a few yards of film haphazardly. With such a method, a machine, for example, would come out as a gray, black, or white spot. The photographer would have succeeded in capturing only the shape of the machine, not its soul.

Life does not allow itself to be captured that way.

The film author should first of all be a specialist in teaching films. They are an excellent school where he will learn how to study, dissect, and collaborate with specialists in the subject to be treated. The author should then study his theme with technicians, spend hours observing each machine in operation, so that he will understand its life and be able to break it down into pictures that will re-create on the screen the functioning of this living organism.

Besides being instructive, such a series of images should offer real entertainment value. In addition to being clearly comprehensible, the image should present a pleasing appearance, charming the eye with its light, surprising it with its novelty. So long as its intellectual content is not affected, it may show the most ordinary object in a novel light, throw it into relief through the use of contrast. This is what constitutes film technique and provides the audience with that element of surprise which attracts and holds their attention, in the promotional film as well as in the teaching film, both of which, as we have seen, draw their inspiration from the psychology of the poster—a common psychology, being nothing more than a profound knowledge of the human soul.

In this genre as in all film genres, the composer's collaboration is of the greatest importance. I once made a film about erecting a skyscraper, for which my friend Jean Wiener wrote a musical accompaniment that was far more eloquent than any spoken commentary would have been! For example, one scene showed a workman climbing way up into the sky as he clung to a girder. His progress was accompanied by a continuous rolling of drums, such as is heard in the circus during a dangerous performance. This accompaniment heightened the dramatic impression created by the shot, right up to the moment when the man, having reached the top of the skeletal framework, allowed a thin spiral of blue smoke to escape from his pipe into the immense void of the sky. Similarly, the tiny, antlike silhouette of the worker emphasized the enormity of the task compared with man's insignificance.

We may easily see that certain lessons can be drawn from this type of film: lessons about things, documentary material, thoughts on the greatness of man. Through constant familiarity with the world that surrounds us, we end up by not seeing it at all. Only a slight correction in our vision is needed to make us discover everything anew.

We could cite any number of industrial advertising films which besides trying to sell a product also teach the spectator something. A film produced by the Sodium Nitrates Company of Chile, for instance, was a real lesson in the growing and harvesting of wheat. In all fairness, it mentioned the advantages of other fertilizers, advising when to use them, and assigned to its rightful place the judicious use of sodium nitrates. This film was shown throughout every country, accompanied by agricultural experts, and helped considerably to increase the yield and quality of agricultural products.

There we have advertising in its finest and truest form, the kind of advertising that should be shown to all who wish to make it synonymous with bluff and falsehood.

The printed bill and picture poster can lie and make good publicity for a poor product, through the imagination of the writer and painter. But a machine cannot be guilty of lying.

A product of man's brain, it performs its prolific evolutions by means of a series of gears symmetrically arranged according to the inventor's specifications. The camera records the machine's magnificent rhythms just as they are, without any opportunity to make them lie. But this same camera must be directed by the brain of an artist and placed at every angle and in every light that will give this mechanical reality a living and æsthetic interpretation.

Whenever there is a question of showing man's tremendous labors in compelling nature's elements to serve him, the very power of reality will brush away all falsehood. For instance, a film might show, as J.-C. Bernard has so well done, the superhuman work of engineers, contractors, and workmen engaged in building a dam, which holds and canalizes the hydraulic power that will give life to entire areas, from the tiniest hamlet to the largest city.

Advertising—the art of making known. What better means of giving man a sense of his power, his greatness, and also of his insignificance in the scale of nature!

Commercial tourist films are not planned and made in complete freedom by artists whose sole purpose is to describe their impressions of the trip. Instead, they are films subsidized by the state or by groups of local interests, such as the hotel business, watering places, and so forth.

If these films are made intelligently, that is, in such a way that their advertising content is based solely on the facts and artistic quality of the scenes, they will accomplish their purpose far better than if they are full of crude advertising that is bound to render them ineffective.

Intelligence of conception, pictorial beauty—all that has been strengthened since the introduction of *sound* into the motion picture. I have already alluded to the importance of the musical accompaniment, but the tourist film may employ sound effects as well as words to advertise through auditory suggestion. For example, the silence or musical harmony of a summer resort, contrasted with the discordant clamor of a big city, will give the audience a longing for peace and quiet. And how feeble the attraction of a poster inviting us to spend the summer at the seashore, compared with the twofold lure of a moving picture with sound effects, which allows us to hear the roar of the surf and watch it break on the shore, inviting us through all our senses to plunge in and be cool!

I can hear someone object that all this is poetry and philosophy rather than advertising. But there is just as much poetry, philosophy, psychology, and dramatic talent in advertising as there is commercial good sense!

All life is contained in advertising! The motion picture and advertising may find their material in all products of human activity and may serve to interpret the life of a locomotive boiler as well as that of a gramophone needle. In trying to persuade us, it may play on all our emotions, taking advantage of our surprise, our joy, and our desires.

Which of man's strongest desires can we conjure up through film? The desire for movement, the pleasure of traveling. The motion picture's role in advertising can and should be to suggest the culture or charm of a country. Like the herald who, in medieval times, used to stride through the streets, calling, "Oyez! Voyez!" its advertising slogan should be "Listen and watch!"

Thus conceived, the advertising film may be used for teaching, as part of that group of films I have called "the classroom window opened on life." It should be recognized, however, that this type of film has been abused, in school as well as in post-graduate education. Without any discrimination, films have been shown which were unscrupulously and inartistically made, which were confusing and overloaded with advertising. A more careful selection should have been made and the diversity of genres taken into account.

Nevertheless, it is true that the motion picture and advertising cover a field limited only by the known universe and that in their purest form they may contribute to making men more conscious of their interdependence and thus promote the idea of community. Occasionally, human beings and their reactions may be introduced into simple lessons about things, machines, and facts. Such films, while remaining frankly commercial, are closely related to the theatrical genre. It often happens that an industrial group will endeavor to widen its market by showing proof of its social utility; for instance, by creating a state of mind suitable to take full advantage of scientific progress. Apart from questions of economic interest, this type of film will aim to create a better organization of social life.

In this case, intellectual conviction must be accompanied by moral conviction. It is no longer a question of making people familiar with an industry: they must be persuaded of its social utility. Emotional conviction can be obtained only through using emotions; hence the intervention of human characters exhibiting their emotional reactions within the framework of a plot.

We have now reached the highest level of the promotional film. And yet, even at this level, it must not repudiate its relationship to the poster. There are posters which, in a single picture, summarize a whole plot. Take, for instance, the poster advertising a certain make of fountain pen, which shows a young man trying to sketch a building with his pen and brandishing the latter in a desperate burst of energy, as though it were an ice ax and he were climbing a mountain — the mountain of daily business.

In this single gesture, there is all the drama of the struggle for a living. A definite atmosphere of human emotion has been created around an object with the aim of capturing our attention more securely through an appeal to our emotions.

It must be admitted that very few films of this genre have been successful, largely due to the fault of the people subsidizing them. I once saw a film on housing. The work showed indisputable traces of the author's talent, but his scenario had been so mutilated by his clients that nothing was left but a puerile and nauseating little tale. Not only had the film been completely spoiled because of this, but the commercial idea behind it had been distorted until it produced exactly the opposite effect to the one it was meant to produce.

Those are the motion picture's relations with advertising. That relationship has resulted in this first film genre belonging to the class of *documentaries*.

But because each of the motion picture's particular tasks is bound up with its general mission, the latter may be said to comprise "advertising," in the finest sense of the word. Every film of whatever kind is advertising for the country that produces it, by the mere fact that it shows that country's landscape, its tourist beauty spots, its automobile makes, its fashions for men and women. For this reason, if judiciously employed, it will be able to contribute, within its own particular sphere, to facilitating cultural and economic exchanges among nations.

5

DOCUMENTARIES

2. The Film of Life

THE TERM "documentary" becomes too restrictive in cases where a film is called upon not only to express man's activities but to transfer life itself to the screen. The universe in which man moves, the visible or invisible beings moving around him, the eternal and constant transformations of nature herself— these are the infinite themes to be sung by the creator of so-called documentary films. Everyone who has devoted himself to this film genre has suffered from the derogatory meaning attached to this far too general term and has sought a more precise definition. I cannot take the time here to discuss the numerous suggestions made by writers who, themselves at a loss for a definition in reviewing a film, would invent their own. Most of the time, the qualifying term used was an accurate one but its significance was not broad enough to designate a genre. Some of the terms invented were quite suggestive, such as that of "Think Films," which Bosley Crowther so aptly picked in his column for the *Times*. But this term has the disadvantage of creating a confusion with the educational film or of approaching the definition for "shorts," a word used—quite incorrectly as a matter of fact—to designate an inferior production.

Following the classic method of "first defining," let me suggest this formula: "What have come to be known as documentary films are those which *reproduce life in all its manifestations*— the life of man, of animals, of nature—without the assistance of

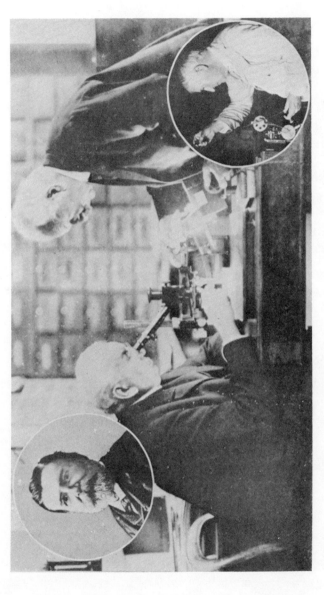

LEFT INSET: Dr. Marey. CENTER: August and Louis Lumiere. RIGHT INSET: Edison.

The motion picture's influence on the poster: Jean Carlu shows a close-up of muscular dynamism (see page 70).

professional actors or studios and on condition that the film represents a free artistic creation."

If we accept this definition, we are led to name this genre *Films of Life.*

Already, we have gone far beyond that designation of "documentaries," which, taken in its narrow sense, ought to include nothing but documentary matter, nothing but facts; dependent in most cases on photographic art. But actually, we are concerned with something quite different, since the chief condition imposed is *free artistic creation.* This condition allows us to differentiate this film genre from all the preceding genres because the latter have certain obligations laid on them at the very start.

Teaching films must observe rules which determine their use for pedagogic ends. Educational films have the responsibility of popularizing very definite ideas or principles. Advertising films must pay heavy tribute to the company or organization subsidizing them. *Films of life* should be real works of art and, like all works of art, be produced in freedom.

If the responsibilities placed on teaching and advertising films are justified, the same cannot be said about the restrictions imposed on the free artistic creation of films of life. These restrictions may result from a political regime, such as those we have noted in countries where authoritarian governments have been established. In these cases, Art is enslaved and forced into serving the cause of propaganda. Before the advent of Nazism and Fascism, Germany and Italy produced some very fine films of life. As soon as the New Order came into being, this type of film went into an artistic decline and eventually expired altogether. This in spite of the fact that film authors were able to make use of technical means hitherto unknown. Sound and photography left nothing to be desired, but the spirit had died; the films were no longer a living art but only a series of photographs, as dead as picture postcards. If, by any chance, the film did live, it lived only to spread faith in the man-god, to exalt the triumph of might over right. This type of propaganda would seize on any pretext. I remember having seen a film in Rome on the harvest. The photography was superb. The composition was excellent. But something kept bothering me all through the film, something I couldn't lay my finger on. I found out what it was at the very end. In a last bucolic scene, the wheat sheaves were stacked into shocks to form a vast tableau intended as a symbol of work in peacetime. Suddenly, a close-up showed the sheaves separating, turning into fasces, and revealing the ludicrous clown face of little Mussolini! This unexpected finale had been bothering me all through the film because the director had not been allowed to create in freedom and had been obliged to work under constraint. Consequently, what the audience saw was not his intention but someone else's.

What a tragic situtaion it is for an artist to be placed in such circumstances! To be in full possession of all the means and yet be unable to give free expression to his thoughts or feelings produces a revolt within the artist which often takes the form of a defense reaction. Dictators are thoroughly familiar with this psychology of the artist and thinker. That is why they persecute intellectuals, artists, and all creators until they have managed to enslave thought. Happily, "the mind" does not allow itself to be thus enslaved; there is no method of persecuting that will prevent a man from thinking. And, if the means of expression may temporarily be subjugated, sooner or later thought will resume its flight into infinite space. The magnificent example provided by the resistance in France and the other occupied countries is sublime proof that thought is incorruptible. In the case of the motion picture, which can be produced only in the full light of the studio or outdoors, the dictators were able to suppress its means of expression altogether, but they could not prevent patriots from thinking, they could not deprive them completely of their means of expression in the clandestine press; never have poets been as prolific as during that time, never have they given clearer expression to the soul of the French people.

Restrictions on the freedom to create may also derive from an economic system. We have seen enough examples of this in the democracies themselves.

It is well known that for several years the film industry has followed the practice of putting out double features, that is, the showing of two major films on the same program. Sometimes, it has even gone so far as to alter the standard speed of projection in order to show three features together. Aside from the fact that this practice is really detrimental to the films thus shown, it also encourages the production of low-grade films and constitutes an obstacle to the circulation of films of life in the larger theaters. The result of this situation is that it has become practically impossible to write off the costs of production and that sooner or later the film of life director is compelled to go back to making subsidized films.

When a film of life does find a place on a program, it is rarely shown in its original form. It is mutilated, condensed, deprived of its vital spark, its emotional qualities. Incredible as it may seem, the industry has not yet realized that the more a film of life is developed the greater its appeal. Whatever is not clear, whatever is incomprehensible, soon becomes boring. We have all been treated to those brief glimpses of human activities in which mysterious machines are momentarily flashed on the screen, in which men are seen going through enigmatic motions. When the film is over, the spectator has no more understanding of what he has seen than he had in the beginning and feels quite certain the whole thing has been a waste of time. On the other hand, when he is given a chance to follow the logical development of a film in which the subject—for instance, some type of professional work—has been treated at length, his attention does not wander and he can absorb the film without getting tired. For that reason it is not a paradox to say that the shorter a film of life is the longer it seems. Only if the subject is treated at length will the spectator's intelligence and imagination be captured and will he be made to lose the sense of time. So long as film of life authors are given the opportunity to respect these essential truths, they will be able to continue, as they have in the past, to produce astonishing masterpieces.

The film industry should realize that in doing this it is acting against its own interests and not carrying out its responsibility toward society.

It is acting against its own interests because in every theater there is a large audience for films of life: *its leaders need only go to movies themselves once in a while* to ascertain this fact.

It hurts its own interests by drying up the purest, most select source of recruitment for prospective film authors and cameramen.

It is not carrying out its responsibilities toward society because it discourages young enthusiasts with budding talents, who have no other means of expressing themselves.

Finally, and most important, it prevents the screen from carrying out one of its noblest aims.

I have good reason to believe that these conditions will change because the economic system itself will undergo a transformation and particularly because the war has everywhere created a network of 16-millimeter projectors, thus forming circuits independent of the theaters.

The young film director, therefore, has in the past found it extremely difficult to work unhampered. Only those with unquenchable faith and well-tempered minds have been able to throw off the shackles, and perhaps to some extent this has been an advantage. The budget problems confronting directors of these films oblige them in many cases to do everything themselves. Consequently, they must be thoroughly familiar with their profession and its technique, that is, with their medium of expression. The scarcity of funds, together with all kinds of difficulties, make the film of life a splendid school through which all prospective film authors should pass.

There is also something else the film maker can learn in this school, quite apart from technique. He will be attending the school of life, which is the very foundation of all motion pictures. Accordingly, he will be able to determine his own particular talents. Not everyone has the gift of being able to create his own imaginary world and give it an objective reality; we might even say that such cases are exceptional. On the other hand, the young film maker who starts his career already endowed with sensibility, feeling, and taste, will find the means to externalize his artistic and creative temperament by coming as close to nature

as possible. In doing this, he will have every chance of trans-
mitting his sensibility to the public he wishes to reach. If he is
incapable of conceiving miracles, the maker of moving pictures
will have a far better chance of discovering beauty if he goes
to nature than if he locks himself up in his study to agonize
over romantic or dramatic lucubrations. I want to emphasize
this point in particular because the artistic future of the motion
picture will depend on the care we take in preparing the young.
This is a question which has always preoccupied me and to
which I have devoted a large part of my time. It is tied up with
the general problem of educating the young. Indeed, it is the
school that should teach the young to regard life with confidence,
faith, and love but at the same time enable them to discover
what path they should set out upon so that their own happiness
and that of the community as a whole will be ensured. For this
to be accomplished, they must be given a taste for work, perseverance, a respect for the knowledge they acquire, and a will-
ingness to receive it from those who already possess it.

I must say that the generation which grew up between the
two wars was quite unprepared for life and little conscious of
the value and dignity of work. The motion picture in particular
appeared to the young as a sort of paradise peopled with brilliant
stars in which, to become a director, all one had to do was to
pick up a little capital at Fouquet's Bar and thereafter relax in
an armchair. Very few of the young people who came to consult
me took advantage of my advice telling them to go to our fine
national school of professions in the rue de Vaugirard and make
a serious study of technique, without which there can be no
free expression of talent. However, there were some who did,
and they are enough for me to retain all my faith in youth.

Evidently, the same problem exists everywhere, for I went
through the same experience in the United States and met with
identical results.

Some time ago, a young man invited me to see a short film he
had made on his own capital. When I acknowledged that his
work had some good qualities, he asked me the following
question: "I know that I'm no genius, and I'm not fooled by my

friends' compliments. I only wanted to ask you what I can do to become a good director of documentary films."

Touched by his sincerity and obvious desire to learn, I began to think out loud in front of him. I recalled my own feelings one morning many years ago when I rang the doorbell of a private house in Neuilly. My hands were shaking, I hesitated before pressing the bell, and it was all I could do not to stutter when I asked the old servant who came to open the door whether I might see M. Louis Lumière. I was shown into a huge room bearing more of a resemblance to a curiosity shop than a laboratory. Among a quantity of apparatus, tools, and notebooks, I finally discovered the master, who was filing a piece of metal, just as a fine artisan might have been doing. M. Lumière, like M. d'Arsonval, himself manufactured the pieces he needed for his work. After he had taken a measurement, the great scientist turned to me and asked, "What do you want, young man?" I was even more frightened, but he smiled at me encouragingly and I was able to tell him that I wanted his advice with regard to my career. Louis Lumière kept me for an hour during which time he encouraged me not to abandon the study of technique until I had fully mastered it. After this, I often went back to ring the bell of that old house in Neuilly. I never forgot my master's advice, which has exercised an influence over my whole professional career, and that is why I, too, have endeavored to help young people who ask me for guidance. Once more I tried to convince a young man that without technique it is impossible to give expression to an art. I defined for him the cardinal points which, in my opinion, form the very basis of all apprenticeship.

"Bear in mind Louis Lumière's advice: don't abandon technique too soon, always keep up with the changes made by progress. Learn the theory and practice of photography and all the problems of shooting and editing. To do this, work your way up the ladder, in the workshop, as cameraman's assistant, as cameraman. But while you are going through all these stages don't ever forget that you want to become a director, and later a film author. Exercise your mind by observing man and nature, develop the psychological sense that you will need so much in order to become a film author. Finally, note down your observations and experiments as practice in writing. Don't think too much about the studio. Become an assistant to some good film of life director. There is no better school.

"When you have got to know your trade backward and forward, you may begin to express yourself; and, if you show talent, courage, perseverance, if you get results with limited means, then you have not lost your time; you will have become an author of films of life, and you will take your place among the numerous crews that will be needed more and more to create one of the finest genres of the motion picture."

Where should the film of life be placed in the hierarchy of animated pictures?

In my opinion, it forms a natural link between the school and postgraduate educational film and the theatrical film.

Naturally, care should be taken not to confuse the teaching film with the film of life. But the latter, which in a way is a lesson without the expressed intent, brings out all the emotional and moving qualities that a teaching film may contain.

But the film industry, which advertises in good faith: "This week, great sensational drama," with the names of big stars from Hollywood or other places, has not the slightest suspicion that the little film of life which tells the story of how live wood becomes paper through man's industry is more sensational than the adventures of an imaginary princess who takes five reels to fall in love with someone not her social equal!

I have often thought about a magnificent film drama that would surpass in power the biggest and most brilliant "world-wide production," a drama that would bring man's intellectual and muscular strength into conflict with nature, at the same time reducing him to what he really is, a poor thing at the mercy of a breeze!

This man builds gigantic machines, subjugates the elements of nature to his will, harnesses rivers and forces them into turbines which will run the dynamos that produce electricity. This electricity will drive man's machines, which in turn will ensure him an abundance of the products he needs.

All this represents the power, the creative energy of man, of the mighty being who would like to dominate all matter and the elements, who has created a civilization which transcends him. But man himself is composed of a fixed number of cells, determined by nature. Should this ratio be upset beyond the limits assigned to it, proliferation sets in and determines his death.

Let this man, whose only strength lies in his mind, catch a simple chill and fail to take care of it. At once, all his organs rush to do battle with the faltering external enemies. But then comes the infinitesimal microbe, hardly visible through a microscope, which saps the man's system until he dies.

And in order to make this a sound film, I would record the clatter of machines, the thunder of waterfalls, the shouts of the man in charge, and, at the same time, I would show the advance of the microbes in complete silence. I really believe that the "silence" of the microbes at work would be more "deafening" to our human ears than the clatter of machines and the fury of elements!

All the elements of drama, poetry, and philosophy would thus be present in these images of life. Of that life to which we must always remain very close, lest we fall into convention or affectation. We have seen so many films which are described as "Moments of pure cinema"! Actually, they are the work of æsthetes who appeal to man's snobbish instincts. They are films directed by the incompetents, the weaklings of the screen, who take great pains to bring together the most ridiculous pictures. These wretched people, some of whom are sincere, believe they are creating films. All they are doing is to show images that are meaningless. And indeed some æsthetes believe that this is a condition of success. But they will never attract the general public, which can be stirred only through contact with life. *For life is always present!*

Therefore, let the film of life draw its substance from certain human gestures which have a wealth of meaning that nothing can equal.

The gesture of a mother protecting her child, the gesture of a priest bestowing a blessing, the gesture of a soldier comforting a comrade about to die. The gesture of a young husband placing the ring on his young bride's finger. The little hands of a newborn child reaching out toward the strange new light. And lastly the creative gestures: the conductor of an orchestra evoking sounds and harmonies with his baton; the humbler hands of the potter, the embroiderer, the cabinetmaker, of primitive craftsmen in distant lands.

Gestures full of life, creative hands, gathered together in a pictorial synthesis of life which constitutes the archetypal film of life.

Films of life are full of potential drama because basically they are documents of life; the most striking proof of this may be found in films that reveal to us the mysteries of animal and vegetable life, in films that teach us things we do not know, that show us what we cannot see for ourselves.

Flashing across a darkened theater, the shining rays light up the screen with tiny creatures who are alive, who suffer, eat, and die exactly like ordinary human beings. In the soft light of these rays, we observe their domestic life, their habits, and their loves. These scenes, though completely unfamiliar, yet seem as natural to us as the various manifestations of human life described in the accompanying newsreel. And we leave the theater deeply stirred by this brief visit to the land of the unknown.

Certain distinctions must be made in this genre as well. There are the films which the great Russian master, Dziga-Vertov, made according to a rigid method. What he called the Cine-Eye was designed to record the concrete reality of things in the cold light of objectivity, without any interpretation. This was really a step in the direction of scientific research, which, though one of the motion picture's great aims, has nothing in common with the film of life, insofar as the latter is an art creation.

On the other hand, some of Jean Painlevé's films derive strongly from the film of life because they obey the law dictating the selection of the Idea and create favorable settings.

For his film on *The Sea Horse,* Jean Painlevé was able to select the dramatic elements in this minute creature's life. The scene showing the animal's reproduction, for example, constitutes a scientific curiosity, due to the fact that, after the coupling, the female slips two hundred eggs into the male's ventral pocket, which, after having fertilized, he will shelter and hatch. But we are also shown the tremendous miracle of the creation of life. A creation which, through one of nature's truly immutable laws, must be made in pain. When the time of delivery is at hand, the male will expel the translucent embryos in groups of six over a period of hours and at the cost of fearful agonies.

Not only did Jean Painlevé produce a work of art through his choice of subject but, by studying the environment, by skillful direction of his natural and unconscious actors, he also produced good theater.

"To make the sea horse feel at home," he tells us, "I used the aquarium in my underground laboratory to reconstruct his environment. There, I spent thirty-six hours observing and film-ing the male's confinement. Toward the end, I was almost as exhausted as he was, but I still had work to do. I wanted to shoot in natural surroundings, so I hurried off to the bay at Arcachon, where sea horses abound. . . .

"In each of my films," Jean Painlevé went on, "I naturally take the most minute precautions. Whether I am dealing with insects or octopuses, I must first acclimate them to the light, protect them from the attacks of other animals, segregate them so they do not destroy each other, and finally curb their normal reflexes so that, when freed before the camera, they will be certain to act as naturally as possible."

There are many different films of life, examples of which could be multiplied indefinitely. Some have delved into the mysteries of the vegetable kingdom. What could be more thrilling than to be able to watch, in the space of a few seconds, the slow and painful growth of seeds forcing their way through the countless obstacles in the soil, to observe the subterranean life of plants in all its hidden wonder!

Thanks to the speed-up, films have also been able to show us the growth of flowers. With wondering eyes, we see their stems and leaves stretch out with graceful movements toward the light!

And so we become aware of all that life which moves about us without our suspecting its presence. Isn't that another principal function performed by the film of life?

It was ROBERT FLAHERTY who first began to make films of life that really answered to the definition I have put forth, that is, they represented a free art creation. Robert Flaherty has always insisted on his freedom, which is why he has clashed with the lack of understanding and even incompetence exhibited by the film industry. When he produced his first masterpiece, *Nanouk* (1920-22), he met with nothing but ridicule, and not a single distributor would accept it. Nevertheless, *Nanouk* was hailed by the public all over the world. Because he had faith in his art, he refused to make any compromises. As a result, the public, which had always enthusiastically acclaimed his works, was deprived of a great many more films that Flaherty would surely have produced. Always there exists this tragic barrier between the creator and his public.

Because Robert Flaherty wanted to remain free, his work is not very voluminous, but this only makes it purer and more significant. *This great artist really created the naturalistic school of the film of life.* He was, and still is, the master of us all, for he created a genre that put new life into the motion picture as a whole.

Robert Flaherty has a thorough knowledge of technique, which allows him to express himself without constraint. Once he has acquired this technical virtuosity, the artist is no longer the slave of technique and will never abuse it. That is why all Flaherty's films and those of his disciples are made according to a basic technique which is so sound that it never intrudes but blends into the artistic expression.

In planning his films, Flaherty spends a long time studying the actions and reactions of human beings in their environment. He knows how to record the gestures and acts of people who seem completely alien to us and brings them closer to us by showing the similarity of their daily existence. His great theme is man and nature. In presenting the vast spectacle of man, he appears to let his camera wander here and there, yet always guided by his will, to seize his dreams and capture life.

Nanouk and *Moana* are definitive expressions of Flaherty's method, æsthetics, and psychology; but, in my opinion, *Man of Aran* is the film most representative of the artist's creative talent.

Off the coast of western Ireland, on the islands of Aran, Robert Flaherty found the most powerful dramatic element of the great theme so dear to him: man's fight against the unleashed elements of nature and against the barren soil. Completely cut off from modern civilization, the hardy islanders snatch their livelihood from the violence of winds and fury of waves. The wretched soil must first be cleared of rocks and then fertilized with seaweed before it can be sown. Flaherty did not have to invent a conflict: he *lived* the great conflict between man and nature; he was able to interpret it through his own feelings and recreate it in terms of images which run the gamut of half-tones and leave a lasting imprint on our imagination and our emotions.

The general public recognizes Flaherty's talent because, though taking his inspiration from life, he never seeks to copy it. He reflects its mutability and diversity, the wide dissimilarity of its manifestations, so that in his films it always appears in its strange and original form.

In the course I give at the New School for Social Research on the philosophy and psychology of the motion picture, I devoted a lesson to Robert Flaherty. After showing *Man of Aran,* I asked my students to describe the nature and quality of Robert Flaherty's talent, and I think it would be interesting to quote one of these essays here. I had great difficulty in choosing it among those submitted by my forty students, for they were all extremely edifying. The following was written by Miss Gladys Toledano, a teacher in New York:

"THE ART OF FLAHERTY"

"The art that can make a man feel most like unto God is that of the motion picture director.* He has in his power all the

* Author's note: Slightly exaggerated!

possibilities for the varied effects that a number of arts can offer. He can be a painter, a poet, a musician, all at the same time, and if he is truly a creative artist can succeed in producing an overwhelming impression. Robert Flaherty is an artist—he has to a great degree exhausted the possibilities of his medium. Thus in his picture, *Man of Aran,* he has raised it, as far as is possible within the limits of its genre, from the commonplace of the documentary film to the higher level of the creative film.

"Flaherty has first of all created mood—foremost requisite for any art. *Man of Aran* is impressive, strong, and full of power. It is presented in sharp, bold strokes and has the depth and sombreness of a Rockwell Kent wood cut. In fact, one is constantly reminded of this form of art—the frequent shots of the dark figure standing silently on a hill or a slope against a light sky, the gigantic waves rising and rising until they dwarf the humans near them into powerless smallness, the jagged and irregular terrain in the background; all these are so much a part of the wood-cut technique. Even the features of the people sometimes acquire that immobility that makes them seem stylized figures.

"But the reason for this atmosphere becomes apparent when the underlying drama of the picture is unfolded—the sharp bitter struggle of Man with the elements for a bare subsistence. It is the sea he's fighting primarily—the most magnificent of all the elements but impersonal, changeable, inexorable. Here he can be musician as well as painter, with crashing sound and lyric stillness. There are several aspects to this struggle—getting the sea-weed to grow a meager harvest of potatoes, fishing for sharks, reminscent of scenes from *Moby Dick,* culminating finally in the terrifying crescendo of the storm. This is by far the most impressive of all and Flaherty builds up the suspense by a constant shifting of scenes from the boat to the anxious family on the shore and back to the sea, always to the sea.

"And so, out of a theme which could be depressing and sordid, Flaherty has fashioned something sweeping and tremendous by a fine distillation of the drama and rugged beauty inherent in it."

Robert Flaherty's influence is so enormous that it has been completely assimilated by film art in general and consequently almost forgotten. For that reason, I would like to make a rapid survey of the magnificent school which he created and inspired.

Robert Flaherty directly inspired JEAN EPSTEIN, who, in his now classic films, *Finis Teare* and *Mor Vran,* also showed genius in painting and interpreting the life of the Breton fishermen among whom he liked to live. The influence of the realistic school is so strong that Jean Epstein's films are completely impregnated with it. In *Coeur Fidèle,* the documentary or, rather, film of life element is so powerful that it makes even the acting of the professional players bow to the exigencies of the "living truth." His country fair, inspired by personal observation, gives birth to a new form of filmic expression that will enable him to come even closer to life through pictorial rhythm and eventually bring him into a very close alliance with music.

JORIS IVENS, a young Dutch artist, belongs to the same school. He knows how to make his images reflect the atmosphere of an environment, how to catch the essence of a landscape, how to make us share with fellow feeling in the harsh life of those who work in the fields and in the towns. His works are stamped with his own impressions, acquired while sharing the life of the people whom he wants to bring closer to us, and with his observations on the environment in which they move. One of his earliest films, *Rain* (1929), is a real poem. Its star is the rain, its setting the city. But a poem can only be the expression of an inner voice, inspired by felt impressions. I imagine that Ivens must have long felt the melancholy effect of the rain and fog descending over the town, and I believe he might perfectly well have created another poem to show the resurrection of spring, the sun dispelling melancholy and allowing man to warm himself in its powerful light.

In his images of life, Ivens also sings the glory of human endeavor; *Zuiderzee* is a magnificent and powerful work which shows us the conquest of land over sea through man's will alone.

Philipps Radio, a superbly orchestrated symphony of industry, extols man's genius in conquering the ether.

One of Joris Ivens's finest works, *Power and the Land,* originated in a request made by the United States Department of Agriculture to promote rural electrification by setting up cooperative power plants. Joris Ivens immediately perceived the human side of his subject. The main idea to be developed, and on which he based his film, was not so much concerned with increasing farm production as with the fact that electricity can alleviate man's suffering. Starting with this conception, he was able to portray a rural scene, not in the style affected by the sentimental bucolic painters of the eighteenth century, but with the sharp edge of an engraver's tool, inspired by rural life.

Joris Ivens was a conscientious artist; he went to live in the country with a family of farmers. He shared in their daily existence, came to be regarded as a member of the family. This approach enabled him to create this remarkable film in which the spectator is made to participate in the life of the American farmer, so similar to that of our own farmer. His natural actors are so accustomed to the presence of their friend that in the film they are seen leading their simple day-to-day lives without the slightest indication that a camera is recording all their actions. The tempo of this rural life is closely followed; there is no concession to studio technique. Life goes on slowly but full of the work that will soon be lightened by electric power and light. There is no scenario, no story in the sense we generally understand, but actually the finest story of all, that which is told by interpreting daily life.

There is no finer example of dramatic progression than that of man's constant advance as he frees himself from the bondage of useless tasks through scientific progress.

The tableau presented by this film is not just a photographic recording but a real work of art, that is, an impression of actuality which the author has drawn from his subconscious and filtered across his temperament. He was helped by another artist, Douglas Moore, professor of music at Columbia University, who provided the musical interpretation of his thought. This musical accompaniment, thanks to which the spoken commentary could be reduced to a minimum, gives the film its elevated tone and often, in a synchronized movement, points up the author's most fugitive intent, such as in the flute accompaniment to the little scene which shows a child momentarily interrupting his father's work to be offered a large cornflower and walking triumphantly off with it through a field, above which after a while only the flower emerges.

Power and the Land was released through a very large circuit; it was shown in hundreds of theaters all over the country. Everywhere, east, west, north, and south, it met with the same success, the same understanding, showing how true it is that everything simple and human carries both an intellectual and an emotional appeal.

When the world went mad again, Joris Ivens took a camera and traveled through China, Russia, and Spain. In these films, Ivens's sensibility has been sharpened by contact with what he saw. His habit of observation allows him to envisage the future consequences of actualities. Today, his observations, seen in the light of tragic reality, appear prophetic.

In 1928, JOHN GRIERSON set up an organization in London to produce motion pictures for the Empire Marketing Board, and gathered about him a group of young people whom he imbued with a consuming faith in the great mission of the documentary film. That organization was soon to undergo a change, becoming, as the General Post Office Film Unit, a central school for producing capable artists.

The young artists in that school enjoyed a kind of controlled freedom which John Grierson skillfully doled out. ALBERTO CAVALCANTI, a subtle and human artist, author of the classic *Rien Que les Heures* (1926), was also an all-around technician and later became a highly valued collaborator in directing the school until the outbreak of war.

PAUL ROTHA, STUART LEGG, BASIL WRIGHT, and many others made films, such as the famous *Night Mail*, which derives directly from the Flaherty school.

There is not the slightest doubt but that Flaherty inspired Grierson and his disciples. Every one of the films made by graduates of the Grierson school shows signs of the humanity, the

Robert Flaherty, genius of motion pictures; one of the greatest makers of "films of life" in our time (see page 89).

The young heroine of *Moana*, Robert Flaherty's fine
film (see page 90).

The native family in *Moana* (see page 90).

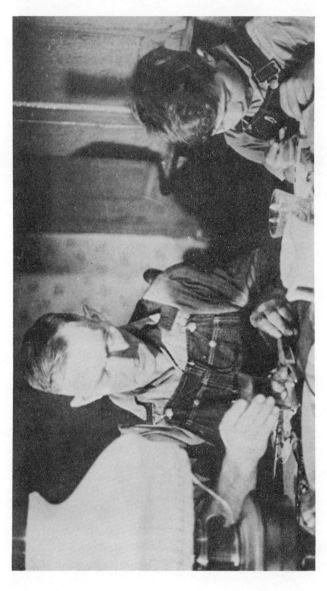

The evening meal: scene from Joris Ivens' remarkable film, *Power and the Land* (see page 93).

interpretation of daily life, and the beauty which form the basis of Flaherty's art. Grierson paid tribute to Flaherty at the beginning of his own career; and, though at present he appears to have turned his back on beauty and feeling, the entire work of his pupils, of those he inspired, is there to contradict him. When Grierson writes, in apology for sins he never committed, "The cross of realism is that it has to do with reality and must concern itself not with beauty but primarily with truth," he is indulging in his well-known love for paradox. In the first place, he is confusing his genres when he speaks of realism in connection with films of life. Although these must be true, it is essential that they be art creations, in other words interpretations, and must not be confused with factual or news films. Furthermore, I fail to see that there is any contradiction in principle between beauty and truth, between an artist's visual interpretation and life! As a matter of fact, the leading film authors of Grierson's school have continued working with beauty, since during the war they have given expression to man's nobler sentiments and attempted to interpret the gigantic effort he has made to repel the forces of barbarism. They have remained under the aegis of beauty because, Grierson's claim notwithstanding, they have kept their faith in the ideal of free men. Likewise, they have remained faithful, whether consciously or unconsciously, to the master's school, to Robert Flaherty. John Grierson, who was their leader, may well be proud of them.

Robert Flaherty's influence has made itself felt all over the world, and a roll call of his disciples might represent a history of the naturalistic school in the film of life. I have no intention of writing that history here. Others, Paul Rotha for one, have already done it superbly. However, I would like to mention a few names, chosen at random from so fertile a stock—RUTTMAN, EISENSTEIN, RENE CLAIR, PIERRE ICHAC, CHOMETTE, BRUNIUS, PARE LORENTZ, VAN DYKE—and pause for a moment to pay tribute to a country which became Hitler's first victim—Czechoslovakia.

For that country made a particularly important contribution to the development of the film of life. It was really a model democracy, and its art was the living proof of its national unity.

Immediately after Hitler's invasion of Czechoslovakia, I received in Paris a visit from a young Czechoslovak refugee, GEORGE WEISS, who was fleeing from the horrors of racialism. He showed me his last films, *The Rape of Czechoslovakia* and *Twenty Years of the Republic*. I was astonished, as much at the technique exhibited by this young film author of only twenty-six, as at his talent in expressing his country's democratic ideal and revealing how perfectly she had realized that ideal in society.

One of the earliest Czechoslovak films of life was PLICKA's *The Singing Land*. This film had the happy distinction of being the product of a collaboration between the director, Plicka, the musical composer, Skvor, of the Prague National Opera, and ALEXANDER HACKENSCHMIED. It is a visual and sound synthesis of the Czechoslovak countryside, people, and folklore.

Bata, the big shoe manufacturer, engaged Hackenschmied and his friends KOLDA, PILAT, and JEAN LUCAS. The first thing he did was to send them on a tour of studios all over the world to study their methods. Then he set up a very modern studio at Zlin, where young directors, besides promoting footwear on the screen, could make some very fine films of life. One of the most moving of these, called *Last Summer,* was about President Masaryk, the great patriot. Masaryk died before the film could be completed. Hackenschmied provided an ending for his film by bringing to life the environment in which the President had lived, with the help of the objects, the furniture, associated with him. Thus, he proved that a sensitive artist could arouse emotion by using "things."

In conclusion, I would like to mention the formation by the Czechoslovak Government of a company called Current Events. This company successfully competed against the current events films made by the German firm of U.F.A. and began to produce exceptionally fine films of life in praise of democracy. Like Grierson's Film Unit in England, this company came to be a school for directors. One of its heads was the youthful HANS BURGER, who, with HERBERT KLINE, was co-author of the last film produced in free Czechoslovakia: *Crisis*. This film was in a sense the protest of a free people temporarily conquered.

This rapid survey of the film of life gives an idea of the vast field it covers. Almost always, it is also a dramatic film, since it contains within it life, which is the basis of all drama. The life of the sea horse, the life of the butterfly dramatically emerging from its cocoon, the life of the plant struggling to force a passage through the tightly packed earth — surely there are no finer dramas than these to thrill us! But what distinguishes the films of life produced by Flaherty's school is the fact that their theme is the life of man himself.

The film of life really belongs in the field of dramatic art when it comprises a story taken straight from life and interpreted by natural actors in concert with the fauna and flora of the region. It is in this sense that some of the younger men have come to rival the master, and the credit for the naturalistic film of life must go to them. One day in New York, I ran across one of these little masterpieces in the following circumstances. "Everyone" in the film-loving world had been urging me to see a great film which had received tremendous publicity. After hearing so much talk about it, one evening I decided to go to a small theater on upper Broadway where it was then playing. Already prejudiced in its favor, I settled back to watch the marvel. The program began with a film announced as a documentary and called *The Adventures of Chico*. From the very first scene, the whole audience, myself included, was held in the grip of a very simple but powerful story about a child who loved nature and animals. This film really brought into play every human and natural element. It was splendid, and the whole theater burst into applause at the conclusion. Once more, my faith in the public's understanding and sensibility was confirmed.

By contrast, the "great film," heralded with such pomp, furnished me with another opportunity to distinguish between true and false film art. The latter was adequately represented by this pretentious film. It was false as an artificial pearl, which borrows its shape and appearance from the true pearl but reflects only the glitter of the lights and setting in the window of an inexpensive jewelry store! Its sole merit lay in having had an excellent cameraman, whose talents, however, had been sadly abused!

Actually, it was the public that had been abused by being subjected to an assortment of childish tricks which might have been amusing twenty years ago. To produce a filmic work of art requires more than placing the camera at the most distorted angles. The real difficulty lies in *being simple.* Because of their talent, their sincerity, and their courage, Stacy and Horace Woodard overcame this difficulty in *The Adventures of Chico.*

The story of this film is an easy one to relate. As a matter of fact, it is nonexistent insofar as imaginative dramatic construction is concerned. Quite simply, it is the pastoral life of a man and his twelve-year-old boy in a magnificent and primitive setting in Mexico. The cast consists of these two human beings and all the fauna and flora of the region. Living so close to nature among his friends the animals, Chico has built himself a world of his own. The birds and the sheep are his friends. Their enemies, the carnivores and birds of prey, are his enemies. He does his best to set right the misfortunes that befall them. In this way, he rescues and nurses some fledgling road runners who have lost their mother. One of these birds, grown up, later repays the young boy by protecting him against a dangerous snake that attacks him while he is asleep. This scene has an intensity and dramatic quality that no imaginative work could have equaled. It possesses this dramatic quality because it was inspired by daily reality. It belongs outside the sphere of the pure documentary, the Cine-Eye genre, because the authors have interpreted it and given it a logical place within a series of actions, the arrangement of which results from their imagination, their talent as authors. It follows that the epic fight between the bird and snake, in which the former comes out the victor, takes place at the climax of the cycle of interest in the dramatic construction. Therefore, we may say that this work, while inspired by reality and employing only natural means, represents a true art creation belonging in the film of life genre and following in the most orthodox tradition of the Flaherty school.

In the same vein was *The Forgotten Village.* John Steinbeck, the great American writer, whose works are to literature what the film of life is to the motion picture, wrote a story which he laid in a small village high up in the mountains of Mexico. Working in collaboration, Steinbeck, Herbert Kline, and Hackenschmied planned and made this other masterpiece while staying in this primitive region, where man's way of life has remained unchanged for centuries. But down below, in the valley, science has brought many changes to the life of the people. Gradually, progress climbs toward the village, where two civilizations encounter each other in a psychological clash out of which progress will eventually emerge. This is the film's main theme. In presenting it, the authors did what Flaherty, the master, and all his disciples had done: they studied the environment, made friends with these primitive beings. And because the natural actors are the same people who had lived the real story, because the story derives its elements from life itself, the audience is deeply moved. If we add to this the fact that Hans Eisler's music is also inspired by local folklore, it becomes clear that this is a work whose sincerity and artistic quality are equaled only by the noble service it performs in helping men to understand one another and to use the fruits of their discovery.

The foregoing represents a rather inadequate attempt to trace the path taken by the naturalistic school of the film of life since its creation by Robert Flaherty. Fortunately, the latter is still with us, vigorous, full of faith, and ready to produce new masterpieces.

If Flaherty is the undisputed leader of the naturalistic school, then John Grierson is the originator of the documentary film, using the term in its nobler sense. He has always endeavored to present the human side of the great political and economic questions affecting the life of men and nations. In this way, he has been able to make the public appreciate the most diverse problems and to provide a civic and a moral education.

Whether he was working with the General Post Office Film Unit in London or with the National Film Board in Ottawa, Grierson has always managed to inspire the younger men with a burning zeal reflected in their films, which have made a deep impression on the public.

6
DOCUMENTARIES

3. The Informational Film

INFORMATIONAL FILMS might as easily have been classed among the educational films, since, as John Grierson so aptly stated, "In a democracy, they represent a means of educating public opinion. They possess the magic power of comprehension. They are capable of establishing a live contact between the individual and the play of gigantic forces at which he marvels." Nevertheless, I prefer to place this genre after the film of life, for it is really a direct descendant of the latter. The informational film is, in fact, made up of documents of life, and by that same token is related to the film of life. However, it differs from this in the sense that it is the result of a different conception and technique directed toward diverse but precise aims.

Moreover, free artistic expression, which is the primary condition for a film of life, becomes limited for an informational film because in the majority of cases the author is obliged to confine himself to presenting facts objectively without having the opportunity to interpret them freely. This does not mean that the informational film cannot be an art, for the great law of selection applies even more strictly to this genre because the aims pursued are more serious and diverse.

Indeed the information disseminated through films must be presented in different ways, according to the particular functions assigned, the common goal of which is to make *known* or *understood*. *"To make known"* is the particular function concerning the events at hand which devolves upon the news film.

In connection with this particular form of journalism, I would like to bring up the name of someone who thoroughly understood its function and served it faithfully and brilliantly. Germaine Dulac was chairman of the French Motion Picture Press, but to us in particular she was a great figure, a pioneer in films. Her masterpiece, *The Smiling Madame Beudet,* will always remain a screen classic; her experimental films were a landmark in the artistic and technical advance of our art. Her firm friendship, generously but discriminatingly bestowed, and her social consciousness made her one of the outstanding figures in the film world. Right after the armistice, she resumed the chairmanship of our union of motion picture technicians, in order to "maintain, work, and start over," a motto which might well remain that of the motion picture as a whole. I am sure that Germaine Dulac died facing the enemy, but she will live on among us as an example of love and devotion for our "fine art."

Germaine Dulac thus defined the aim of the news film: "By affording a means of communication between all kinds of people, the news film encircles the world. Does it not reveal to each individual the truth about other countries and people, behind the official mask of tradition and historic invention?"

It would be difficult to find a more accurate definition for this marvelous means of interpenetration, this powerful instrument for overthrowing prejudice, ridding people's minds of antiquated traditions, and delivering men from the ties binding them in unconscious servitude to their ancient history.

The current events film pictures the everyday life of the world, knowledge of which cannot be gained by reading commentaries, books, papers, or textbooks. Taken in this sense, the motion picture becomes an individual experience, enabling each person to see, to live, and to know, rather than to guess. Through the current events film, classes and races are brought together directly without the need for an intermediary. News is made up from day to day; it is never premeditated. It takes hold of events, reflecting them accurately. News is the mirror of a country, of its thoughts, its work, and its play. In the remotest haunts of man, news is a segment from the true life of the world, in its beliefs, its struggles, its hopes, and its ideals.

Such is the function of the newsreel. Obviously, its presentation involves a certain amount of danger, and in this connection La Rochefoucauld's maxim comes appropriately to mind: "Truth does not do as much *good* in the world as its semblance does *evil*." If we desire the newsreel to accomplish its basic mission, which consists of helping individuals and peoples *to know one another* better in order to understand one another better, it behooves us to *select* with great care the fundamental truths beneficial to all.

This selective process is extremely difficult and delicate in general cases involving artistic material, but it becomes exceptionally important when it concerns *facts* with which the public is to be acquainted. The writing press has not always been fully aware of the responsibility incumbent upon it. It must also be said that a news commentary by a journalist, however conscientious he may be, is always influenced by his own beliefs, that is, exposed to the inevitable human error. But a newspaper reader can always take time to reflect on what he has read or turn to other papers expressing different opinions.

The newsreel offers no such opportunity. It is full of congenital defects, structural faults—if I may use the term—due to the fact that the motion picture depends on mechanical means.

A film projected at a standard speed of twenty-four images a second does not provide any opportunity for reflection or going back. The moving image makes an immediate and indelible impression on the spectator's mind.

This gives an idea of the responsibility that falls on the men who make newsreels. They must select the facts and limit their commentaries to mere explanations identifying the images flashed on the screen. They must do a job of reporting and avoid any attempt at interpretation or editorializing. To accomplish this, there is no need to have a system of censorship and police measures. On the contrary, the film press must be given complete freedom—real freedom, protected from the influence and dictates of hidden powers serving private interests. To be more precise, I might say that until 1940 the Havas Agency had a concession for newsreels in all the principal theaters of France. I do not have to describe all the disadvantages resulting from this situation; the least that can be said is that this apparent freedom actually concealed the worst possible kind of oppression. On, the other hand, it is the government's duty to protect freedom by assuring the newsreel an opportunity to fulfill its mission within the exact boundaries that make this possible. Since the informational film can easily become a political weapon, it is important that the Ministry of Information direct that freedom to the advantage of the nation's real interests by keeping a close watch over its privilege of presenting facts impartially.

The prewar situation might perhaps not have been so tragic if the world had consisted, in accordance with Kant's proposal for perpetual peace, of "republican states." There might then have been cause to hope that the democracies, through force of public opinion, could have guaranteed a minimum of sincerity in their exchanges of information.

But unfortunately this was far from being the case. The totalitarian states used the newsreel for propaganda purposes. In this they were initially successful with their attempts to inject the slow poison of Nazi ideology. Later on, there was a shift in tactics, and they used propaganda in the form of power demonstrations which had the effect of frightening other countries. The technique employed is all too familiar, differing from that employed in democratic countries in that it makes no appeal to individual intelligence. Instead of presenting real documents for the spectator to interpret, the Nazi technician distorts the information in a commentary and subordinates the fact to the needs of his propaganda. Not content with this, the Nazi technician assembles propaganda films, using newsreel shots purposely inserted to support his thesis. In other words, he seizes the truth, wrings its neck, and forces it to proclaim lies.

This artificial, lying propaganda should have been countered tit for tat by proclaiming the truth. The vindication of might, the destruction of libraries, should have been answered with facts showing what all that really stood for: nothing more nor less than the annihilation of a civilization.

We should even have gone beyond the purely intellectual sphere to show, as brutally as possible, the progressive and rapid destruction of productive wealth, the regression of man's status in life. This was the task that the democratic newsreel could have accomplished without going outside the limits of its own genre, remaining strictly in the field of information and facts.

If the newsreel had been given access to free screens, if the democracies had realized the power of the motion picture to the extent that the dictators did, they would have won an easy victory over falsehood solely through the power of truth. I believe in the future of the newsreel because I know that a truly democratic world is taking shape. I have confidence in it because this film genre possesses the finest technical crews in the motion picture industry.

Cameramen have the noblest and most thankless profession of all. Always on call, in a state of daily alert, they are ready to rush toward the most dangerous tasks. Having none of the technical facilities afforded by the studio, they must be all-round technicians, completely self-sufficient. Anonymous workers, they carry on their work without glory, while their material compensations are far below those of their studio colleagues. At present, both in and out of uniform, they are risking their lives to gather the material with which history will be written.

The fathers of the "newsreel" would be proud of their distant disciples!

It was in June 1895, six months before the Cinematograph performance at the Grand Café, that Louis Lumière completed the first "newsreel" ever made and showed it that same evening at a banquet. One year later, in May 1896, Louis Lumière sent one of his young apprentices, Francis Doublier, to film the coronation of Nicholas II. Doublier almost lost his life in the disaster at Hodynsky, where 6,000 people were crushed to death while fighting for the gifts distributed by the Czarina. Doublier continued his epic career across the world and at the time of this writing he is working in a New York laboratory.

At the same time, Félix Mesguish also made a trip around the world. He had so many adventures, brought back so much material that he acquired the nickname of picture hunter. Thanks to these picture hunters, the newsreel will be able to spread to all the world the big and little news about the daily life of men so that eventually they will discover they are all alike.

The essential aim of the newsreel is to make the facts *known;* it is the function of another film genre to make them *understood.* *The March of Time* created this genre, which the informational film lacked before Luis and Richard de Rochemont conceived it.

Differing from the newsreel, which presents the news of the day, *The March of Time* borrows its narrative methods from the radio and is related to modern pictorial journalism. *The March of Time* takes an event and dramatizes it rather than describes it. It catalyzes opinion about a fact. By means of a happy formula, it presents a single topic at a time, in a rhythm synchronized with that of the contemporary world. This formula, which is to the newsreel what the editorial is to the newspaper, exposes the fact and attempts to make it *understood* in terms of the present and its immediate or future consequences. These films, by providing enlightenment, are an indispensable complement to the newsreel, so long as they keep to the same fundamental principles based on a respect for the truth. *The March of Time* has successfully achieved its aim because its creators were conscious of its importance and have always preserved their sense of responsibility. Richard de Rochemont, the present director, was before the war responsible for all European productions of *The March of Time.* He lived in France and did not leave the Continent until he had gone through the bombing of Warsaw. In other words, he lived through one of the most troubled periods in the history of the democracies and had to show great discernment in revealing and explaining events that were to alter the course of history. Richard de Rochemont was upheld in that task by his ardent faith in the intrinsic value of facts and by his distrust of everything that might resemble rumors, trial balloons, or exaggerations. Because Richard de Rochemont knows how difficult it is to take the truth and make it shine in living images, he has made it a rule to *choose* only known facts. First making sure that his choice conforms to the truth, he groups his facts around a single idea and achieves dramatic effort solely through the editing, the rhythm of which blends in with the music.

Using this method, *The March of Time* was able to present the American public with *The Refugees,* a film based on true facts and showing the persecution of free thought, of intellectuals, and of a whole race by the Nazis. The works of great thinkers are burned in public squares to the acclamations of a barbaric people. The enslaving of science, the looting of laboratories, the police roundups, the concentration camps, the long lines of refugees struggling toward a welcoming France and toward the United States—all these scenes were true, horribly true, and every one of them was amply authenticated.

The creators of *The March of Time* showed their artistry by building this documentary material into a dramatic structure based on the idea to be put across, and by assembling it into a rhythmic unity of sound and image. The resulting work remained within the rigid framework of facts, of truth, while art intervened only to capture more surely the imagination and feeling of the audience.

The March of Time exercised a considerable influence on public opinion in the various democracies, but could not capture it all alone. Other, more underhanded forces were working daily to bemuse people's minds; and—I always return to this question— the lack of civic education resulted in the individual being unable to draw any firm conclusions from the intellectual stimuli provoked by the pictures in *The March of Time.*

Rehearsal for War in Spain, for instance, produced in 1937, should have provoked free peoples to action if they had not already been obsessed by the fear of communism which Nazi propaganda had skillfully distilled and spread like a poison. Despite all this, it may be said that *The March of Time* founded a new school and exercised a marked influence, particularly on the British motion picture. John Grierson acknowledged this not long ago, stating that he had been obliged "to dramatize public information." This is precisely what he achieved with the National Film Board in Canada, when he originated the fine serial entitled *The World in Action,* directed by Stuart Legg, one of his disciples.

The March of Time and *The World in Action,* the rhythm of which seems as inexorable as the steadily advancing hands of a clock, will, I hope, soon be striking the painful but happy hours of deliverance for the enslaved peoples.

This deliverance, this victory, must be won with all the weapons at the disposal of the United Nations. In his long and minute preparation, which no one saw fit to interrupt, the enemy made ample provision for psychological weapons. Among these, none is more powerful than the motion picture.

In the preceding pages, I have tried to discuss the informational film's function in peacetime and the various ways in which it may apply. That peace, to which we sacrificed everything without making provisions to guarantee it, has now been broken. The normal evolution of progress has been halted by a tidal wave of hate, of mass murder, of spiritual and material destruction, which has threatened to wipe out civilization itself. Only if all the forces of democracy are mobilized can this raging flood be stopped, and among these forces we must give the motion picture at least as much importance as the enemy has given to it.

Therefore, it is necessary that we consider the role of the informational film in wartime in connection with the specific aims it should achieve. It is equally advisable for us to consider the different techniques that may be employed. These techniques are not new; they are related on the one hand to the technique employed by newsreels to make the facts *known* and on the other to that used by *The March of Time* to make them *understood.* The wartime news film is no different from its counterpart in peacetime, except that it should present the facts even more objectively. By this I mean that the choice of material should be made with complete impartiality and utter realism. There is no need to gloss over the horrors of war for an adult people; their morale should be healthy enough to support the truth. The significance of the newsreel in wartime is increased by the fact that the public is eager to be shown the true facts on the screen when the actors are its loved ones.

Sometimes the news film becomes an epic piece of reporting, as in the case of *Desert Victory*. Although a few of the scenes were shot subsequently in order to obtain an orderly sequence and the editing gives it the quality of an art creation, the film is really a great piece of reporting, designed to make the *facts* known about a campaign of liberation.

The film was produced by the photographic and motion picture services of the British Army and Air Corps. Its setting is the desert battlefield, starting sixty miles west of Alexandria. It stretches across 1300 miles of pursuit and combat to the streets of Tripoli. The cameramen were combat troops, carrying both their arms and their cameras. These hunters of pictures and Nazis moved forward with the advance guard of engineers who removed the mines, and very often would precede them. Four dead, seven wounded, six captured was the score sheet of this army of heroes who were recording history while they made it!

The informational film, considered as a psychological weapon of war, must possess certain special characteristics, depending on how it is to be used. Different objectives may require the informational film to be either an *offensive* or a *defensive* weapon, but in each case it will follow the *March of Time* formula; for it must not only make the facts understood but also, with the help of the truth, exalt natural feelings of duty toward the nation and civilization.

In proof of the foregoing, I would like to cite some examples. First, however, I want to state clearly that they in no way constitute a qualitative selection from the splendid collection of films made by the United Nations in the course of the war.

France, before 1940 and I hope in the immediate future, England, Russia, and the United States have done a magnificent job in the field, and it is by no means confined to the few works I am about to mention.

The Film as an Offensive Weapon

Its general function is to combat enemy propaganda abroad.

Among others, its particular functions may be to establish the truth about events previously shown in their false colors, to show the courage, calm, and energy prevailing within the nation, to give information to patriots in occupied countries and keep their hopes alive.

At a time when England was holding out alone against the avalanche of barbaric forces, during the worst moments of the blitz, the whole nation came together as one; from the youngest to the oldest, from the strongest to the weakest, each individual, according to his strength or his ability, joined in the defense and salvation of his country. It was then that magnificent films were born, showing the imprint of the heroic times.

The battle of England was illustrated by a series of brief sketches showing the mobilization of a great people. Thousands sought refuge in shelters, even more stayed in bed, but the majority had night tasks. The latter watched the skies, fought incendiaries, rescued the injured, and guided the homeless to shelters. Others served antiaircraft batteries. And, while the bombs fell, the incendiaries sputtered, the houses crumbled, each person calmly went about his work, following the example of the great pilot who stood at the helm: Churchill, the soul of the nation.

There is no need to go into any further detail to show what a tremendous impact these films made all over the world. The facts speak for themselves, but they are facts altogether different in spirit from those apparent facts exploited by the enemy, who tried—with success, it must be admitted—to make the world believe that England and her empire were done!

Later, in March 1942, when the country was armed for her defense but still exposed to bombing and the danger of invasion, it was thought desirable to show the real face of the nation. This appeared in Humphrey Jenning's little masterpiece—*Listen to Britain*. The sounds, the vibrations of the activity and the soul of a people at war can clearly be felt across this blend of sound and image. Sounds and images of work: factories, trains, ship sirens. The sounds and images of rare moments of leisure: music and song. Sounds of combat: antiaircraft batteries or bombs. This audio-visual poem constitutes the finest heroic symphony ever created, one inspired by a people doing super-human work, relaxing in order to work harder, and fighting to save the world! An offensive weapon worthy of the cause for which the United Nations are fighting, wielded with the strength that only truth and noble deeds can give it.

Lastly, films may be used as offensive weapons against the enemy in a special type of newsreel which brings the facts to oppressed peoples.

The United Nations Newsreels regularly edits, on 16 mm. film, a summary of extremely condensed news, condensed because their audience has very little time to see them. In fact, these films are dropped by parachute into the occupied countries and picked up by patriots who are avid for "truthful" news and who project it at the risk of their lives.

Our dear friends in France and elsewhere, brothers all in suffering, will tell us later whether these films have accomplished their mission, but I would like to believe they have had some effect, when I think of the comfort and hope they must have brought.

The United States, by showing the progressive growth and blossoming of her productive strength in tools of war, the almost miraculous building up of her tremendous army; Russia, by communicating her legendary heroism and by recording on end-less film the glorious and yet so human scenes of her own epic, have at the same time justified the peoples' faith and created the epic film, made of tears, of blood, and of glory!

The Film as a Defense Weapon

The fact that we contemplate the motion picture's use as a defensive weapon does not mean that we attach a static quality to this function. On the contrary, the films making up this type of weapon must be planned and made according to well-defined aims but must also be a dynamic force. They must defend the

Crisis, the film made by Hans Bruger and Herbert Kline (see page 96).

The Adventures of Chico, one of the most moving films ever shown on the screen, made by Stacy and Horace Woodard (see page 97).

nation against enemy propaganda on the inside, keeping up the people's morale by glorifying patriotism and the democratic ideology. A citizen army does not fight without ideals; the home army, the production front, needs them just as much. In order to instill these ideals, the informational film must be entrusted with a special, well-defined mission the scope of which would not be suited to documentaries planned without method, without faith, and without ideals. Let us consider certain aspects of that mission and their application.

Three hundred years ago, Oliver Cromwell proclaimed that "the soldier-citizen must know why he is fighting." The British Army of today still follows the great principle enunciated by Cromwell. In 1941, the Military Division of Current Affairs was set up as an experiment and became a permanent branch of the Army. The chief aim of this branch is to organize within every unit groups of free discussion about every conceivable subject without resorting to official propaganda or compulsory lectures. These groups answered the need for discovering the truth by substituting a knowledge of the facts for the daily rumors that circulate in barracks and camps more freely than anywhere else. The topics discussed generally fall into two categories. They have to do either with military operations taking place in the various theaters or with questions of more general nature, such as "Why are we fighting?" or else with social problems or city planning, both now and in the future. A short film has been made which records a few of these discussions. It conveys a fine impression of these meetings, held in complete freedom, at which the officer delegated by the Division merely acts as chairman to answer questions. Other films have been made to answer the public's growing interest in problems of international security. These films, crystallizing as they do the multiple problems of peace, represent a potent source of information for the discussion groups in the Army. One of the most important is *World of Plenty,* which takes up food problems and goes into questions of production, distribution, and consumption on a world-wide scale.

Such vital topics provoke discussions of a sort to promote confidence and sustain the will to fight for a better world.

The informational film has also and very effectively been used as a defense weapon by the United States Army. The great director, Frank Capra, now a lieutenant colonel commanding the motion picture unit, is at present directing serials, such as *Know Your Enemy* and *Know Your Allies*, whose educational value is on a par with their artistic merit.

Each of these films is based, according to the *March of Time* formula, on a central theme and relies for its effect entirely on the power of the truth contained in its images. However, it must be made clear that this effect could not be produced if the rhythm of the editing, synchronized with the musical rhythm, did not provide this defense weapon with the dynamic qualities necessary to hold the spectator's attention and arouse his enthusiam.

The dynamic effect of the informational film may also be applied to the army of workers who manufacture the materials of war. To keep these factory troops in action and bring them close to the front, war films are shown on the premises. During the hour of rest, in the work shops or dining halls, the magic screen suddenly transports the workers to the vivid realities of combat. No sooner has the worker whose job is adjusting a part on a tank or an airplane laid down his tool for a much-needed rest than a screen goes up on the wall and he suddenly sees that same tank or airplane, or its twin, taking part in the action. The fate of friends or brothers who are using it depends on how well he has done his own particular job. The outcome of a battle depends on the number of these weapons.

All this seems vivid, tragic, urgent. By showing the realities of war, films have brought the factory closer to the battlefield, and the workers go back to their jobs to work at a new pace, the same pace as that of the battle which must be won. Among the numerous films that perform this function, I would like to mention, for its moving beauty, *The Life and Death of the Hornet*. This deals with the birth, life, and heroic death of the aircraft carrier *Hornet*, from which the American airmen took off to bomb Tokyo on April 18, 1942, and which was sunk on October 26 of the same year.

The film really makes the spectator share in the life of this great ship, which becomes a kind of symbol. We may imagine what a powerful effect it would have if shown in a naval ship-yard during the rest hour, toward three o'clock in the morning, before all those men who are busily making new warships.

As a defense weapon, the informational film has a more general role to play with regard to the vast audience of theater filmgoers. In addition to newsreels, films should be shown which make their appeal to the audience's reason and sensibility. But the greatest care must be taken in appealing to that sensibility, and the psychological factor determining the expected reaction must be taken into account. The natural tastes and tendencies of the masses must be known in order to avoid false interpretations that would run counter to the aim sought. Here again we come up against the danger of "the semblance of truth" about which it is well to be forewarned. I would like to take a typical example.

The first film made in the United States as a defense weapon and shown by the federal government, *The World at War,* was designed to counteract the German propaganda which flooded the country before its entry into the war. It was a failure for this reason: the makers had not defined the film's specific aims, whether offensive or defensive, for use at home or abroad.

The basic theme—the forces of democracy reacting against the Nazi ideology—had not been determined. The makers merely used scenes that had been manufactured and assembled by Goebbels' office, adding a commentary to alter their meaning and arouse public opinion against displays of force.

The task is not that easy. Words are not as powerful as pictures. Adjectives cannot fight against visual facts.

This film had retained its Nazi character. The technique of the regime's Propaganda Ministry remained unimpaired, its dynamic quality was all in favor of German might. Watching this magnificent spectacle, which showed none of the horrors of reality, the public experienced a kind of admiration for the organization, for the people who had filmed such powerful scenes, against which the commentary could do nothing.

The film had exactly the opposite effect to the one it was meant to have because it encouraged the natural sentiments of the masses, who admire technical perfection in any form, yet furnished no antidote, no elements capable of awakening other sentiments of generosity and pity in the masses.

Finally, the display of Nazi might provoked a reaction on the part of the democratic forces in answer to that other natural sentiment which derives from the first: the desire to be strong in order to avenge and conquer.

In 1942, the Canadian National Film Board produced *This Is Blitz*, which had aims identical with those *World at War* had failed to achieve. Stuart Legg, to whom we owe so many fine films, went at it a different way. Using all the captured German films, he composed a dramatized version of the blitz which was more frightening than anything the Germans themselves had made in *The Campaign in Poland* and *Victory in the West*. The audience sees the lightning conquests of Poland, Norway, the Low Countries, and France, the systematic enslavement and stifling of thought in the conquered nations. The film has been so edited that all these conquests are shown at a headlong pace; then, little by little, the action slows down, becomes quieter, and the film begins to show how the democracies mean to counter with even more powerful methods. There is no lecture, no appeal for confidence, but simply a demonstration of the lesson learned from all this, a statement that this lesson has already been put to use in producing the means to conquer. Confidence is imparted by the fact that, having analyzed and discovered the reasons for the enemy's success, the democracies have perceived the way to vanquish him by using the same methods, with the added weight of moral force. *This Is Blitz* accomplished its purpose because it touched the natural sentiment requiring that confidence be restored before a show of strength can be made.

We are now going through an experience which emphasizes the necessity for obeying the law of genres, the law of selection, and the normal reactions of human beings if the motion picture is to achieve its various aims. As soon as competent men had undertaken the responsibility for guiding the destinies of the war film, it can be said that in the majority of cases these aims were magnificently attained. In the United States, thanks to Frank Capra, William Wyler, Anatole Litvak, and their collaborators, the screen arsenal produced extremely efficacious weapons of offense and defense. *Battle for Russia* gave a lucid, objective, as well as emotive picture of the Russian campaign. The epic of Russia, pictorially transcribed in all its tragic reality, triumphed over the lying campaign with which the enemy tried to split up the Allied powers.

A final aim of the wartime informational film is to keep the nation in permanent touch with its army. This was thoroughly understood by Colonel Calvé, the head of the Motion Picture Division of the French Army, who was not only a great soldier but an animator and a technician in teaching and informational films. Every week, he edited *The War Journal of the French Army*, patterned after the *March of Time* formula. Each film was based on a central idea, around which clustered all the details of the soldier's daily life.

I remember one film entitled *The Phony War*, a term invented by the Fifth Column to lull the nation into a sense of false security. After seeing this "phony war" on the screen, the spectator did not find it at all phony. He was shown the life led by men who struggled against the cold, worked long hours, fought and died in the advance posts. All this was presented at a pace, a rhythm, calculated to inflame, to exalt patriotism, to create and sustain that warlike spirit so necessary to victory. It was an impressive sight, *planned* and *executed* with the intention of bringing the French people closer to their citizen army.

We must conclude that this *War Journal of the French Army* constituted a source of grave danger to the enemy and to the traitors working for the defeat of France; for, in spite of the commanding general's orders, it could never be shown on any screen in France.

But already, as I write, the army of the Republic is preparing to take part in the decisive battles and to continue the fight which, thanks to General de Gaulle, it has never abandoned.

I would like to mention two of the many films linking the

nation to the army. One of them is very short and simple. An Australian soldier takes a few minutes to paint a visual and oral picture of the dangers and hardships he and his comrades must face on a Pacific island. The atmosphere is stifling; mosquitoes torment them; they wade in mud, under a warm rain; men fight, die, and are wounded. The audience actually shares in this life evoked by the pictures and the simple commentary of the narrator. It is a true film of life, giving parents and friends at home a vivid idea of what their loved ones across the seas are doing from day to day. These men are very near to us; they are heroes because, though hating war, they fight as a duty, to defend their traditional life of liberty and humanity.

The other example is *The Memphis Belle*. This magnificent film was made by the cameramen of the United States Army Air Corps, under the direction of a great film author, Lieutenant Colonel William Wyler.

It is the story of a Flying Fortress and her crew, in whose daily chores as well as most heroic deeds we are allowed to participate.

The never-ending work of each man, the scientific preparations for each flight, the calm courage and ever-present consciousness of danger in action, comprise the elements of truth with which the film manages to make the audience share in the life of these heroes of the air.

Because the film narrates the simple yet splendid life of these men, because the author's art, though never in evidence, succeeds in making us share their hopes and fears, we may say without fear of exaggeration that it is a masterpiece in the film of life genre, with which all informational films of war are closely connected, being themselves living documents. It is these living documents which make the documentary motion picture great, for they are the marks of man's activities and noble deeds.

7

ORGANIZING THE PRODUCTION AND DISTRIBUTION OF TEACHING, EDUCATIONAL, AND INFORMATIONAL FILMS

IN THE preceding pages we have rapidly reviewed the motion picture in the various fields of teaching, education, and information. We must now determine how these film genres may be constituted in such a way as to survive and expand according to a harmonious system.

I had always dreamed of an ideal organization that would polarize individual achievements, bring to light new talents, and guarantee a methodical distribution of teaching and educational films. This dream was realized in Canada by my old friend John Grierson, thus providing me with a perfect example to study in order to draw certain conclusions.

The Canadian Government first began to produce motion pictures in 1917, when the Ministry of Commerce founded the Bureau of Exhibitions and Publicity.

For the next ten years, Canada led the rest of the British Empire in making the fullest use of films within the various government departments. The services rendered by the motion picture were soon recognized to be so important that the administration created the Canadian Government Motion Picture Bureau. The activities of this bureau were seriously restricted by the budget reductions necessitated during the terrible years of depression, but in spite of this it continued to keep pace with progress, installing sound recording equipment in 1934. However, the Bureau did not seem to be properly organized to answer the growing needs of the various government departments. In 1938, the Canadian Government called John Grierson in to investigate the situation. That same year, Grierson submitted his report, in which he reached the following basic conclusions: The Government would have to enunciate a Canadian policy regarding motion pictures; the Government needed a strong central organization that would be capable of co-ordinating the motion picture activities of all government departments.

A decree passed by Parliament and promulgated on May 2, 1939, sanctioned Grierson's report by setting up the National Film Board.

The law prescribes that the National Film Board be administered by a committee the composition of which is of considerable interest. There are two members of the Government, one of whom must be the chairman. Three officials and three prominent individuals, chosen outside the administration, make up the rest of the Committee. Insofar as the latter three are concerned, Article 5 of the constitution contains a provision the importance of which cannot be too greatly emphasized. This article eliminates any candidate who might have direct or indirect financial interests—either as an outright owner, as a stockholder, or as having any connection with the production, distribution, or showing of films or the manufacture of equipment.

A fair balance is thus struck between the executive power, the administration, and the public.

The administration of the Board is placed constitutionally under the authority of the Government Film Commissioner. The latter controls the production and distribution of all films relating to the activities of governmental departments and, in general, all films of national interest. The Commissioner must be consulted on all expenditures to be made for the purchase of material and for maintenance; in addition, he is the government adviser on all matters relating to information.

The Commissioner's powers are very extensive and in particular include authority to hire temporary personnel in all cases where the type of film to be produced requires the assistance of foreign artists or technicians.

It would take up too much space here to dwell upon the nonetheless extremely interesting articles contained in the constitution; but the latter does set a primary aim for the National Film Board's activities: "The National Film Board guarantees its entire film production to the Government, save when the Commissioner deems it more advisable to have recourse to private assistance."

In order to gain some idea of what the National Film Board does, let us look at the accompanying chart (see pp. 120-1).

The administrative bodies include:

The Administration, whose permanent members are the Government Commissioner, John Grierson, and the Deputy Commissioner, Ross MacLean.

The general departments are set up in such a way that every section receives the financial and technical assistance it needs and is relieved of all administrative cares.

The Division of Film Production is under the permanent direction of the Commissioner and is composed of different units each of which is assigned to a specific film genre. These units are made up of permanent elements as well as technical personnel assigned to those in production.

The production staff includes a responsible head. The latter is chosen from those individuals whose previous work entitles them to be considered as complete film authors, that is, capable of planning, shooting, and editing a film. His three assistants are alternately charged with the preparation, shooting, and editing, under the constant guidance of the chief.

Obviously, a system such as this will have great interest from the standpoint of apprenticeship. The younger men are given an opportunity to learn through experience and to become complete authors themselves. During the first few years of the Board's existence, John Grierson took advantage of his authority to hire temporary collaborators and called in his former disciples

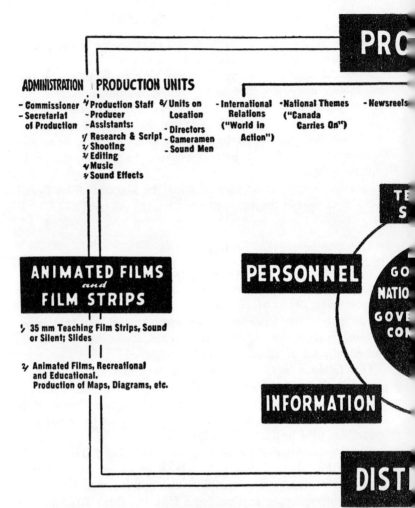

PRO

ADMINISTRATION | PRODUCTION UNITS

- Commissioner
- Secretariat of Production

√ Production Staff
- Producer
- Assistants:
  √ Research & Script
  √ Shooting
  √ Editing
  √ Music
  √ Sound Effects

√ Units on Location
- Directors
- Cameramen
- Sound Men

- International Relations ("World in Action")

- National Themes ("Canada Carries On")

- Newsreels

ANIMATED FILMS and FILM STRIPS

√ 35 mm Teaching Film Strips, Sound or Silent; Slides

√ Animated Films, Recreational and Educational. Production of Maps, Diagrams, etc.

TE S

PERSONNEL

GO
NATIO
GOVE
CON

INFORMATION

DIST

CO-ORDINATOR   **ADMINISTRATION**   **THEATRICAL DISTRIBUTION**
(35 mm)

- Reports and Statistics
- 16 mm and 35 mm Film Libraries
- Preview Library
- Liaison with Production and with Laboratories

√ National Distrib
- Film Libraries
- Program Plans
- Rural Circuits
- Industrial and Trade Union Se
- Volunteer Proje Service

CTION

T ASSIGNMENTS

| | -Industrial and Labor Relations | -National and International Economics | -Public Health -Industrial and Rural Hygiene -Housing and Town Planning | -School Films | -Cultural Relations -Human Geography | -Agriculture -Sociology -Education |

CAL CES

IAN MENT M BOARD NT FILM IONER FILM ONER

LIAISON

ACCOUNTS

PHOTO SERVICES

-Production and Distribution of Stills
-Photographs to Journals and Magazines and Other Publications

DISPLAYS

-Production and Distribution of Displays, Posters, Publications and Photographic Exhibitions for Public or Academic Information

UTION

16 MM DISTRIBUTION

| Liaison with Armed Services Navy Army Air Force | Distribution in the U.K. and Br. Commonwealth | U. S. Distribution | Foreign Distribution |

to make up his units. Stanley Hawes and Stuart Legg still head units and, with Grierson, teach the "fine art" of film making to young Canadians who appreciate their good luck in having a school that is unique of its kind. The Commissioner has also called in experienced foreign cameramen, editors, and sound technicians to teach motion picture technique through experience. The preparatory and editing stages determine a different time of shooting for each unit. The excellent administration of the National Film Board has organized production so that technicians are methodically distributed among the units ready to shoot their films. This system ensures the presence of a permanent technical personnel, familiar with the film genres produced and, in particular, thoroughly imbued with the spirit which permeates the entire organization.

Film genres produced by the National Film Board. These genres are clearly marked on the chart, so that any further comment is unnecessary. However, I would like to draw special attention to the "Productions for French Canada." This is actually a separate department, which is growing in importance with each passing day. Its head is a young French Canadian belonging to the new intellectual elite in Quebec, which has made a very favorable impression on me.

By constitution, Canada is a bilingual nation; therefore, one of the first tasks of the National Film Board was to make French adaptations of all films having English commentaries. But it was even more important for the Board to respect one of the aims set forth by its constitution: "to produce and distribute films of national interest calculated to help Canadians in all the provinces understand their way of life and their mutual problems." So that the motion picture might carry out its mission of national unity and solidarity, a French Canadian section was needed to strike a balance with the Anglophile production.

This section, then, endeavors to familiarize the other provinces with the life of Quebec by producing films carefully planned to that effect. Let me emphasize at once that there is no question of propaganda here, since this would be extremely ill-advised in a country which possesses national unity. The task might seem to be a particularly delicate one to the observer who judges only by appearances and accepts superficial statements without carefully analyzing them. Actually, it consists of honestly pointing out and explaining certain peculiarities in order to make them respected.

All Canadians, whether consciously or not, feel very strongly about national unity, so that once this great concept has been brought into the open, it becomes a relatively simple matter to use animated pictures showing it in all its varied forms through the sole power of truth. To take an example, French Canadians represent the most touching proof of the permanence of French culture; their love for France is the sign of a stubbornly persistent atavism, but, aside from this, they are as uniquely and profoundly Canadian as their Anglophile compatriots.

Not all the genres shown on the chart are rigidly separated from each other. Frequently, a unit will split up, either temporarily or to form a new cell in this hive of industry, and concern itself with questions engendered by the constant evolution of human civilization.

Lastly, I find that neither a chart nor anything I can say is adequate to describe the spirit which reigns among all these young people. Every one of them is driven by some force deep within him to crusade in the cause of educational films. They will become not only good film authors but also good citizens, accustomed to showing respect for the public weal. Their modesty will be dictated by the sense of responsibility which derives from the fact that they are using the most powerful means of dissemination man has ever invented.

Distribution. The chart shows two kinds of distribution:

Distribution of 35 mm. films over commercial circuits, that is, films planned and made to be shown in motion picture theaters to the general public. These are distributed by agreement with the distributing companies. For instance, this is the case with the serial *World in Action,* which is distributed in Canada and abroad by private industry. In the United States, the films in this serial are distributed through United Artists to over 5,000 motion picture theaters.

When the commercial field has been covered, this type of film is distributed over circuits handling educational films.

Distribution of 16 mm. films. This is done either by the sale of copies to local or specialized film libraries or over circuits controlled by the National Film Board.

The National Film Board provides film libraries with documentary material regarding foreign productions and gives them sample copies which its services have been able to obtain either as a loan or even by buying them. Local teachers, who are often very far from Ottawa, can thus thoroughly acquaint themselves with the material before placing their orders.

The distribution circuits established and controlled by the National Film Board consist of two specialized groups: one for industrial centers, the other for rural communities.

This organization for direct distribution follows the same system of using units. It is remarkable to note that the young heads of the distribution units are imbued with the same spirit which possesses their colleagues in production, even though the stimulus of creative work is lacking. As a matter of fact, the Commissioner has provided them with another incentive for their youthful enthusiasm. Each unit chief is put in charge of a light truck, an electric generator, and a projector. He and his unit are assigned to operate in a specific area, and every night they give a free performance with the educational films made by the National Film Board. This schedule may seem simple, but actually the unit must negotiate for the use of the municipal or parish hall, show the films, and often direct the discussions that are always promoted and encouraged. In short, these young men and women must be diplomats and educators. Nor should we forget the tremendous energy and physical stamina they need. The distances are tremendous, the climate harsh. In winter, they have to take the train and carry their equipment by hand from the station wherever the film is to be shown. But here again it is their sense of responsibility, the knowledge that they are daily performing a great service, which gives them strength and keeps alive their enthusiasm. In setting up these groups, the Commissioner was fully aware that they would develop individuality and promote rivalry.

I had the privilege of attending a small conference held by the chiefs of these mobile units at a camp beside one of those colorful and charming Canadian lakes. For four days, this tiny parliament deliberated on the best means of serving the public's education.

Coming from every section of this vast country, all these young people were united by the love they had for their work. They were all eager to exchange information that would help them perfect their jobs. They were all seeking to serve their country by promoting this marvelous means of education, in which they were discovering new possibilities every day. What a salutary lesson this would have been to that army of skeptics and ignoramuses who still regard the motion picture as a toy, a kind of side show! They would have seen that all these young people were crusading in the cause of public education, for the programs shown had no recreational or entertainment films but only films designed strictly for educational and informative purposes. The National Film Board's task is made more difficult precisely because of the fact that the Commissioner very properly rejects all proposals tending to introduce so-called "entertaining" films into the programs. The aim is to educate, and this is attained through arousing interest by the quality of the films. Since I had only too often attended postgraduate performances, dubbed educational, where certain films were shown that would have been banned to children in Belgium,* I was all the more able to appreciate the Commissioner's firmness in resisting all attempts to deviate from the aim for which the Canadian Parliament created the National Film Board.

Foreign Distribution.

Another function of the National Film Board is to disseminate government films abroad so that other peoples will get to know what Canada is really like. To this effect, it communicates directly with foreign embassies or official agencies and is tending more and more to set up its own offices in the great capitals of the world. But the Commissioner has realized that this cannot be a one-sided proposition; he favors and hopes to develop

* See Belgian censorship, p. 205.

exchanges of educational films between Canada and the other film-producing countries.

Animated Films and Slides.

The National Film Board has established a workshop for animated cartoons and puppets which does all the work required by the production units. One of this workshop's creations was the charming and delightful serial of Canadian songs.

This last section also makes and distributes the slides that form a part of visual education.

Finally, the National Film Board has workshops for making and reproducing photographs, drawings, and posters designed for the information of the public. This far too sketchy outline may give some notion of the work done by this unprecedented organization in producing and distributing educational films. But I want most particularly to emphasize the fact that the National Film Board constitutes a splendid school where the young not only learn their trade but also become eager to serve the public weal with the help of an art which they are fortunate enough to be able to practice.

Such an organization might be held up as an example for other countries, given a certain amount of adaptation to local conditions. In France, for example, it would be advisable to obtain the help of the producers, who have long specialized in educational and documentary films. But the organization should remain a school for the young and, for the government, an expression of its national activities, over which it has a responsibility and a duty to exercise control.

I hope that some day very soon all nations will have their own national film boards and that, by federating them, it will be possible for the educational film to achieve its great aims. This is not the place to go into the aims and activities of the future "International Federation of National Film Boards"; but its foundations have been laid, and the people who, for so many years, have crusaded in its cause are ready to build the framework of this new League of Nations designed to further the general education and knowledge of all peoples.

PART II

THE MOTION PICTURE IN THE ART
OF ENTERTAINMENT

8

POETRY, FANCY,
AND COMEDY

THE MOTION PICTURE has rapidly won for itself a preponderant place in the art of entertainment. Some people are surprised, others deplore it, but most are delighted. In reality, the true reason for the success of this seventh art lies in the very simple fact that the place it occupies was vacant.

As a matter of fact, an art was needed which, involving new concepts of technique and artistry, would furnish a means of creating "entertainment for everyone." The motion picture filled this gap because it was an art in its own right and because it had tremendous potentialities for diffusion. It would be suicidal for it to imitate the theater or attempt to substitute for it.

All the genres which make up the art of entertainment are based on the general laws common to all arts, the essential aim of which is to procure visual or intellectual satisfaction; but these genres must obey special laws which are dictated by the structure and aesthetics suitable to them.

The motion picture, therefore, should never be permitted to take the easy course, which is that of producing canned theater and music hall, but should, on the contrary, preserve its own individuality so as to accomplish its great and noble mission.

Where should we put the entertainment film in the hierarchy of genres?

Occasionally we hear people saying, rather scornfully, of a dramatic film: "It's a good documentary." If they mean that the film brings "documentary" material to the public, then they are paying it a valuable compliment. The best dramatic films are those in which the action unfolds amid true surroundings. A dramatic film may be given a documentary character by the environment it studies and an educational character by the idea on which it is based. I cannot believe that this detracts either from the interest or from the emotion. On the contrary, I am certain that it provokes them.

There are times when even an object can take on dramatic significance or become one of the actors. Not only does the lens record the life of mobile objects but it also brings inanimate objects to life.

A telephone, for example, may appear differently in each of several shots. First it may be shown in its true proportions, within reach of our hand. Then, as the camera travels, it gradually expands into a close-up until it spills over the edge of the screen, which no longer contains anything but partial images of the ringing bell, the receiver glued to an anxious ear, the switch jiggled by an impatient hand. The camera lens analyzes the object; by panning, it can cover it from every angle, tilt over it or beneath it, revolve around it as if the better to guess its secret, and once more draw off to contemplate from afar that THING which gleams in a light as bright as day with an air of being alive.

The linking of the entertainment film with the educational film through the intermediary of the film of life makes of the motion picture a unified whole, since the finest dramatic works of the screen are most often those which are bathed in a documentary atmosphere and take root in the full light of day.

The motion picture may be an art of life, of truth, or of fantasy. When we go to a motion picture theater, we must be careful to choose between the various genres according to the mood we are in at the time, lest we make an unfair criticism of the film we do see. Just as we do when going to see a play, we should decide whether we want to see a comedy or a tragedy before making our choice and should refrain from criticising a work except as the representative of its genre.

Like the educational and documentary films, the entertainment film comprises several different genres; but whether it be comic, dramatic, or fanciful, a work can have significance and be capable of stirring the emotions of human beings only if it is itself concerned with human nature. I don't mean that its story must be kept within the limits of absolute realism. The most fanciful dream, as well as the most down-to-earth fact, can furnish an excellent theme for a film. Nor is there any law against expressing the poetry of the commonplace. Those dramatic stories which are closest to life should not forcibly be deprived of the poetic element contained in everyday occurrences.

Nevertheless, it is true that the public, though capable of being deeply moved by reality, is equally desirous of forgetting it and occasionally escaping into fantasy.

THE FILM IN POETRY AND FANCY

The poetic film permits a transferral into the unreal world of fairyland and affords man the opportunity to escape into the hazy realms of fantasy, into a world of fabulous fauna and flora, into a nature created by the poet's imagination. So that he might transport the mind into these ethereal regions, Walt Disney made himself the high priest of the poetic film.

The poetic and fairy genre sprang from the genius of Georges Méliès, who was the first real film author. He invented quantities of technical details and brought to the screen those qualities of verve and fantasy which later enabled it to develop its fairy-like aspect. Méliès' career and character were such as to prepare him for becoming a great pioneer in motion pictures. While a student at the Ecole des Beaux-Arts in 1880, he was attracted to the art of prestidigitation, in which he became a virtuoso. With the invention of motion pictures in 1895, he discovered all the potentialities contained in this new art to satisfy his magician's imagination. He established the first studio, he invented single frame photography, which later on made animated puppets and cartoons possible. He never stopped working until in 1938 death put an end to his long and heart-rending career in pursuit of chimeras. *The Exorcised* (1899), *A Trip to the Moon* (1902),

The Palace of Arabian Nights (1905), *The Conquest of the North Pole* (1912) were the stages in Méliès career, and are as precious to the motion picture's history as the primitives are to the history of painting. Even today, his films are the delight of children and adults whenever they are shown at the Museum of Modern Art in New York or at the British Film Institute in London.

The fantasy film received a wealth of new technique, thanks to the efforts of Ladislas Starevitch, natural history professor and director of the Kovno museum, who at that time felt the need for using motion pictures in his courses. He first tried to record animal life by ordinary processes; but the equipment available at the time, particularly the big arc lights, interfered with the natural reactions of his subjects, and because of this the films he obtained were lacking in any scientific value. Starevitch was thus compelled to invent animal "puppets" which he used to reproduce his own observations for the purposes of his course. Gifted with the temperament of an artist, this scientist soon turned to the realm of fantasy as a means of self-expression. He perfected his technique, simplifying his puppets as time went on. Each figure consisted of a framework covered with a specially prepared fabric, while the various parts, such as teeth, tongue, and limbs, were mobile. Later on, he used a plastic material for the face, which enabled him to obtain a whole range of expression through the breakdown of the movement recorded frame by frame. By making his characters move around on a set, he managed to give a queer impression of human comedy transported into a world of fancy.

Starevitch's particular achievement lay in bringing to life the fables of La Fontaine, thus using his talents as an educator, which never deserted him. For his first film, *The Grasshopper and the Ant*, he was rewarded by the czar; one of the last films he made in Russia was *The Revenge of a Motion Picture Cameraman*. After the revolution, he came to live in a little house near Paris, where, together with his daughter, he worked unremittingly to produce little masterpieces such as *The Frogs Desiring a King*, *The City Rat and the Country Rat*, and *The*

Adventures of Reynard, the first full-length film of this type (8,200 feet), which had a superb musical accompaniment. A talented, courageous, and conscientious man, Starevitch made a great contribution toward blazing the trail along which the fantasy film would soon triumph.

But before this genre could achieve success, another artist came along to mark one more of those painful stages which seem to be required of all creations of the human mind before they reach the point where they are accepted by the world.

To Emile Cohl goes the honor of being the true originator of the animated cartoon.

Emile Cohl began as an apprentice jeweler; his hobby was caricature drawing. He became a pupil of André Gill and collaborated on a number of humorous periodicals but only became interested in motion pictures toward 1905, when he produced several films with animated puppets. Finally, in 1907, he made the first film to use animated drawings: *Mr. Stop.* This was the story of an inventor who had discovered a way to suspend motion. A second film was shown in the Folies-Bergères. Others followed in quick succession, among them *Phantasmagoria* (1908), *The Neo-Impressionist Painter,* etc.

In 1912, Emile Cohl was sent by the *Eclair Journal* to New York, where he acquired a number of pupils. Fortified by their master's experiments with the process, these pupils lost no time in commercializing the production, which was soon to expand to the point at which we now know it.

Returning to France in 1914, Emile Cohl produced other films, but he could make no headway against an organized production.

The cartoonists Gros, O'Galop, Lortac, and Benjamin Rabier made films of great charm, bearing their own personal style. Not one of them was able to break away from the routine work that took up all their time, which led Emile Cohl to remark one day: "Our finances are in a deplorable state; but that is a consolation to the French artist, with his hypertrophied self-respect, which makes him prefer to drink out of his own cup, small as it is, than become a cog in a picture factory." * Further on, we

* Arnaud and Boisyvon, *Le Cinéma pour tout,* Garnier, 1922.

shall see that it was possible to relieve the artist of doing mechanical work so that he could create more freely and more rapidly. However that may be, Emile Cohl was the first to make and to show a film belonging to this genre.

In France, Max Pinchon; in the United States, Winsor McCay with *Gertie the Dinosaur* and Pat Sullivan with his famous *Felix the Cat* were among the pioneers who, with Cohl, prepared the ground for Walt Disney, the founder of the poetic genre. But whatever improvements the latter may have brought, the technique of animated cartoons is based on Méliès's invention of single frame photography, first put into practice by Cohl. Moreover, Walt Disney himself generously and forthrightly acknowledged this fact. In 1936, the French Consul General in Los Angeles decorated him with the Legion of Honor; Walt Disney expressed his gratitude to the two Frenchmen, Méliès and Cohl, who had, in his own terms, "discovered the means of placing poetry within reach of the man in the street."

Walt Disney is a great poet whose works have brought beauty and a few precious moments of happiness to the world. Thanks to him, all of us have often felt ourselves transported into the world of the unreal and the fanciful.

Gay and serious by turns, like our own La Fontaine, a medieval troubadour of *chansons de geste,* a composer of symphonies in color, that is Walt Disney, the poet of film art! For years, his films have delighted millions and imbedded themselves deep in the heart of man, who is ever eager to escape momentarily from reality. Through the magic of his art, Walt Disney has made this escape possible, bringing joy and beauty and love. Walt Disney represents a crowning achievement of Art, whose everlasting aim is to draw inspiration from the life of man and of nature and transmit that life, interpreted by the artist's sensibility and talent, to the people with whom it is in touch. Never has this been done more perfectly than in the work of Walt Disney, who brings to man that joy of living which he himself possesses. Never has an artist's mission been more humane or more sympathetic.

This ray of pure sunshine even now lights up a devastated

world, bringing momentary relief to millions of tormented souls. Indeed, his magical creations come so close to our hearts that we find it hard not to believe a miracle is taking place. If we may conceive of a miracle as being man's faculty for dreaming and imagining, then it is very true that Walt Disney's work constitutes a miracle which is performed before our eyes when we find ourselves suddenly transported to the laboratory of ideas, of dreams, and of magic where it takes shape. It is in the studios of Hollywood that so many poems are born that will fly all over the world.

Walt Disney and his collaborators dream, imagine, think out loud. They create joyfully, as though inspired by thought vibrations from the millions of people for whom they are creating new masterpieces. Together, they form a kind of orchestra of minds, to which each individual temperament lends its own harmony, all blending into the one score directed by the maestro. As a matter of fact, the theme that later on will inspire the cartoonist is first set to music. And so the perfect cycle between creator and living universe is accomplished, so the miracle of art is achieved in its purest and most complete form.

I do not intend to analyze Walt Disney's fertile work, from *Mickey Mouse* and his *Silly Symphonies* to *Snow White*, *Fantasia*, and *Dumbo*. This would require a separate book. However, I would like to note that Walt Disney would have failed in his mission if he had lost himself in dreams at the most tragic moment in the history of a civilization which millions of men are sacrificing themselves to preserve. Fortunately, he felt that, while keeping alive the poetry which the world will need so badly when the nightmare is ended, he should devote most of his time to making instructive films for the army and navy. By making it possible to accelerate the training of young soldiers and sailors, these films contributed in large part to the miraculously rapid building up of that huge and splendid American Army.

During our last encounter, while we were naturally speaking of France, whose greatness Walt was extolling, I asked him to write me a message which I could broadcast to my compatriots.

Whereupon, without any further ado and showing a sincerity that touched me, he dictated the following lines:

Twenty-five years ago in France I saw the Republic rise from the crushing heels of a ruthless enemy to a glorious triumph. Today the steel of that same enemy is again trying to crush the life and spirit out of your glorious country but the free spirit of France will never die.

The blood of your youth spilled on your verdant fields will flower again into the liberty and equality every Frenchman reveres. That day is not far distant. The weapons and the men are being forged in America to forever sever the chains of your oppressor.

In Hollywood we are making pictures to hasten the training of these men and to teach them how to handle the unending stream of weapons pouring out of our factories. We are also looking ahead to the days when the mantle of peace again falls over your beautiful country and we can bring to you the food, the clothing and the shelter our enemy has taken from you. We are planning for pictures that will help your hearts forget the anguish of your travail. Our boys and girls are with the youth of France in spirit and deeds and when the blood of our youth mingles with the blood of your people once more on the field of Flanders, then will come the day when France will forever be freed of the fear of war and terror.

Vive la France!

Walt Disney

December 30, 1943

To permit a sufficient production and enable it to reach a world-wide audience, it was necessary to set up a powerful industrial organization. Walt Disney planned and built a modern workshop where some two hundred people work at sketching, filling out, and coloring fanciful drawings, as well as sound recording studios of unrivaled excellence, the function of which is to ensure constant technical advances; but his most notable feat was to found an industry without affecting the ability to do creative work. The machine and the mechanical gesture are made subservient to thought, which in turn directs and nourishes the machine. Walt Disney thus proved that art and industry could be happily associated, provided the latter intervene only to bring man a little happiness, either by enriching his mind or by bettering his condition. And this is particularly important for the motion picture, which, as we shall see later, is an art-industry.

This, then, is one of the motion picture's primary aims in the art of entertainment: that of providing fantasy, magic, and poetry.

THE FILM IN COMEDY

There are numerous other film genres whose principal function is to divert. Comedy relaxes the mind through laughter or smiling. The dance and music, allied to the art of scenery and costume, satisfy this natural taste for spectacle, guiding it toward the beautiful, and provide the spectator with an unconscious visual education in art. The motion picture has made it possible to bring within reach of all those lavish spectacles hitherto reserved for the privileged populations of large cities. For this reason it is in a position to perform a social function by providing *diversion*, which, together with *work*, constitutes an essential element of equilibrium. This equilibrium can be maintained only if the element of diversion preserves an artistic or moral quality calculated to elevate man.

Comedy or vaudeville should provoke laughter through the healthy mirth contained in situations and through the imagination of the actors. In no other genre do the actors have as potent and responsible a part to play. The success and quality of these genres depend on the intelligence and imagination that go to make up the art of the comedian. Max Linder, the founder of the genre, for years provided the relaxation of laughter. He won his audience over from the very start by his fancy, by his imagination, and especially because the situations he conceived were scenes from daily life transported into the realm of fantasy. He was very close to his public, yet he never made base concessions to it. Since his day, we have delighted in the antics of the Marx brothers, Laurel and Hardy, and a few others worthy of carrying on the genre created by Max Linder. In this sense, the art of the comic actor is very closely allied to that of the clown. In pointing out that relationship, I mean it as a rare compliment to the comedians of the screen, for to my mind nothing in this field can equal the talent of such truly inspired clowns as Footit, Chocolat, the Fratellini brothers, Grock, and the delightful Porto, to mention only those I have seen. Moreover, it should be noted that the Circus and cinematic Comedy are brothers in entertainment. Both are based on observations of life and people which they transpose into fantasy. They bring out the comic in everyday acts and gestures, magnifying them through the distorting mirror of their interpretation. The comic effect thus results more from the situations and the interpretation of character by expression than from the quality of the dialogue. For this very reason, film comedy differs from theater comedy.

The purely spectacular genre, so well represented by the "musicals," is designed to bring to the screen the rhythmic cadence of the dance, the tuneful quality of song, and the brilliant coloring of scenery and costume. This genre will achieve its aim so long as it remains filmic, that is, so long as it is not satisfied to imitate the musical comedy of the stage but exploits all the possibilities offered by its fourth dimensional quality. The American motion picture industry is past master in this type of film which is particularly adapted to the tempo of its own national life.

Hollywood, which is unjustly condemned, has made possible the production of films whose lavishness it alone could guarantee. Hollywood is unrivaled for its artistic and technical resources. On this little piece of land, virtually a separate state, the greatest artists in the world are gathered — writers, composers, stage designers, directors, actors, dancers — all of whom have been judiciously hired by producers seasoned in the technique of the film spectacle. The result is that all over the world people have delighted in film spectacles such as *Broadway Melody, Bathing Beauty,* and many others.

The standard type of American film spectacle, in my opinion, is *Yankee Doodle Dandy,* whose spectacular quality coincides with the personality of the leading character. The story is about a family of actors whose upright, honorable lives, full of devotion to their profession, emphasize the importance of the social role, so often unrecognized by the pleasure-seeking public!

All honor is due the American motion picture for having enabled the greatest cities as well as the smallest hamlets of the world to benefit from these magnificent spectacles.

It is only fitting that we should revise our opinion of Hollywood and acknowledge the excellent quality of its productions in this genre. Generally speaking, it is particularly important that a film should be judged as an example of its genre. If, for instance, on seeing a musical, we look for an idea or a problem to discuss, as we often do, we are bound to find the film stupid; we are doing it a serious injustice. Indeed, this film genre cannot be confused with the dramatic film; its sole function is to divert, and it should be discussed solely from an artistic standpoint. Let me repeat that it all comes down to being *willing to select,* among the different genres of film entertainment, that which is best suited to the mood of the moment. Each person should be careful to decide whether he wishes to be amused by a comedy, escape into fantasy, or stimulate his intellect with ideas. He should give himself a searching cross-examination.

Once he becomes aware of the limitations of each genre, he will acknowledge, even though he may not admire the film spectacle as a genre, that it possesses artistic merit and plays an important part in contemporary social life.

By providing man with the means to escape into poetry, magic, and fantasy, the motion picture will have assured him an equilibrium which is as necessary to his moral health as to his physical health.

9
THE ART OF THE DRAMATIC FILM

AN IMPORTANT element would be lacking in the individual's equilibrium if the motion picture did not provide, in a different form, what the theater has so generously dispensed for centuries. This is the intellectual element, in the form of "food for thought," which is as necessary to the human brain as nourishment is to the stomach.

This function is performed by the *art of the dramatic film,* whose importance and seriousness require from those who serve it a very lively sense of the heavy responsibility incumbent upon them.

Film authors who are responsible for planning and making dramatic films must be particularly careful in exercising the law of *selection* and measuring the consequences of the subject matter they offer for the reflection of the public. Above all, they must take into account the psychological reactions determined by the screen, the very power of which may convey a double meaning.

Goethe had clearly envisaged this power of the image in the following verses,* the truth of which has now been proved by the motion picture:

> *Many stupid things are often said,*
> *As well as written;*
> *They do not kill the flesh or soul,*

* *Zahme Xenien.*

Nor any change effect.
But something stupid offered to the eye
Exerts a magic force:
Because it chains the senses
The mind remains a slave.

That stupidity of which Goethe speaks is to be avoided in all fields covered by the art of entertainment and in all genres of the motion picture, but it becomes especially dangerous in dramatic films for the very reason that they are intended to solicit reflection. The author of these films has an imperative duty to present subjects that are capable of elevating and enlightening the mind.

The field of the dramatic film is a vast one, but more often it conveys everyday life, made up of joy, love, and suffering. It derives its principal source of emotion from the simplest actions, common to all men. Every individual, no matter what his environment, goes through certain motions every day that are common to all other individuals. These daily motions lead to a series of infinitely varied actions. By co-ordinating these actions, a dramatic structure may be obtained. This dramatic structure will have true emotional value if the actions it co-ordinates are motivated by an idea, if it places them in a truly alive environment.

It follows that the basic principles on which the conception and creation of dramatic films must rest are the *Idea* and the *Environment*.

Above all, the idea must be capable of supporting a dramatic film construction. Some ideas belong more particularly to the field of literature, and in such cases the screen could only betray them. Every art has its own means of expression; these must be distinguished so that the idea may be presented more clearly. For instance, in order to conceive a good dramatic film, more is needed than just finding "a story": an idea must be found which can be developed naturally by filmic means; this idea must be sufficiently powerful to be worth the trouble of putting it on the screen. The dramatic motion picture should only make use of ideas that are human and alive, that reflect the fundamentals of filmic art.

It is only fair to point out that the choice of idea is not as easy as one might believe. Apart from the ability to appreciate its proper value, which is always subject to human error, the film author must be possessed of vast experience and tremendous technical knowledge to determine whether the central theme is capable of sustaining a dramatic film construction. These are qualities which are at once natural and acquired. Natural, because the critical and appreciative sense is an innate gift. Acquired, because one must know how to go about *choosing*. This technique can only be acquired through exercises performed in accordance with certain methods. For my part, I try to exercise my pupils' minds by asking them to determine the central theme of a book and to trace the framework that supports it. The idea, thus stripped of the seductive finery in which the author's talent has clothed it, can be appreciated for its intrinsic value. If it is deemed worth while, it can grow another framework, one capable of sustaining a dramatic film construction. Thus, the original idea will have been adapted from the field of literature to that of the motion picture. By following this method, the film author will be able to appreciate the central theme of the work being considered for the screen, or to choose one of his own ideas from the many rising out of his subconscious mind.

Once the qualities of the central theme have been appraised in connection with the dramatic construction, the film author must make sure that he can develop it without being obliged to rely on the conventional methods of the theater. This statement should in no way be construed as disparaging the latter. The theater and the motion picture are two separate arts, in the conception of their works as well as in their execution. The theater has behind it a long and glorious career, and its future is assured. The motion picture is a very young art but sufficiently mature for its laws and aims to have been determined.

The fundamental difference between the two arts is that in the theater the footlights are postulated. The audience concedes that everything which takes place on the far side of these

One of the earliest animated cartoons: *A Trip to the Moon*, by Georges Méliès (see page 131).

The Road to Life, by Ekk (see page 146).

footlights is, by the very fact that they exist, the result of a convention. By definition, the word theater is the physical location where an action, an incident, an event, takes place. Therefore, the stage of the dramatic theater represents a set point for the development of a plot which, by the same token, is compelled to observe the unity of place.

On the other hand, a dramatic film is four-dimensional and can change scenes by means of dissolves which constitute the punctuation of its visual text. Furthermore, a motion picture projects its animated images directly onto a screen, from which there is nothing to separate the audience. The latter, therefore, is put directly in touch with life.

In this connection, let us refer once more to what Canudo wrote in 1927:

"The theater has come to occupy a preponderant position in this and, by the aura of glamor that surrounds it, has managed to distort everything that touches it. Some of the greatest French artists who have made their living in the theater have come to grief in films. Truth in the theater is impossible. It is indispensable to the motion picture. When an artist has spent his entire life working wonder with 'the illusion' of life, he finds it most difficult suddenly to start working wonders with life itself.

"In the theater, actor and director can only be workmen, for they are working with the material of Art. In the motion picture it takes a true artist to handle his materials and his workmen."

And later: "A photoplay must not imitate theatrical methods, whatever they may be; in this senile Europe, decaying with traditions and yet full of health and imagination, the film remains the preposterous slave of the theater. The general inferiority of its technical achievements, compared with the American film, cannot be disputed. The fact is that the Americans, who are a mingled race, a race yet not a race, a product of mankind, admirable as it is, rather than a race, loathesome as it has been, have no intellectual traditions, are bound by no cultural shackles. They were born esthetically into the Art of the Screen, just as the entire old world was born into the Art of sound or color or stone. They have nothing to forget in order that they may plunge wholeheartedly into this new creation of himself which man has conceived."

These fundamental differences should be taken into consideration at the time of choosing. Since the motion picture provides a direct contact with life, films should be human and true to life, that is, they should take hold of their audience through the material of its day-to-day, hour-to-hour existence. They will have succeeded in this whenever the audience is heard to remark: "Oh, that's so true!" or "Why, he acts just like So-and-So!" These reflexes represent the final great verdict, the only one that counts, the verdict of the people, with whom one must never lose touch.

Finally, the film author must believe in the idea before he takes on the responsibility of spreading it. He must believe in it so that he may be able to protect it from all the distortions which it may so easily undergo during the period of gestation. He must believe in it so that he can communicate his faith to everyone who works with him. Finally, he must believe in it because faith and sincerity are necessary to creative inspiration and constitute elementary principles of integrity required in dealing with the people who come under the powerful ascendancy of pictures.

Unfortunately, it happens all too often that a film author, driven by material needs, will agree to make a film based on an idea in which he does not believe or, even worse, a film having no idea at all. In that case, "the fine art" becomes one long calvary without hope; the artist is merely doing a job; he has become a skilled worker, using his technical knowledge to "manufacture" images without a soul.

Some film authors are incapable of giving shape to an idea in which they have no faith or even to a simple story which has no central idea. This state of mind has not had a very happy effect on their careers, while it has cut down on the number of films they were able to make.

This does not mean that they were lacking in ideas, but, as luck would have it, the ones they did believe in would often hold no interest for the producers. On the other hand, they themselves could rarely get up any interest in the ideas that were suggested to them. In most cases, any discussion was impossible because they did not talk the same language. They were thinking in terms of the idea, while the producer was thinking in terms of the billing. Even before taking a look at the scenario timidly handed to him, the producer would invariably ask, "What stars have you got in mind for the cast?" In other words, the important thing was to get the cast lined up and then find a "vehicle." These producers were such poor businessmen that they did not realize that all great dramatic films which have met with world-wide acclaim were built around a universal theme, developed within its environment.

The second basic element necessary to dramatic films is *Environment,* for the selection and study of the environment are as important as the selection of the idea. I mean that the selection of the idea represents the human motive embroidered on the fabric of the environment. The study of this environment provides a store of true details, noted from day to day, a thousand and one realistic touches, a veritable human synthesis that surrounds, strengthens, and prolongs the action and, far more than the actual set, roots it firmly in everyday life.

The environment is the broth culture wherein the embryonic characters gradually come to life. They take on a living human shape; a skeleton forms and becomes covered with flesh; finally, a mind awakes and manifests its first reactions on coming into contact with other creatures born of the same matrix. In this way, they become human beings, whose appearance and character will be molded in accordance with their mental make-up and the environment in which the story places them. They will be given clothes befitting their estate and their character; they will be lodged and furnished with possessions of a sort calculated to create that environment, a real biological fluid, out of which they could neither breathe nor move, in a word, live.

The environment, so necessary to the development of the idea through the dramatic action, cannot be reconstituted unless it is first carefully studied. To do this, the film author himself must live in the environment before he starts to write his scenario. This brings us to the relationship that exists between dramatic films and films of life, for here, too, the author must go to life for his material the better to interpret it on the screen.

All great dramatic films have a universal theme and are drawn from observations of life. We need only consider a few classic examples to be convinced that this is true.

Ekk could never have created his splendid masterpiece, *The Road to Life,* if he had not first been inspired by the idea of vagrant children, whom the war had thrown on their own resources, and by the idea that it was the nation's sacred duty to save these little ones who had reverted to a state of nature. Ekk's work would not have been successful if he had not made a study of this tragic problem, if he had not suffered in the same hopeless environment and witnessed the dawning of new hope, if he had not, day after day, observed his subjects, and especially if he had not loved them. His love for these unfortunate children is so evident, even when they are committting their worst crimes, that the spectator never condemns them but always understands them, feels sorry for them, loves them. This film author was able to build up a strong dramatic construction entirely out of elements that were true and human because he had been inspired by an idea and because he had shared the existence of the people he brought to life. He would never have been able to portray this existence if he had not lived it himself.

The entire work of Charlie Chaplin, as a film author, testifies to the value of the idea and the environment as fundamental bases of the dramatic film.

Chaplin was able to put his philosophy into images because his genius had allowed him to draw out the substance of the environments in which he had lived. A product of the people and remaining in close touch with them, Chaplin was able to observe, understand, infer, and express what his subconscious mind had noted down. Through his own feelings, he recorded the suffering and joy, the greatness and folly of man, and each of his works is inspired by observations of life which, in every case, he concretizes around an idea allowed to take form within the environment most favorable to its growth.

Chaplin's is a smiling philosophy that brings tears to the eyes.

His caustic wit strips away the sham to reveal defects of character; but, more often, his faith in human kindness allows us to discover within ourselves the secret garden common to all men, wherein a few fine flowers grow, needing only a sprinkling of kindness to make them bloom. Chaplin's genius affects our innermost feelings because he draws his strength from the power of the idea developed in an environment which he re-creates for us through his own interpretation. A courageous observer of people and events, Chaplin has every right to be harsh and biting with the people at whom he directs his shafts, because he does it with wit and integrity. But his genius almost always takes the form of that smiling kindness, that sensibility without sentimentality which has marked all his work from *A Dog's Life* and *Charlie the Soldier* up to the great cry of outraged conscience expressed in *The Dictator*. In this last film, Chaplin uses the sharp edge of satire to triumph through ridicule. In *Modern Times*, he uses his own methods to fight against the exploitation of the individual by those who control for their own profit the machines which are really a part of the natural evolution of progress for the betterment of man's condition.

The diversity of Charlie Chaplin's work finds unity in the fact that it is the product of a talent which has been put to work serving the cause of ideas made up of human kindness and drawn from observations close to life in an attempt to make the latter better and finer. Under these conditions, the social aim of the dramatic film is superbly achieved. Charlie Chaplin's work, like that of Molière, to which it is akin, will never die because his genius enabled him to draw universal conclusions from his observations of the human environment.

Every film author naturally expresses himself in accordance with his own temperament and sensibility. René Clair, for example, though apparently in a lighter vein, nevertheless draws his inspiration from the same sources. He allows an idea to take hold of him only after he has judiciously examined it in the mirror of his conscience. And, when he has once allowed himself to be convinced, won over to its cause, he cultivates it through his observations of the environment suitable to it or by recalling certain incidents which justify his selection. *Sous les Toits de Paris* and *Le Million* are the works which seem most characteristic of his particularly brilliant and intellectually stimulating talents. But *A Nous la Liberté* shows the true depths of his feelings, reacting to the same social problems as Charlie Chaplin; indeed, the one almost certainly inspired the other. Similarly, *Le Dernier des Milliardaires,* made in 1934, pictured the tragic folly of dictators.

In his lighter moments, René Clair's vivacity and sparkle, his imagination, are nonetheless always directed in the cause of a central theme and reveal an environment that has been carefully studied. The author's temperament, the characteristics of his talent, are still in evidence, whatever the genre, the idea, or the environment. In *It Happened Tomorrow,* René Clair's wit, always effervescent as champagne, dominates the whole film, yet he uses the utmost tact in disclosing a great idea, attracting the audience to it by the rhythm and beauty of his images.

Numerous similar examples could be cited, all apparently different, because a variety of talent has gone into them, but all faithful to the principle of *selecting* the central idea and to the study of environment. First of all, D. W. Griffith, and then, in the modern school, Jean Renoir, Frank Capra, Julien Duvivier, William Wyler, Serge Eisenstein, Raymond Bernard, André Berthomieux, Marcel L'Herbier are authors who, along with many others, exemplify and illustrate that diversity in art, while at the same time respecting the fundamental laws which constitute its greatness.

Perhaps it will not seem amiss if I mention a few personal experiences in an attempt to justify the foregoing.

The modest contribution I was able to make to the French school of motion pictures was based on the choice of the idea, the faith which led to that deliberate choice, and the study of environment.

In *Hélène,* the theme was faith in life. It showed a human being's will to triumph over daily vicissitudes, the story of one woman whose shining courage brightened the lives of the young people around her. "One must believe in life," said Hélène, thus voicing the film's central theme, which we selected among the quantity of ideas contained in Vicki Baum's profound and varied work.

To bring this idea to life, we studied the environment in which the story was laid. At Grenoble, we took part in the life of the university students, made character studies, noted all the details and sites. Later on, we returned with the characters we had created in the image of those we had studied in their environment.

La Maternelle was meant to illustrate the idea that the sentiment which comes naturally to every woman—love for children—can lessen the mental and physical misery of an unhappy childhood. The film's whole theme is summed up in the reply made by Madame Paulin: "You've got to love children, if you want them to love you!"

For the treatment and scenario, we already had some splendid material in the seven or eight stories by Léon Frapié, themselves documents of life. But we could not possibly have planned the film without that direct observation which alone can put one in tune with life. Therefore, we spent a few months living in different schools in the most crowded sections of Paris.

We settled down to watch the children live. Once we had gained their confidence, we were able to analyze them psychologically. We lived in these nursery schools that constitute a kind of paradise for children, an oasis of happiness for those among them—far too many, alas—who know only misery and moral abandon everywhere else. Among others, I remember two good little children whom no one came to fetch when their hour of happiness was at an end. So the maid accompanied them home, where she found the parents had fallen into a drunken stupor, though not without having had the "touching" forethought to leave a bowl containing some queer-looking mess for their children's nourishment! We saw countless scenes like this, and I see no excuse for the society that tolerates them; but at least during the day the nursery school brought these children a few hours of cleanliness, happiness, and, more especially, the unstinted affection with which they were cherished by women who love children and know how to make themselves loved in return. The nursery school is a place of love, in the finest sense of the word.

It was in this heart-warming atmosphere that we noted down all the details for our film. We took all our material from life because, though one may interpret and transpose life, it can never be invented.

This child, for instance, who did not know how to smile, was a poor little foundling whom no one had ever kissed before he came to us.

There was little Roland, six years old, who came to school in a pair of pants that were as full of holes as a sieve but whose fly was hermetically sealed by a zipper.

Amusing, picturesque, tragic details which we brought to life in our scenes, portraying a splendid theme, a great universal law: the law of love, the interdependence of man, which some day will take the place of that ignominy known as "charity."

The splendid women who devote themselves to this little world, the teachers and nurses, perform their daily tasks, quietly and matter-of-factly, with never a thought that they are doing an act of charity for these little beings who are no different from any other children. And the public does not fail to appreciate their work. It senses the truth, recognizes the observations made from life, shares in this pouring out of love which deeply moved the makers of the film—the technicians, workmen, and actors—communicates with them! We received many proofs of the happy effect made by our film. I would like to quote from a letter I received one day from a rather tough fellow who had never felt any particular attraction for children. "I saw *La Maternelle*," he wrote, "and it opened my eyes to children; last Sunday I stayed with my own more than I was accustomed to doing." A man like that would never have been moved by a technically brilliant production or a skillfully written scenario. The film struck home to him solely because our scenes were taken from life, because they were charged with love and humanity.

My film *Ballerina* originated in an idea which had obsessed

The inimitable Charles Chaplin in a memorable scene
from *Gold Rush* (see page 146).

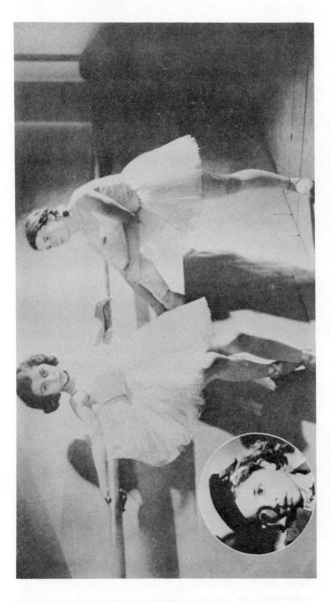

The "natural actors" in Jean Benoit-Levy's *Ballerina*. INSERT: Micheline Boudet. CENTER: Janine Charrat and Jacqueline Queffelec (see page 150).

me for some time. Indeed, I am convinced that *love for his work* is the most solid foundation of man's happiness, the element most calculated to instill in him a love for life. I found this notion particularly well-developed among the people who practice that glorious and ephemeral art known as the Dance. This gave me the two basic elements—the idea and the environment—and I was fortunate enough to find a point of departure for the dramatic construction in a novel by Paul Morand. But in order to build up the story and people it with flesh-and-blood characters, we were obliged to study the real environment.

For this purpose we spent a few months living at the Paris Opéra, in this temple of dance, this academy, this training school. Like every theater, the Opéra has two sides to it: one made of velvet and gold, magic and pleasure; the other of dust and painted canvas, reality and work and self-sacrifice. It was the latter side we wanted to portray, and to do so we had to live among real people and breathe the same backstage air that they breathed. Accordingly, we set to and took a hand in everything that went on, in the prompter's box and in the highest flies, in classes and rehearsal rooms; we shared in their joys and in their labors; by following the creative artists and performers of the dancing school and the Corps de Ballet in their daily tasks, we got to love the ballet and all the people in it. By observing the thousand and one details of their daily life, we were able to write our scenario and bring it to life through the veracity of the details we had noted down from day to day. The things that went on before our eyes were the daily manifestations of human nature: laughter and song, love and hate and jealousy. But Music and the Dance brought all these people together around a common ideal—love for their work, the dance. And with all this human material, observed in its natural environment, we created living characters to portray the central theme of the film.

But the public cannot be won over just because the rules of art have been observed. Talent, technique, all the basic elements necessary to the artist, are lifeless if he himself is not imbued with a burning zeal which he transmits to his work. This faith which possesses him is as essential to his creative powers as it it to his physical existence. An ideology is as indispensable to an individual as it is to a nation. Without that faith which inspires creation, no work will penetrate the feelings of the audience or gain its support. One must believe passionately to convince; one must have profound faith in the idea to make other people receptive to it.

And so these works of faith, consecrated to ideas that are noble, generous, or quite simply human, bring us once more to the motion picture's great educational mission. Without deliberate intent to educate, even obeying a strict rule to avoid anything that might resemble a lesson or a sermon, the dramatic film, thus conceived, is essentially educative, for it induces the mind to reflect and serves as an education in art.

The dramatic film would not be an art if its realism were confined merely to copying life. On the contrary—and I cannot repeat this too often—it must be an art creation, that is, inspired by real life but interpreted by the artist. It is equally important to note that the motion picture possesses great powers of suggestion which should be exploited. Thus, the public will be led to meditate on facts or conclusions that are suggested rather than specified and will have an opportunity to make its own deductions from the proposals set forth by the images on the screen.

But in the last analysis the dramatic film can carry out its mission only if it is presented by film authors who know how to *choose* the idea, who believe in its greatness, and who always remain in contact with that life without which the motion picture would not be an art but simply an artifice.

10

INTERPRETATION

IN THE LAST CHAPTER, I tried to give some idea of the "constitution" and conception of dramatic films. The problem of the interpretation remains to be considered. What system should we follow in selecting the people who will have the job of bringing the characters to life?

We have now reached the exact moment when the film author, after having selected and fully considered his central theme, studied the environment in which it is to be developed, and gathered in a mass of observations, facts, and details, shuts himself up in his study and begins to write his film. From that point on, he lives with his characters. They become real people to him, and he shares in all their psychological and physical reactions. He thinks, suffers, or enjoys himself with them, depending on the situation in which all of them—author and characters—have been placed by the logical unfolding of the story. Although this story is merely a product of his imagination, it becomes a dynamic force to the author because he finds himself constantly associating with his characters. The latter never leave him, and henceforth he will be holding conversations with them day and night, even in his deepest dreams. This identification of the author with his characters is indispensable if the resulting story is to have a logical construction, and it requires complete freedom of mind. Any attempt to impose a cast at this stage of the creative process would tend to distort the personality of the characters who already have their own lives and to give a hopelessly artificial personality to those who are just being born.

Once more we have come up against the great natural law which every art must obey, so true is it that no art creation can resist a choice imposed from without.

Therefore it is better to forget about the interpreters until the characters have matured and carried out their share of the imagined plot in presenting the idea. This amounts to saying that the interpreters should be chosen for the scenario and not the scenario for the actors.

I use these two words, interpreters and actors, designedly, for they are very characteristic of filmic art. As a matter of fact, we feel that the word *actor* is a misnomer when applied, not to acting, but to interpreting. The term actor implies the act of playing a part in accordance with rules that must be learned. In motion pictures, the more art an artist puts into his part the less sincere he is, for the close-up will magnify the slightest details of his art. Besides, it is not so much a question of physically creating a part but far more of expressing a "temperament," a depth of feeling. What we ask of an artist who interprets one of our characters is that he materialize him, make him live intensely. A film artist can do this successfully only if his powers of concentration are such as to enable him to put himself in the character's position and, through his sensibility and plastic resources, externalize the psychological reactions induced by the shock of the circumstance, event, or problem that may present itself. There is no subterfuge, whether artificial tears or skillful make-up, that will take the place of the true emotion felt by an artist who blends himself body and soul into the character he is given to portray.

During the period of silent films, the selective process operated automatically. There was no magic of words to conceal with deceptive charm a lack of feeling or of plastic sense. The primary requisite for anyone going into films was to have a "personality" and be able to express it. The silent film undoubtedly marked the beginning and decline of a pure art which required that its interpreters possess very special talents deriving from their own natural gifts. D. W. Griffith, the great exponent of the senior art, was the first to recognize the different values of shots, thereby giving birth to true filmic expression. Griffith took the single view or angle of the action which the theater or pantomime affords and decomposed it into its elements. Shown as a whole, from head to foot, the body was to express the progress of the story. A little closer, half length, the character was to use the upper portion of his body and his arms. Another shot, framing the face and shoulders, concentrated more on facial expression. Then the face shown alone was responsible, with no other help, for the expression. And finally, only the eyes were to show expression, while the face remained immobile, giving the greatest value of dramatic expression. All these shots, representing the notes of the dramatic scale, provided authors and interpreters with a more powerful means of self-expression than the words of any language.

Charlie Chaplin, whom I mention this time in his capacity as an interpretive artist, succeeded better than anyone else in voicing what seems to be the epitaph of the silent film:

"The talkie ... negatives everything that we have ever learnt in the way of film technique. Action and movement must be subordinated to speech, to the careful and lifelike reproduction of sound, which in my opinion, the spectator is capable of conjuring up in his own imagination.

"Slowly, step by step, our method of acting has become a recognized art form. Film players learnt that the camera could reproduce ideas, though not words. Ideas and feelings. They also grasped the alphabet of gesture, the poetry of movement. Gesture begins where words leave off." *

This quotation serves in passing to characterize without any further comment the talented artist who can happily combine imagination, fancy, "the poetry of movement," to make masterpieces that are pregnant with meaning.

It was in *Broken Blossoms* that D. W. Griffith made the finest use of his scale of shot values to permit Lillian Gish to express

---

* *Film*, Rudolf Arnheim (London, 1933). Translated by Sieveking and Ian Morrow.

herself. Griffith animated and inspired her to such a degree that she became a veritable photographic plate on which he could record his own thoughts and reactions. The one transmits his thought and the other receives it through the intermediary of the character she portrays. But, if Lillian is able in her turn to transmit all her emotions to the audience, it is entirely due to this scale of filmic notes, to the shot values that Griffith imposes on her to communicate the most delicate nuances of her feeling. Talent, real talent, alone counted in an art so stripped of non-essentials. Sincerity was relentlessly demanded; for, just as truth was recorded on the sensitive film, so the slightest falsehood, the slightest affectation, would be magnified out of all proportion. At that time, it was impossible for the motion picture to tell lies by using sound. Often, I find myself thinking that if a film must lie it might better be silent, for its great aim lies in capturing life so that we may find the latter more beautiful, and it has no right to deny us this splendid gift.

Fortunately, Chaplin's epitaph is not yet needed. The motion picture, after having lived through a period in which sound was used indiscriminately and stupidly, now seems to be emerging once more from the flood of words in which it almost drowned. People are gradually beginning to realize that films must be given the means to express themselves in their own language, and at the same time be allowed to keep the new advantages brought to them by sound. If we agree that film characters should be made to talk only when they have something really important to say, then the motion picture will be enriched with new and greater potentialities and its marriage with music will become more and more closely knit.

But in that case the talents required of the artists who brought glory to the silent films must be carefully safeguarded if the motion picture's character and own particular art of expression are to be preserved.

On the other hand, we must also consider that freedom of choice which comes into play whenever there is a question of art. For example, if we take a dramatic scene played by two characters, a dialogue occurs which will not only be verbal but visual as well. To shoot this dialogue, the two characters should be taken in two complete shots, either full or three-quarters face, the speaker in each case being only partly visible. In this way, two strips are obtained which must be edited to get a shot of the dialogue. The nature of the editing will depend on the choice of the most interesting *moments* from the dramatic standpoint, intercalated in a tempo synchronized with the story. If the interpreters are capable of externalizing their reactions by their expression, the author will, more often than not, pick out silent shots of the listener on which the speaker's words will be mounted, the speaker himself either being left out altogether or partly appearing within the frame. This involves an extremely delicate choice which cannot possibly be made unless the author is completely free to exercise his own judgment. He must be sheltered from all pressure exerted in favor of casting this or that star or in connection with the direction or editing. The fate of a whole sequence will depend on this choice, and ten or twenty images too few or too many are enough to destroy its tempo or dramatic quality.

The film artist must be able to interpret an entire sequence by means of his plastic talents and the depth of his feeling. Very often, silence can be more dramatic than the finest dialogue. Lillian Gish's pitiful smile in *Broken Blossoms* is far more tragic and emotive than a display of oral grief penned by the most talented author and recited by a famous actress. A character's psychological reactions to the sound of footsteps mounting a stairway, to the striking of a clock which sounds the mysterious hour, to the far-off whistle of a locomotive which indicates an irrevocable departure, are pure motion picture art. We are gradually coming back to the latter, by a kind of natural law resulting from the instinct of preservation in an art that refuses to die. To enable the dramatic film to survive and develop further, we must make certain that it has its own interpreters and that they are chosen in accordance with the qualities it requires.

The film artist must forget the profession he learned in order to liberate his natural talents. He will then be able to work at developing his plastic talents and do everything in his power to concentrate on studying the character to the point of identifying himself with it. In that way he will succeed in *living* the part rather than *playing* it, thereby communicating that life to the public and making the latter share in it.

The film author will have a better chance to approximate the ideal interpretation if he seeks artists whose personality, tastes, and way of life are similar to those of the characters he has conceived. In that case, the artist will have to make a great effort to remain natural while adapting himself to his new personality, but he will be more likely to give the latter a completely true interpretation, free of all professional artificiality.

For instance, I chose Madeleine Renaud to interpret Rose in *La Maternelle,* not because she was a member of the Comédie Française, but in spite of that fact, and because I knew, perhaps better than she, that her personality was identical with my conception of the character. It was apparent from the very first meeting that we would have a hard time getting the artist to be herself. Accustomed as she was to reciting plays, she thought my script very poor in dialogue, and she did not at first realize that the delineation of the story she would be living was more important than the words.

On the set, she had to struggle against all the mannerisms that were perfectly natural in the theater, until one day, after having successfully rid herself of everything that was not a natural reaction, she said to me: "I understand. You want me to forget about my profession." From here on, we were able to establish that communication between artist and author which is so necessary, and proceed with a lifelike creation of the part.

People will tell me that I gave Madeleine Renaud two very different characters to interpret: the part of Rose, the serving woman in the nursery school, and the apparently quite dissimilar role of the young medical student, Hélène. My answer is that man is a complex creature, made up of several characters, and that talent lies precisely in blending together these different aspects, provided they are not inconsistent with the individual's true nature. It is most important that the film author should not make any mistakes about that nature at the critical moment of choice, for it represents the living and sensitive plastic material which he must shape to the mold of his thought; and, by the same token, all external influences or even personal sympathies must be warded off.

When I made *Hélène,* I spent a long time looking for an artist who could "live" the part of Pierrot. A great many candidates turned up; and, though there were some whose talents drew my attention and others whose personality I liked, I felt that none of them had any real affinity with my character. None of them was naturally endowed with that strong artistic personality submerged beneath a complete contempt for life. One evening, I happened to see a film in which a young unknown actor had been given a bit part. In one sequence, he expressed himself with such sincerity and charm that I felt he must resemble my Pierrot very closely. I had a number of talks with him which confirmed my first impression, and Jean-Louis Barrault turned out to be identical with the character I had created after Vicki Baum's original inspiration.

Before the war, it was particularly difficult to choose interpreters because we had very few artists who devoted their talents exclusively to the screen. In most instances, we were obliged to resort to the theater for artists who regarded motion pictures as an inferior art, to be utilized only for supplementing their incomes, for providing them with luxuries and publicity. But those of them who really liked films found it very difficult to adapt themselves from one art to the other. Madeleine Renaud, for instance, should be given great credit for returning every morning to the part of the humble servant after having played a Musset character at the Comédie Française the night before. Such a change-over, from the conventional art of the stage to the natural simplicity of life, requires of the artist a division of personality which few are able to achieve. When the Musset character, which she had so well interpreted not so many hours before, tended to creep into her characterization of Rose, I had only to say, "Madeleine, you're being just too *charm-*

ing," for her to realize the artificial implications of the word and return to a more lifelike interpretation.

The motion picture is an art which demands much from those who claim to be its disciples; they must perforce devote all their time to it. Already, there is a tradition behind it, made up, not of craft and artifice, but of sincerity, of sensibility in rendering life and truth. So that screen artists can really practice their art, they must be placed in natural surroundings. To do this, we must take people from real life.

Apart from the interpreters of the principal parts, we should do our casting from the environment in which our film is laid, choosing people who are accustomed to living every day the bit part or profile they will be assigned in the film. Just as Marie Coeuret's friends in *La Maternelle* were real children, coming straight from the suburbs, so Hélène's friends were real students.

I have often heard doubts expressed on the practical value of using "amateurs." I am told that "they will not know how to act." No, thank God, they won't know how to act; but, when they are made to feel at home, *they know how to live.* It is true that one isolated individual who is snatched from his familiar surroundings and exiled to the studio, where he is thrown among strangers, far from his regular haunts and way of life, will freeze up and become incapable of the slightest natural reaction. The only emotion he could express would be an acute embarrassment. But put him with a crowd, let him jostle elbows with a hundred and fifty others of his own sort, and he will contribute his own bit of reality; he and his friends together will bring the entire life of the laboratory and operating room into the studio. As a matter of fact, the danger does not lie in using these "amateurs" but in the fact that they set the pace to which the professional actors must adjust their interpretations. The latter must be very great artists, in close contact with life, before they can be given such lifelike collaborators. The smallest convention, the least little trick of the trade, rings out like a false note amid such natural simplicity.

My real students began by overwhelming Hélène with all the

admiring respect due to a great star, to a member of our national theater. But in a few hours they were treating her as a boon companion, as just one member of a friendly group.

I want to emphasize the fact that I am speaking only of the background, the bit parts and profiles, and that I do not believe it possible, as a rule, except in the case of children, to use amateurs to interpret roles in dramatic films, in company with professional actors. Though it is true that dramatic films derive their strength from the documentation of environment and are thereby related to films of life, and though it is also true that films of life made without professional actors and outside a studio can be dramatic films, it is essential not to confuse the two genres.

Dramatic films, as opposed to films of life, are films the success of which is not determined by natural elements alone. Professional screen artists have largely concentrated on developing qualities indentifying them with the inner life of the characters they interpret; they have become accustomed to moving about in front of the camera and know how to make full use of their plastic resources. Because of this experience, they have acquired, not a craft, but specific qualities exacted by the dramatic film, which cannot be demanded of occasional interpreters. Actors for dramatic films are ideally recruited from real life, but they will need time and a great deal of work before they can acquire the qualities necessary to the development of their talent.

The American motion picture industry, with its superior organization, was able to give its casting departments the advantage of a permanent and continuing production. The studios are in a position to guarantee these artists the material and mental conditions permitting them to devote all their time to motion pictures.

Hollywood has become a magnet attracting all the world's great talent. Its producers are constantly on the lookout for new talent to promote. This has the effect of facilitating the choice of interpreters for a cast. To fill the biggest parts as well as the smallest, film authors have only to take their pick of the dazzling array of talent lying before them. Apart from the question of stars, it happens very rarely, under these conditions, that a part is badly filled, in other words that an artist is not suited to the personality of the character he is to interpret. This is particularly evident in the case of short parts, which must be distinguished from the bit parts or profiles chosen from the extras. One of the most striking examples was the part of the President of the Senate in *Mr. Smith Goes to Washington,* Sam Wood's great film. We may be certain that without Harry Cary's brilliant interpretation of the part the sequence could not have been included. It was entirely due to the dialogue shot of the President and the orator that the interminable speech could be physically tolerated. But the powerful interpretation rendered by Harry Cary, who really lived the part, gave this sequence its proper place in the scale of values of the dramatic construction, which rose to a climax at that point.

It would seem that under such conditions the interpretation of dramatic films might always be carried out to perfection. I must note with regret that often, despite superb organization and a wealthy reservoir of talent, a film's basic idea is not followed through or the personality of an important character is irreparably distorted. The fundamental error, which I shall discuss in a later chapter, lies in the persistence of a complete misconception regarding the public's psychology. Indeed, it has been decreed once and for all that the public demands to be shown an artificial life of luxury as an escape from the tedium of its daily existence. By virtue of this law, it has become an axiom that houses should always present a certain amount of luxury, while the people who dwell in them, particularly the women, should all be clothed, made up, and have their hair done according to a standard pattern, in order to preserve a no less standardized type of beauty. The result of this has often been to shift the emphasis to such an extent that the idea loses all significance and the physical aspect of the characters becomes so distorted that the interpreters are unfailingly led to act and, what is worse, to act badly. Operatic peasants, little country teachers made up to look like vamps, characters coming out of tragic situations with impeccable permanents are a few of the many classic examples that have unfortunately prevented many fine and great ideas from possessing any emotional appeal for the audience. Because it is not true to life, because the dramatic film should draw its art from true life, the audience cannot admit the artificial representation of people like themselves. Experience has proved the falsity of the artificial theory; one need only study the public's reactions to be convinced of this. The public has been deeply stirred by Russian films that were made with human material. It shares in the life, the reactions of men and women, reproduced in English films. The English do not hesitate to show, as in Noel Coward's splendid film, *In Which We Serve,* completely natural women without boudoir make-up and dressed like any other woman who suffers, and sometimes smiles.

Once again we find the genres being confused. The law of artificiality, so dangerous for dramatic films, is on the contrary perfectly sound when applied to imaginative or comic films, for the sole function of these is to divert the eye by presenting a spectacle specially designed for that purpose. I admire the impeccable clothes, the dazzling brilliance of the girls who create such marvelous rhythms; but I shudder to see Michele Morgan, as a little waitress in a bar, heavily made up and, ten minutes after the story opens, dressed up to look like a great lady through some trick or other. When the film is based on a great theme such as the French resistance, great care must be taken not to make the people who represent it artificial and false.

I believe our friends would find it advantageous to revise their theories if they took the trouble to make a closer study of that public which they have underestimated and which, in the last analysis, is the master of us all. If this were done, a great many marvelous artists would have an opportunity to display their talents according to their lights, while on the other hand the industry would have found a means of raising American dramatic films to the very high level which it has attained with the other genres.

The problem of extras, who are so essential to the creation of atmosphere, would be ideally solved if we could seek them among ordinary people. Unfortunately, it is impossible to use this method exclusively, since we cannot go around asking people engaged in other activities to hold themselves in readiness for the occasional demands of the screen.

In France, we tried as often as possible to call in people who had no motion picture experience, but in the majority of instances we were obliged to draw on the "professional extras" who, every evening after five o'clock, could be found in the cafés of the Boulevard de Strasbourg. This system was not as bad as it might seem. There was a nucleus of professional extras who were fine, conscientious, sincere people, convinced of their "artistic talents." This touching and respectable conviction unified these minor artists into a disciplined and plastic nucleus around which could be made to perform those who were recruited from the majority of candidates sitting in the cafés. The latter group was fluid in the sense that it consisted of men and women who joined the group temporarily, either because they were unemployed or merely because they were curious, and who gravitated away as soon as they had found a job or satisfied their curiosity. In this way we had every opportunity to obtain a certain percentage of the natural elements which, I repeat, are so necessary for creating the atmosphere. Moreover, this picturesque crowd would occasionally yield individuals whom we could begin to entrust with a few lines and who might eventually become real artists.

The problem is quite different in Hollywood, where the enormous production calls for thousands of extras. It was found necessary to set up a system that would answer, on the one hand, the requirements of the producers, who had to be able to count on a sufficient number of extras at all times, and, on the other hand, the need to secure salaries for these extras that would enable them to remain at the disposal of the producers.

There is a union in Hollywood called the Screen Actors' Guild. This organization is similar to our own *Union des Artistes* except that it also includes professional extras. The Guild reached an agreement with the Film Producers Association to set up a Central Casting Corporation. This office, besides listing the 8,000 members of the Guild, keeps files on the independent or occasional workers, classified as to children, boys and girls under eighteen, Negroes, Orientals, and various special types who can be employed only in specific cases determined by the requirements of a production.

This organization functions in an extraordinary manner, and, although I have tried to avoid technical details in this book, I would like to make an exception in this case.

Every day before five o'clock, each studio notifies the Central Casting Corporation by teletype of the casting for the productions to be run off the following day. The sheets are passed on to the casting directors, who are seated around a large table. All these directors have memorized the names of the actors or extras that are written down. At five o'clock the Guild members begin calling the central switchboard of the Corporation, giving their names. All names are broadcast over a loud-speaker to the room where the directors are sitting. If one of these picks out a name, he takes the receiver off one of the telephones before him and gives the man his instructions: the studio he is to report at in the morning, the costume required, type of film, period, etc. If he is not chosen, the applicant merely calls back the next day at the same time. In special cases, the director knows where he can reach the individual requested by telephone. All this work is carried out with remarkable order and precision and shows Hollywood's splendid organization at its best.

Central Casting thus allows the producers who have teletyped their casting to count without fail on getting the number of people they need who answer to the description typed on the the sheet given to the directors.

Moreover, Central Casting has done away with the pitiful lines of people wandering from studio to studio begging for work; it has eliminated the chance of an individual's missing a job in one studio while vainly waiting in another. The organization has made it possible for this extremely interesting class of film collaborators to acquire a new dignity, while at the same time it does everything it can to ensure a fairer distribution of salaries. The very diversity of character and atmosphere required by dramatic films makes the task of Central Casting extremely difficult; but, all things considered, I think it represents the maximum advantages and results that can be expected from such an organization in finding a close solution to so difficult a problem.

11
NATURAL ACTORS

NATURAL ACTORS ARE those who approach closest to nature; they are creatures whose minds have not been cultivated, who have kept their psychological reflexes independent of any control by will or reason.

Children are the ideal natural actors of the screen, but I have found the same freshness of mind, the same innocence, in the Schleus tribes of the Atlas. The primitive life led by these nomad warriors had kept their intellectual development at the level of that of a normal child who has not yet felt the impact of reason and education. We are now dealing with completely virgin material that reacts spontaneously to events and circumstances in the environment favorable to it and capable of making an impression on it. We must, therefore, arrange the sequence of events in such a way as to obtain a logical story that can make an impression on these primitive creatures, placing it in the environment to which they are accustomed.

Children are potentially endowed with all the diversity of the human character. Heredity or environment often orientate the component parts of this diversity in different directions, but a basic criterion remains, represented by the degrees of intelligence and the purity of the environment that will have sheltered that intelligence from premature adult influence.

For that reason it becomes extremely important, when casting children for a film, to be guided in the selection by methods of examination based on a profound knowledge of child psychology, and to make certain that their minds have not been distorted by surrounding influences. The first to be avoided, then, is the little professional actor who has already "proved himself" on the stage or screen. On the contrary, real children, quite unspoiled, must be sought in the streets, in school, or at home, children who are leading normal lives.

For example, in *La Maternelle* we had to pick out the two hundred and fifty children required by the scenario. For two months, one of my assistants paraded countless children before me, in groups of twenty or twenty-five, whom he had recruited among the real people, from suburban families or nursery schools. Occasionally, however, parents, lured by some mistaken notion, would come to me of their own free will, accompanied by their progeny, and do their best to convince me of their offspring's unique talents. In that case, I would invariably hear the stock phrase: "Come on now, recite something for the gentleman!" In general, I would make up my mind right then and there, since the child's personality had already been distorted.

Among others, I remember one little girl who, in obedience to her mother's injunctions, launched forth into some interminable poem. With all the artificial mannerisms of an aged actress, she swooned over the "lily of the valley" and the "stars in the Milky Way." Fortunately, an urgent physical need suddenly interrupted her and sent her scampering off without any further literary flourishes.

Blessings on Mother Nature, whose demands will ever be triumphant over all worldly influences!

My usual procedure was to hold the interview without the disturbing presence of an adult. I would receive the child alone; we would get settled and I would proceed to put him at his ease. Once I had made a friend of him, I would choose a topic having the most appeal to his natural tastes, and in the ensuing conversation I could determine how quick-witted and sensitive he was. The length of time I kept him would depend on how difficult it was to draw him out. Naturally, there were times when I would make a mistake, for a child's personality is often concealed under a veil of shyness which requires a certain amount of time to brush aside. One day, I interviewed a candidate who seemed to

Madeleine Renaud in a scene from her splendid interpretation in Jean Benoit-Levy's *La Maternelle* (see page 158).

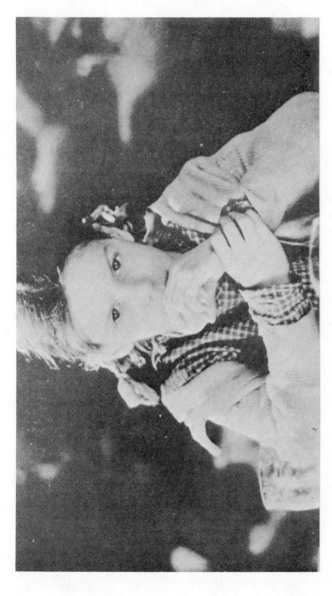

Little Paulette Elambert in an unforgettable scene from *La Maternelle* (see page 158).

me to have nothing to extract, so I gently dismissed him after a very brief session. A few minutes later, I heard someone crying and wailing. It was my little visitor, who said to me through his sobs: "You sent me away sooner than the others; you don't like me a bit!" He had waked up! I took him, and later on he did a fine job with a bit part.

Gradually, we sifted out all the children who had already "acted" and obtained sensitive, natural children whom we could train to the point where they would be living the parts of the little children in the story. In this way we recruited all the children for *La Maternelle*, including Paulette Elambert. We found the latter living with her mother in a cheap rented house near the Porte de Charenton. Shy and modest, she came to see me one evening in a group of twenty little friends; and, though I immediately noticed her quick mind, her eager look, and her well-developed sensibility, she did not turn out to be Marie Coeuret until after the screen test.

After all the children have been selected for a film, there remains the task of choosing among them the ones qualified to play the big roles or merely to speak a few audible words.

For the first time these little children will find themselves in a studio, at the mercy of lights, projectors, and microphones! Their confidence will have to be restored, while their mothers, whose emotional outpourings constitute the worst danger, must at all costs be kept out of the studio. This involves carefully setting aside a waiting room for the parents and making it as comfortable as possible; from this room each candidate is brought in separately.

In my film, *Feu de Paille*, I inserted a sequence which was an exact reproduction of the way I gave a screen test. I even asked my good friend and colleague Jean Renoir to exhibit his profession in the part of the film author. He agreed enthusiastically, but the exigencies of his own production prevented him from taking on the part, and we obtained a very fine actor, Henri Nasset, to do the interpretation.

In this scene, the film author is seen receiving a child dressed up in his Sunday best, with a stiff collar, tight jacket, and well-polished shoes. The author has him remove his collar and shoes, which are bothering him, and then says something like this to him: "We're friends. All those people you see in the studio aren't here at all; there's only you and I." As the boy regains confidence, he and the film author really do appear to be the only two people in the studio. Then occurs that phenomenon of suggestion, that transmission of thought, which permits the film author to communicate with the child. There is a real visual dialogue expressed in alternating close-ups of each one as seen by the other, which enables the child to be placed in exactly the same situation as the character whose reactions he is externalizing. In this way, the author can almost invariably make his choice, which, in the last analysis, depends on the child's sensitivity to coaching and his receptivity to the film author's mental reactions. The latter must have powers of concentration strong enough to practice that telepathy which, while enabling him to direct his adult and professional artists, becomes indispensable when natural actors like children are involved. Children must remain unconscious of their actions, or they will turn into monstrous little prodigies. Only when the film author decides that the child is responding sufficiently to his inner impulses should he run the risk of confiding a part to him. I might say that the chief difficulty in selecting a child lies largely in the fact that almost all children make excellent natural subjects and that often there is very little to choose among those who come through the tests satisfactorily. In such cases, the selection is based on some factor such as physical appearance.

When everything is in readiness to start shooting the film in the studio, the delicate problem arises of making sure that the children will be working under the most favorable conditions, from both the mental and physical standpoints. This problem must be solved satisfactorily, not only because it constitutes an obligation toward the children for whom we are responsible but also because it is indispensable for creating an environment in which their natural talents may be exercised.

First and foremost, all hygienic precautions must be taken. In *La Maternelle*—which I use as an example because it involved very small children—a governess, assisted by a nurse and several maids, remained constantly in attendance on the young actors and spared no pains to see that they were given the same care in the studio that they received at school. To keep them from becoming needlessly tired and to maintain their balance, the governess would hold classes in a building next door to the studio and, when everything was ready, would bring them onto the set in single file.

In this way, the proper environment was created and the children's mental balance ensured. In addition, it was particularly important for them to continue their schooling, which motion picture making must never interrupt, whatever the child's age. In France, the necessary precautions were generally taken and arrangements made to shoot films in which children were cast during their vacation periods. In Hollywood, the producers are compelled by law to set up classes in their studios, which are taught by specially designated teachers. The shooting is timed to fit in with their classroom schedule, and the children are not permitted to work more than four hours a day.

Lastly, from the material standpoint, the child's parents or guardians must be prevented from exploiting the just remuneration he receives for his work. Apart from the professional child stars, for whom I hold no brief, there are all the children who may occasionally collaborate on a film. The money earned by such a child can materially contribute to the support and comfort of a needy family. For my part, I have seen too many striking examples to regret having secured such a windfall for numerous children or to feel they should be prevented from ever making any money. But I do think that parents should be obliged by law to open a savings account in their child's name and put part of his earnings into it. This would constitute a small reserve for the future, but most of all it would set a limit to the ambitions of parents who try to get as much as they can out of the studios by forcing their child to follow a career which should preferably be made as short-lived as possible. The fact that he is earning money does not in itself do the child any harm. On the contrary, his first pay check gives him a kind of unconscious dignity and pride, generally manifested in a delightfully picturesque manner. Such was the case with a four-year-old boy nicknamed Patachou, whom I overheard in conversation with his father, come to fetch him:

The father: "Come on, let's go have a drink!"

Patachou: "No!"

The father: "Come on, let's go!"

Patachou: "No, I don't want to go to a bar."

The father: "Say, who's giving the orders around here?"

Patachou: "Listen, who's bringing home the dough, you or me?"

And every evening this same Patachou would bring his "wages" home to his mother, as if he had decided to back up the latter's weekly attempts to get those of his father.

It is relatively easy to provide proper working conditions from the physical and material standpoint; either a sense of responsibility or the protection of the law will suffice. A more delicate problem involves creating the proper psychological atmosphere. Far more care and a greater effort to understand are needed in dealing with the mind than with the body. First of all, the adult must be certain he likes children before undertaking to direct them. A child's instinct is unfailing; he knows full well when he is really liked or when he is merely being treated with the politeness affected by grownups, and he will only confide in or be himself with people who like him naturally and without affectation. This inherent liking is revealed in the way we look upon and treat children. It compels us to talk to them seriously, to start treating them as responsible individuals as soon as they can understand, and always to avoid that baby talk which makes us seem ridiculous or contemptible in their already penetrating eyes.

The author must love children so that the entire studio group will also be won over to them. He must build up that atmosphere which is so indispensable if their freshness of mind is to be preserved. Most important of all, the ultimate justification for using children is that their message may be conveyed to the world of "grownups." That message will not reach its destination unless it is charged with love for the most sacred cause of all: the cause of these poor little children of men. Every child who is plunged into an atmosphere of love feels happy to be alive and reflects his joy on the people around him.

Given such conditions, all the members of the production group, all the studio workers will come closer and closer to these little natural actors and become an ideal family to them. Take the case of Jeannot, a little "hero" of twelve, who, in between takes, had formed a partnership with old Tanase, one of the stage hands, for carving airplanes out of left-over bits of wood. Their business association developed into one of those firm friendships that exist between men, and endured far beyond the shooting of the film.

When the final day of shooting for *Ballerina* arrived, three or four of our most sensitive young ballet students began to snivel at the thought of the good-bys they would have to say that evening. Before long, we were obliged to give up trying to shoot a supposedly gay sequence with some sixty little girls who had all given way to tears.

The quality of the atmosphere is, not alone sufficient to keep these little ones in the natural state which is theirs by right: certain elementary precautions must be taken. Chief among these is to avoid the danger of isolation. A child who is placed among other children of his own age will remain a child. But a child who is left all by himself among grownups will be in danger of losing his childhood, of being formed too soon. We have always taken care not to isolate a child. Even on days when we only needed one, we had all the others come, too, so that they would always be together. A single, isolated child feels lost, is paralyzed by shyness and deprived of all life; or else he tries to imitate the grownups. But in a crowd, their numbers give them strength. Their confidence restored by this collective security, engrossed in themselves and unaware of the adults surrounding them, they begin to live intensely as though they were alone in the world.

Everyone who feels any sense of the responsibility he incurs by using children in films has gone through the agony of fear that he would make them into little monsters, matured long before their time. Father Maillet, director of the Choir School for Young Singers at the Croix de Bois, who loved and understood children so well because he had lived with them so long, was one person who shared this anxiety. He managed to avoid the danger by always having his soloist remain anonymous, hidden among the other members of the choir. One day, after having returned from New York, where he had given a series of recitals, he told me that on the opening night, when he himself had a strong case of jitters, he had been reassured by the calm and natural behavior of the children, who were peaceably playing with a yoyo, as though they were still on the streets of Belleville rather than on the stage of the Metropolitan Opera, five minutes before curtain time with a packed house. As always, their very numbers had prevented them from being affected by this change in environment.

That is why we must be so very careful to re-create the atmosphere that will keep them within the compass of their everyday existence. The studio set will reproduce as closely as possible the real classroom, playground, or dining hall. I remember the happy surprise of the little ballet students when they found the studio set to be an exact copy of the rotunda in the Opera, where they were in the habit of practicing every day to the music of an old piano and, during pauses, looking out of the oval windows at the panorama of Paris spread below them. By making the setting realistic, by faithfully reconstructing the framework and atmosphere of everyday existence, we shall be able to keep the children in their natural element, that everyday existence outside of which they are only poor little puppets without a soul.

Once the familiar environment and atmosphere have been re-created, we must also take care that our natural actors adhere faithfully to the personality of the characters they represent and keep within the limits of the dramatic story conceived by the author. Above all, we must satisfy that feeling of curiosity which children exhibit so markedly before something new. For them, the novelty lies in the personnel of the production group, in the

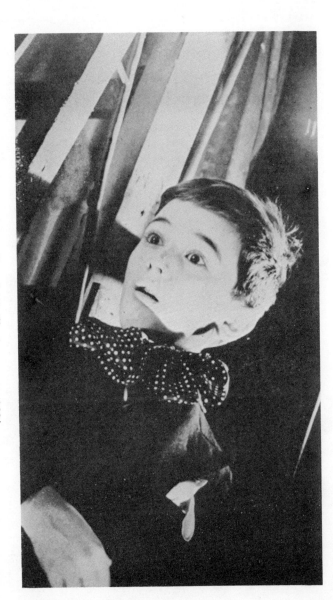

Jean Fuller in Jean Benoit-Levy's *Le Feu de Paille* (see page 169).

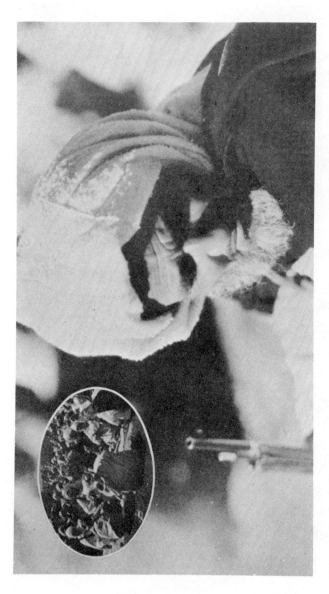

A great chief of the Moroccan Atlas in *Itto* (see page 214).

studio, but most of all in the camera, which appears always to have a penetrating eye fixed on them, and the mysterious microphone, which follows everywhere they go. To satisfy that curiosity, we must take the time before really starting on the film to see that friendly relations are established between children and grownups. After this the children should be allowed ample opportunity to look over the camera, microphone, projectors, and the rest of the studio equipment. Once they have made firm friends with their co-workers and become thoroughly acquainted with these strange new machines, they will begin to feel really at home and may then be asked to live out the story of some little children who are just like them.

This story will be given to them in the form of very short outlines, so that they may more readily enter into the situation and, insofar as possible, be required to exhibit but one reaction at a time. Children should also be prevented from having to learn dialogue by heart and recite lines which possess no deep significance for them. Special care should be taken not to distribute scripts in advance. Their parents or neighbors, fine connoisseurs in the art of recitation, would unquestionably use them to "rehearse" the children and thus saddle us with little prodigies whose real nature had been lost beyond recall.

The written dialogue in the scenario should in reality serve only as an indication, a point of departure. The important thing is to familiarize the children with the part of the story they are to interpret and prompt them to find spontaneous replies, using their own words, the words they would use in real life if they were faced with the same situation. In this way, we obtain dialogue which may be very far removed from academic language but is extremely true to life. By going ahead piecemeal, we are able to preserve that spiritual freshness of the child which can survive only in unawareness. Little Paulette Elambert, who lived the part of Marie Coeuret with such dramatic intensity, actually never realized what she was doing. On the day the film was shown to the artists, she was naturally sitting on my lap. Suddenly she burst into tears. As I was anxiously trying to find out the cause of her distress, she said quite simply, "I didn't know I had been so unhappy!"

If all these necessary precautions are taken to safeguard the child from any influence that might disturb him, he will live his own life with an almost animal-like sincerity that leaves the spectator speechless. Only nature herself can rival the sincerity expressed on the screen in a close-up of a child's spontaneous reaction.

There are times when we have waited several hours for the shadow of a cloud to pass over a field of wheat or, similarly, waited for the shadow of grief to pass over a child's face. One of the most touching memories I have in this connection goes back to my film, *Peau de Pêche*, suggested by Gabriel Maurière's novel and made in the days of silent films. The story took place during the war. The main character was a nine-year-old child who thought of war in concrete terms of the games he played with his friends or in terms of his passion for cutting out pictures of soldiers from toy catalogues. The death of his close friend, the son of the farmers whom he regarded as his parents, brings him to a military cemetery. Faced with the forest of crosses, he discovers the horror of reality, which he expresses tragically by the mere depth of his look, without a word except to murmur to himself, "So that's what war is!"

All I did was to take a close-up of a child's profound disillusionment on discovering the evils perpetrated by man.

On the other hand, the film author will find it greatly to his advantage to study that little world and its reactions to life, for in it he will find the inspiration that imagination alone cannot provide.

For instance, in *Ballerina*, when a little girl of seven refuses to go on stage and bursts into tears at the sight of Faust's devil, we may be certain that this is not an agreeable invention of the author's but that actually one night the curtain of the Paris Opéra was delayed for five minutes because of just such a "dramatic" incident about which the public knew nothing.

The motion picture in general is an art close to life, but the dramatic genre, more than any other, requires us to stick closely to nature to avoid the artificial and conventional. Very small children and young people will form a natural link for us with the sources of life, provided we know how to treat them with infinite care.

A child possesses irresistible charm so long as he is unconscious of himself. But this divine unawareness is a fragile thing. The slightest thing threatens it and may destroy it forever. It is a state of grace, which, once lost, can never be regained. In the theater, the repetition of the same gestures, day after day at the same time, makes it completely unattainable. On the screen, only a child's first film is able to capture it; with the second, in most cases, it is already gone. The incomparable grace of a little animal enjoying freedom has been replaced by the mechanical skill of a frightful little puppet.

No one has the right to say that a child who appears to have hidden gifts is talented. Before it can be manifested, talent requires a maturity of mind and an amount of work that cannot be achieved before adolescence. Only then will it be strong enough to resist outside influences and blossom forth at the same time that the individual's personality begins to assert itself. Thus, an artist in full possession of his means can, through the power of his feelings, controlled by his will, exert such an effect on his public that he brings it to share in his own emotions. For the time being, the child must return to his childhood, to his games and his schoolwork. In short, he must preserve that freshness of mind in which talent is cultivated.

Being in contact with natural actors exerts a powerful influence on professional actors. The teeming activity and turbulence of children impose the severest kind of test on adults. The least imperfection, any professional artificiality or convention, are immediately high-lighted by the superb unawaresss of children. The naturally mischievous little faces of the latter make it impossible for anyone about them to wear any make-up. In *La Maternelle*, nobody wore make-up, and this led to a rather amusing incident.

One day, while Alice Tissot, the directress, was sitting in a corner of the studio waiting for her cue to go on set, a fine lady, excessively made up, came and sat down next to her. Thinking that she was one of the cast, assigned to interpret the part of the inspectress, Alice out of kindness advised her to go and wash her face "to avoid a scene with the boss." Whereupon a scene really did take place, which reverberated through the entire studio. It appeared that the fine lady, instead of being the film inspectress, was actually a real inspectress of day nurseries for the city of Paris. She sailed out of the studio in a rage at having been taken for "an actress."

Similarly, children oblige grownups to cast off all mental make-up. The former, I repeat, set the pace for the professionals, and the latter must keep in step, lest they become conventional and throw the children off. Actually, the children dominate the actors and, generally speaking, the latter are forced to bow to the realities of life. My smallest children never for a moment imagined that they were associating with actors. Whenever one of them needed help, he would call Rose, never suspecting that Rose was anything more than a servant whose job was to kneel down beside him and wipe his face or blow his nose.

It may be said that a screen player's ambition should be to equal the unconscious talent of natural actors, since in the last analysis he will not achieve the fullest development of his art until he is able to express the emotions that he himself experiences. His talent will then enable him to concentrate on not letting professional technique distort the unconscious reactions of his personality, which he will transmit through the delicate range of his feelings.

12

THE CREATIVE GROUP

AFTER HAVING so often alluded to the film author and the other people participating in the making of a film, it is time I introduced the real creators of the dramatic film. I do not intend to elaborate on the definition of *producer,* as this would only lead us into an endless discussion deprived of all interest. I shall merely sum up this burning question by saying that the producer's role varies with each case and according to the personalities of the men bearing the title. In France, the producer was generally the businessman who gave an author the job of making a film or else an individual who undertook to form a corporation for producing films.

In the United States, the title of producer varies in meaning, according to the degree of responsibility conferred on him and the ability of the man himself. The producer may be a film author himself. He may be the writer, in which case he becomes co-author. He may be merely an employee of the corporation and act as its representative to the film author. He may be an important figure in the corporation or an independent producer and thus have authority to take on responsibilities.

In the latter case, the producer belongs to that great line of creative leaders who have inspired so many fine films. So long as the producer does not attempt, even unconsciously, to take the place of the film author whom he has nevertheless hired at a huge salary for his talent, then he may be considered the head of the enterprise and will co-ordinate the creative elements from the standpoint of the financial problems, which he alone can judge.

I must be very careful not to underestimate the producer's role in the motion picture industry; it is a highly important one. But, except for those instances where he himself steps in as writer, composer, or director, he has no right to claim the position of author.

The film author who signs his work will in the long run take all the artistic responsibility in the public's eyes. Therefore, he has the right to demand freedom of expression within the limits of the financial budget laid down by the producer.

The true creator, then, becomes a film author, provided the latter term answers the definition of its use, because he possesses the requisite qualifications and because the producer leaves him free to exercise them.

What, then, is the definition of a film author? Before going on, let me specify that the title generally accorded this function (in France, *metteur en scene;* in Germany, *regisseur;* in America, director) actually applies only to one phase of the creative work, namely, that which is concerned with directing the actors on the set. The designation *film author* comprises a far more extensive role, for it denotes the creator of a complete work.

The film author selects an idea which he himself has conceived or which he has extracted from an already existing literary work. After having observed the environment, he imagines the dramatic structure and brings the characters in his story to life. Then he translates the original idea into motion picture terms. In other words, he writes his film sequence by sequence, with all the dialogue and technical notations. Finally, he enters the shooting phase and takes charge of the studio artists, whom he will have to set in motion; from then on, he will be directing a group of people. But at all times he is a creator, an author, for he will have selected the idea and given it plastic form.

The poet first thinks of what he has to say, of the idea, then he selects his words. The film author must have something to say, think of the idea, and then select his images. In transferring the thought content to the screen, he is doing creative work, using all his feelings and the gift he possesses for composing vivid images. He imparts his style, he makes characters live who up till then were imaginary. He will continuously animate these characters, placing them in situations that correspond to the fragment of the story they are to live.

Indeed, it is fitting to consider that a great difference in method exists between the work done on the stage and the work done in the studio. In the theater, a play is recited and acted out according to the logical progression of the story. The motion picture, on the contrary, for the very reason that it is confined to no spatial limitations, requires that the sequences be grouped according to sets. Moreover, it is usual to divide each of these sequences into as many shots as are required by the tempo, the value of the dramatic expression, and the filmic punctuation. From this it results that the actual shooting of the film will never follow the logical progression of the story and will be done in extremely piecemeal fashion. It will, therefore, be up to the film author constantly to live the central story in order to place the artists in the circumstances dictated by the situation in which the characters find themselves at the precise moment in the sequence or episode which is going to be taken.

Not only will the film author have to bring human characters to life but it will often be his job to bring objects, noises, and even nature into the story. The ticking of a clock might suggest a death watch or mark the passing of time. A raging flood that destroys man's work, while defying it, may, if the images have been well assembled and edited, represent the climax of dramatic interest. Talent, purpose, imagination will allow the film author to take and direct men, objects, and nature to the advantage of the idea he wishes to express and of the work he is bringing forth. The supreme aim of the film author is to produce life and, through his style, evoke a feeling for beauty.

The great master, D. W. Griffith, long ago determined the essential condition for creative work in the following lines:

"A film author must be able to reproduce, in its integral beauty, the simple effect of the wind moving over the water or through the branches or tops of trees, or again the powerful contrasts in a ravaged countenance, seen under appropriate lighting; then and only then will he have succeeded in doing something that the theater, the best theater, can never give an audience. And that very fact is in itself an artistic creation."

The film author cannot give his work concrete form unless he is thoroughly conversant with his means of expression, that is, with his technique. No art can find expression without the help of technique, the motion picture less so than all others. There is no question of the film author's doing everything by himself but of freeing himself from the shackles of technique by acquiring complete mastery over it. The cameraman, for example, is one of the most important members of the studio group, but the film author must be able to point out to him and control the photographic values he requires. The photographic palette is composed of an infinite variety of shades, running from black to white. Out of these different values, a shade must be made up that will best correspond to the mood of a sequence or the personality of a character. In order to achieve this effect, the film author must speak the same technical language; he must know how to "read" lighting effects and modify them when needed. In short, the film author should possess technical mastery, so that he may escape the influence of his closest collaborators when their suggestions run counter to his intentions, and, primarily, because authority can only be justified by artistic and technical superiority.

Once the actual shooting of the film is completed, the film author still has a part to play. He must sit in the projection room and *select* the best from each sequence. This leaves him with hundreds of short, numbered film strips which must be *edited*. Editing is just as important an operation as the others, since it, too, is creative. It provides the film with its tempo, its life, its ultimate form. The fate of a sequence may often depend on a few images too few or too many, on a dialogue in which the choice or timing of the shots is good or bad. For this reason, the author is always highly keyed up when for the first time, in the dark of the projection room, he sees a small part of his work materializing on the screen. Rarely nowadays—and this cannot be too greatly regretted—does a producer's exigencies allow the film author to do his own editing. At any rate, he should be capable of doing it so that he may control it with authority.

Such, then, is the "fine art" of the film author; but, as André Lang wrote in his book, *Malaise au Cinéma,* "The author dreams up his film while writing it. And in the studio, within five or six weeks, he builds the multiple facets of that beautiful dream which, in the cutting room, often becomes a nightmare." Actually, this fine art is rendered extremely difficult by the fact that the motion picture is an art-industry the organization of which is determined both by the economic laws common to all industries and by the freedom necessary to all creative art.

A writer, a painter, a sculptor, needs only paper, canvas, or a little clay to practice his art. But the film author lives through a drama from which he is seldom liberated because the only way he can obtain mental release from the idea that preys on him is through the help of the vast machinery of industry or finance. He spends a large part of his life trying to convince people who rarely understand him, for they do not talk the same language. Once he has succeeded in convincing them, he must waste his strength in defending the idea when he should be doing all he can to materialize it.

Moreover, once he has finished his scenario, the film author no longer works alone: he takes on the responsibility of directing a group. From then on, he can no longer allow himself the luxury of reflecting, experimenting, and redoing, which is the painter's privilege in the privacy of his studio.

On the other hand, the teamwork exhibited in a film studio gives the motion picture its characteristic high-mindedness. True, all human activity makes men live, but at no time does intellectual and artistic work rival manual work for interdependence except during the filming of an idea which has been translated into pictures.

For instance, in order to represent a nostalgic day by the rain streaming down a windowpane, we not only need cameramen and sound men but also men to hold the sprinklers where they will produce the desired effect, others to catch the water beneath the level of the window, against which still others will direct the floodlights so that the shower will glisten; meanwhile, after three takes, the rain has watered the glue in the flats and the carpenter and painter must be called in to make the necessary repairs before the fourth take, which may perhaps be the last. There, where a pictorial poet needs a whole group of people, a verbal poet will take up his pen and write:

> There are tears in my heart
> Like the rain in the streets.

But it is precisely this teamwork that constitutes the strength of the motion picture, morally as well as materially. There is greatness and beauty in the common effort of so many diverse workers. The title of the film which the "clap man" would call out at the beginning of each take as he held up the number to the camera may well be taken to symbolize the link binding all these men together for several weeks in the pursuit of a common aim.

For several weeks, the great composer and the construction chief, according to their respective ability, will be no more than parts of the same team with different functions. It is a little like a long trip that a group of people make together, isolated from the world of reality.

The titles preceding a film always seem irksome to the audience, yet to the professional they are thrilling and always incomplete. So many precious collaborators left in obscurity and never mentioned! All those splendid fellows who can always be counted upon to perform any task without a murmur! They never think in terms of "the boss's" film but of "their film." Each one is proud of "his" film, for he has put his whole heart into it.

This state of mind can be found in every case where the film author is a true "patron," in the noblest sense of the word. It is not enough for him to have talent, to know his technique. He must win the hearts, the sympathy, and the interest of his group, create a bond of friendship between its members that will endure, provided he can strengthen it by promoting a feeling of community spirit with regard to the work to be produced. If he wishes everyone to contribute his own share, he will have to

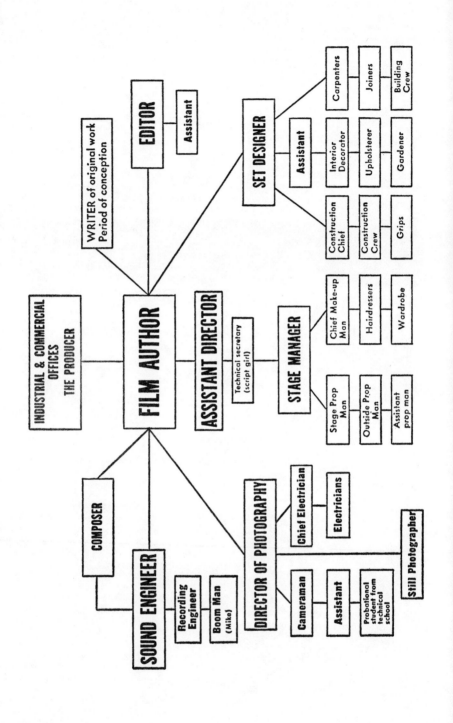

speak to all of them, including the most insignificant grip, and explain the idea, the scenario, and the characters of the film so that the group will function intelligently and not just mechanically.

In short, we are no longer dealing with motion pictures alone but with a general definition of the leader's role in society, which may be applied in every circumstance where one man is burdened with the heavy responsibility of directing other men.

It is the production group that makes creating a joy. In addition, it provides the film author with an ever-present segment of the public, whose reactions he may observe at any time. Often, while rehearsing a dramatic scene, we would catch a smile pass over the honest face of an electrician perched in the flies. When we would ask him what had made him smile, we would rarely find the criticism unjustified. A simple observation made by a grip may result in a very serious error being avoided. One day, I hired a little girl whose delivery had unfortunately been completely spoiled by conventional methods of recitation and who, I thought, would marvelously suit my purpose of contrasting a ham actress with normal children. While she was reciting, I overheard a grip murmuring, "Why, that kid's good!" That was all I needed to realize that the public might misunderstand, and I cut out the scene.

The devotion shown by the members of the group knows no bounds when they really enjoy the film they are working on and when they are treated on a par as intelligent men.

Some idea can be had of the normal composition of the creative group if we take a look at the accompanying chart. Chart II. The titles born by each participant have not always meant the same in one country as they have in another, but the basis remains the same. Depending on the individual case, the functions of some of the workers may differ vastly.

For instance, in the United States the *assistant director* is more often a company official who is responsible for organizational details. In France, he really does assist the director, from start to finish of the production. The position of assistant director provides the younger men, on leaving technical school, with an opportunity to make their practical apprenticeship at the side of a film author who later on will help them get started on their own careers. In some cases, the assistant director may become a real collaborator of the film author.*

We see, then, that the title of each position may have a different meaning, depending on national practice, on the ability of the individual concerned, and particularly on the conception held regarding the importance of the share contributed by each member of the group.

In cases where the film is adapted or suggested from another work the original writer is not included in the creative group for the following reasons.

I believe that writers would make a great contribution to the motion picture if they were only to conceive of their own role in its true light. As a matter of fact, some writers rely on motion pictures to give them a substantial increase in income by selling the rights of their novel or play. Again, others claim to have written complete scenarios, and thereby destroy all the qualities their creative talent might have in doing work for which they are unsuited. Neither of these two groups are working for motion pictures. All we want them to do is to let us have a central theme capable of supporting a dramatic construction and a setting in which that idea can be developed, all condensed into twenty-five or thirty pages. The rest is up to the film author. It must be said that writers who might produce works of this nature have been discouraged since producers prefer to buy works which have already made a hit on the stage or in the bookstore.

As matters stand now, the film author has the greatest interest

---

* If I may be permitted, I should like at this point, by way of dedication, to pay a grateful and affectionate tribute to one who has been my precious collaborator and who remains a very dear friend, both to myself and to my family. When she read these lines, I would like Marie Epstein to feel that all the professional joys and sorrows through which we have lived together are reflected in this essay on the art we both love. I am certain that, over there, in the country of tragic heroism, she, like myself, retains the hope that soon we shall be able to revive our old group and, through our "fine art," attempt to express what we feel we have yet to say!

in consulting the writer of the original work about the dramatic construction, provided the latter is agreeable. In every case, the film author must make certain that he is not betraying the writer and distorting the idea by interpreting it too freely. This collaboration or control must come to an end, once the period of conception is over: in other words, the moment the film author takes charge of the creative group, he alone must be the boss on whom the ultimate responsibility for the work will rest; he must be invested with the authority which logically accompanies the position.

With very few exceptions, relations between writers and film authors have always been excellent. For my part, I hold only the happiest recollections of the relations I have had with the authors of original works which have inspired me, notably Gabriel Maurière, Léon Frapié, Vicki Baum, and Henri Troyat.

But the reason I am able to look back on these relationships with such pleasure is that they all realized that they ceased to have any rights once they entered the studio, where, of course, they were always welcome as guests.

The *composer* occupies a position very close to that of the film author, though unfortunately custom does not allow him to intervene until after the film has been shot. We attach special importance to music because, with the motion picture, it forms a close union in which neither of the two must be sacrificed. These two dynamic arts demand to be linked together from the moment the work is conceived, in such a way as to form a single whole. A score which is slapped onto a finished film, without the author having participated in a common creative effort, will seem a stranger to the idea which it, too, should present. A song which expresses a character's state of mind, a symphony which sets the mood in a scene from pure filmic art, or musical sounds which are suggestive rather than pretentiously imitative of nature, are all musical compositions which form an integral part of the filmic work.

I have said that characters should not be made to talk unless they have something to say, as in real life. But in real life, complete silence rarely occurs, which is why we always try to "fill the silences." Besides natural sounds, such as footsteps, the closing of a door or a window; besides intentional silences which often build up the intensity of a dramatic scene—there is also the auditory mood, which only music can create. The principal function of this music is to prepare us emotionally for the impact of the image. The composer himself, therefore, must be attuned to the emotions felt by the film author and, as a result of collaborating with him, prepared to translate these emotions into musical sounds. This is an extremely difficult and thankless role. The composer must be a great artist, willing to make sacrifices. In my opinion, the music in a film should have the greatness and humility that are needed to *serve*. Whenever an audience begins to pay more attention to the music than to the story pictured on the screen, the music has exceeded its role. We should be able to hear the music in order to see more clearly; but the moment it compels us to listen, our eyes wander from the screen, and we lose the sense of the story. Film music is successful when it cannot be told apart from the work itself.

Goethe wrote that "music should only be a prop for poetry." Even if we grant that there might be truth in his analogy with the poetic art, we may still be permitted to doubt that Goethe would have held the same theory with regard to animated pictures. Dramatic film art needs no prop but calls on her sister, music, to collaborate jointly with her in the creation of a harmonious work.

The *director of photography* is the film author's principal technical collaborator. A master of values in half tints, he must translate into lights and shadows the angles into which the author has decomposed each sequence. The author must be able to count on him as the painter relies on his palette.

Sound engineer is a term which should be applied only to the radio-electrical engineer. In reality, the sound engineer should be assisted by someone who would record the music. It might be possible to call in a young composer who had taken courses specializing in sound recording. This would give him a technical knowledge of both music and recording. The music recorder would then be in a position to make a faithful transcription of the music, the words, or the sound. I do not have to emphasize how valuable such an artist-technician would be.

The *set designer* is also an artist, who has charge of building and maintaining the sets. I have already mentioned the importance of the atmosphere to the dramatic element and to the behavior of the actors. The set designer, primarily an architect, will execute the sets in accordance with the author's exact specifications, taking into account the angles at which the shots are to be made and the different foci of the camera lens. In other words, he must be an artist who specializes in the technique of filmic stage setting.

I do not want to take up the composition of the production group in detail. In confining myself to the chief participants in the intellectual creation of the work, I have no intention of slighting the studio technicians and workers. All the members of the creative group are equal in the sense that they have the right to claim a share in the creation of THEIR FILM.

A film author's dream would be always to work with the same group. This dream might come true if certain economic conditions, which I shall discuss later, could be brought about.

The life of the creative group is as ardent as it is brief. On the last day of shooting, the whole group is photographed around the "clap" which bears the film's title like a coat of arms. And then each one goes his own way, toward other productions.

Sometimes, men who have worked in the same group will run into each other in another group. They are glad to see each other. For a while, they still talk in the dialogue of the last film. They laugh together at the same recollections. But soon all that fades away. The completed task gives way before the task at hand. The new group takes everything they have: faith, enthusiasm, hard work. Shoulder to shoulder, they strive once more for a few months to produce an hour or two of projected film which the public will watch with interest or boredom and go away saying, "Not bad, but it could have been better." The public is right, for masterpieces are seldom made, and the true artist is always dissatisfied. That is why he starts over again to try to do better!

13

THE MOTION PICTURE
AS AN ART-INDUSTRY

CREATIVE GROUPS similar to those I have tried to describe may be found everywhere, and all are imbued with the same spirit. They remain the same, even when magnified on the fabulous scale of American industry. I have had the same pleasure in meeting John Smith, cameraman, electrician, or grip, in a Hollywood studio that I experienced in working with my old friend Totor in a Paris studio. I have found the same spirit of solidarity in the group, the same interest in the film being made, and the same good will toward the boss, when the latter is a true patron.

Despite all adverse conditions and vicissitudes, this team spirit exists all over the world because the power of the motion picture and its tremendous future exert an influence, which is often unconscious, on all who participate in its creation, in whatever capacity. But, if this is true, then what is the reason for the trammels which exercise an invisible but no less powerful restraining influence on the full blossoming of that beneficial pride in a noble work? These trammels derive from the fact that the motion picture is an art-industry and the eternal, stupid conflict between creators and organizers has been treated no more objectively in the case of the motion picture than it has in other industries which are essentially artistic. The effects produced by this basic cause have been reflected in the motion picture's artistic and intellectual development. On the other hand, the failure of industrial leaders to understand the laws of natural evolution followed by every human society has prevented outworn economic procedures from being adapted sufficiently to the requirements of the motion picture.

This major art, so full of life and promise, is kept confined, its growth arrested, within a rigid framework and a style long dated. It would take an entire volume to attempt a description of these causes and their multiple effects. However, I would like to bring up certain essential questions which have a direct influence on the destiny of the dramatic film.

In France, the conflict became most bitter at the time the industry lost its "patrons." By now it must be clear that I use this title in its loftiest sense, for it presupposes the bearer to be possessed of certain technical and intellectual qualities. During the period when the French film industry was headed by great patrons, such as Charles Pathé, Léon Gaumont, and Edmond Benoit-Lévy, there was no conflict in the proper meaning of the word. By this, I mean that film authors would have the usual arguments with leaders of the industry to make their ideas prevail, but they would be up against men who spoke the same professional language and who, like themselves, felt pride in their work. There were fights over ideas and technical arguments, but professional unity was preserved by a mutual esteem based on ability. The businessman who was afraid of a subject because of the financial repercussions it might have would often allow himself to be convinced by arguments based on artistic grounds or through fear of not promoting a progressive step that might mark an important stage in motion picture history.

When these great patrons, for diverse and sometimes regrettable reasons, had ceased their activities in favor of motion pictures, the situation changed completely, and a tragic rupture took place between the industry and the art.

The former fell into the hands of financial speculators who regarded the motion picture as merely another excuse to make money. They immediately set about making their stock go up and down according to the needs of their speculations, exhibiting no interest in motion pictures other than that of attending "great premieres" in the company of people who were important to their "business." That was just the trouble: it had become purely a matter of business; the owners changed with the fluctuations of the stock; they all had a profound contempt for the profession. I remember suggesting to one of these ephemeral leaders that he stay with me during a production so that he might at least acquire some idea of the profession. This important individual replied condescendingly that if, by any mishap, he should have the slightest knowledge of either the art or the technique, he would feel incapable of running his business. As a matter of fact, in view of what he meant by "his business," he was perfectly right, for to him it was merely another name for scheming and bluffing. Given these conditions, we may easily see that there could be no happy or effective collaboration between such businessmen and the artists and that the latter deserved great credit for the way in which they managed to preserve their intellectual and artistic integrity in the face of such hardships.

It was in this fashion that the two great industrial concerns which had exercised a regulative effect—Pathé and Gaumont—soon disappeared and the French motion picture fell into the hands of short-lived combines which, in most cases, did not last out a single production.

The situation was no better off from the economic standpoint. The advent of the talking film had considerably reduced the value of French motion pictures on the international market, while production costs had quadrupled. The French market itself, badly organized and lacking any control over box-office receipts, was not turning back the sums that production had spent. The motion picture statute which the entire industry had proposed would nevertheless have brought about an improvement in this situation, to the extent of allowing production some measure of profit in the French market alone.

Despite all these obstacles, the French motion picture produced some fine works, and was thereby enabled to retain its very high position among other countries. Perhaps it was precisely on account of those difficulties that a greater effort was made and the will to create strengthened.

To start work on a film, and particularly to finish it, involved something of a miracle. That such a miracle could be achieved was due entirely to the faith and creative energy of the Ideal Production Group. It is the latter that will enable the French motion picture to resume its rightful place among the nationally diverse motion pictures of the world.

In the United States the situation is altogether different.

There is already in existence a strong, powerful industry, in many instances headed by the same men who created it. These men have kept their spirit of enterprise and their pioneering courage. They have passed on these attributes to their followers. Hollywood possesses the finest technical and artistic organization in the world. Its studios are equipped with the last word in electrical and photographic improvements. The tremendous acreage owned by the companies enables them to reproduce entire towns of every kind. California has an ideal climate, while its variety of terrain makes it possible to find almost any type of natural setting for a film. Hollywood attracts all the great talent of the world, as well as excellent artists for the smaller roles. Fine orchestras and superb choruses are always on hand for any musical. Hollywood's resources are immense, its funds limited only by the enormous reservoir of receipts from the world market.

Such is Hollywood, uncontested capital of the film spectacle. What does this metropolis lack that prevents it from becoming a mecca, a place of pilgrimage from which the visitor may return with all his illusions intact? Let me answer this question which I have asked myself by saying that it will appear to lack nothing if we do not take care, once again, to distinguish between the genres.

The American motion picture industry was created and developed with a specific goal in mind which certain film genres should aim to attain. The pioneers intended to create an industry that would "manufacture" products designed to be sold as escape entertainment, as diversion. This involved organizing production along industrial lines with a high rate of profit by obtaining the best technical talent. The whole of Hollywood's vast machinery was planned and built up on this basis, and I am glad to say that in this field it has been a complete success. All specifically American films of the fanciful, spectacular, or comic genre reveal a technical and artistic perfection that is unequaled. They all have the effect of resting the mind and delighting the eye. The founders of the American industry believed—and experience has proved them right—that these film genres could be adapted to a multiple creative collaboration, high-lighted by a wealth of resources, beauty of sets and people, all co-ordinated by the industry. Ingenuity and organization accomplished this miracle.

Too many people are prejudiced against Hollywood so that it gives me pleasure here to pay tribute to its brilliant organization, sincerity, and technical knowledge. Most of these lamentable critics will be the first to go and enjoy these native products, which have no other pretension save that of diverting by means of a skillful blend of visual and musical harmonies.

Let us now consider the film genre which really belongs in the field of dramatic film art and which I have tried to define in the preceding chapters. Here, I am compelled to make certain criticisms which, I am sure, our American friends will not hold against me. Each of these criticisms derives from the fact that Hollywood is organized to produce film genres which, in their conception, are able to support the collaboration of many people. Though always in evidence, good will alone is not sufficient for a personal work to be adapted and developed in purely industrial surroundings.

A dramatic film is the work of an author who, at the end of the conceptual phase, surrounds himself with a group of technicians and artists whom he will direct and inspire. The film author is both an artist and a craftsman, in the sense that he first does the creative work, all by himself, and then puts this work into concrete shape with the help of his family of craftsmen.

The mind must be free, or at least preserve the illusion of freedom, before it can give birth to ideas. In general, Hollywood has not taken sufficient note of this. With very few exceptions, the dramatic genre has been assimilated to the other genres; it has been forcibly cast in a standard mold, made to bow to the exigencies of mass production, whereas in reality it should rise out of a living matrix, bearing all the marks of a creative mind. The division of labor, as it now exists, is unsuitable for personal creation.

In the vast majority of cases, a producing company purchases the motion picture rights of a successful play or novel. The work is turned over to a series of writers who take it through various stages of transformation in accordance with a standard pattern presumably dictated by public taste. After countless modifications, the shooting script is placed in the hands of the director, who will have nothing to do but direct the artists on the set. The author of the original work will have nothing to say in the matter, even if he fails to see any resemblance between the script and his play or novel. The film author's role will be reduced to that of an agent who executes a plan. The former will have sold the raw material, which may be altered at will; the latter will not even have been allowed to bring to the work his own originality of talent. The collective brain of the company is never capable of selecting the idea and evaluating it. That is why it so often happens that B pictures contain first-rate ideas which should have been given the benefit of all available resources.

I hasten to say that there are a few top-notch American film authors who have been able to get around this rule, either with the help of far-sighted producers or because they were producers themselves. That is why Hollywood occasionally puts out some very fine personal works. But even in such exceptional cases, there are obstacles which no one can avoid, for they are the product of intangible rules.

We have seen that the dramatic film is very closely allied to the film of life; therefore, it must contain certain natural elements. Here again, Hollywood has set up standard principles which, though suitable to other genres, ought never to have been inflicted on the dramatic film.

For example, the standard make-up and hairdress worn by the girls in an American chorus are commendable because they provide a homogeneous general effect and unity of visual rhythm.

Conventionalized compositions are suitable for comic or fanciful characters.

Dramatic films, on the other hand, must avoid anything artificial. Compelling a film author to use country girls wearing heavy make-up and a permanent, fresh from a four-hour session with the hairdresser, results in falsifying the entire dramatic story of a film.

The setting and mood of the fairy-tale or fanciful film may, and in certain cases should, leave reality far behind. But dramatic films require a setting and a mood which have been imagined by the film author to bring his story closer to life.

The most serious limitations arise from a misinterpretation of the public's tastes. Their effects are reflected in the selection of the idea, the treatment of the idea, and the choice of interpreters.

It would seem that the industry's acceptance of an idea should be based solely on the latter's value and its quality of being universally comprehended. In Hollywood, the selection and treatment of an idea are governed by a kind of intangible but extremely artificial law which results from an imaginary poll of the public. Thus, for instance, it appears that the public insists on being shown every conceivable form of luxury—houses, clothes, and so on.

As a matter of fact, the poll is not always imaginary. From time to time, some companies have instituted a kind of inquiry into public opinion. On one occasion a number of film authors adopted a splendid idea for a film, conceived by a famous author. The company interested in buying the motion picture rights sent out a specialist to take a poll of the public. The following question was asked: "Would you be interested in seeing a film the story of which takes place in a market?" Naturally, the reply was negative because the people were thinking of a documentary, which would hold no interest for them as they went to market every day. The experiment was basically unsound, for a work cannot be judged until it is completed. Only then can the strength of the idea and the artistic worth of its presentation be appraised. In any event, the film was never made and undoubtedly never will be.

It is not hard to imagine the confusion created by such methods when applied to the selection of the idea, the reproduction of the environment, and the dramatic construction itself.

As to the choice of interpreters, the law of Box Office decrees the use of stars who are idolized by the public. Unfortunately, it is only too true that a direct ratio exists between the rise of box-office receipts and the degree of fame attached to the stars who are billed. But it is equally undeniable that this situation was created by a rash policy of excessive publicity designed to promote these stars. It was not the public that invented the stars but the industry that imposed them on the public through the power of publicity. A name was "sold," just like any other product, and the effect has been identical.

Altogether different results might have been obtained if this publicity had been more equally distributed among all the creators, particularly the film author, who is in general completely sacrificed and consequently unknown to the greater public. Most important of all, the genre and subject of a particular film should be announced. This involves giving the public an education, an education that will benefit dramatic film art and all who serve it. In the meantime, the casting of a film's lead parts is limited to a few stars whose talents are undeniable but who are often obliged to take parts they are unable to play. Because of this, a great many talented individuals are marking time and may never have an opportunity to prove their merits.

In France, my colleagues and I never made a film without running across someone in a bit part who had talent we wanted to promote. In Hollywood, there is a whole crop of fine screen actors waiting to be picked from all the talent and diversity of character that may be found in every film. They form an immense reserve of capital and an artistic gold mine as yet untouched.

America is fortunate in possessing independent film critics, some of whom occasionally take the trouble to chart a course. The critic's role is a beneficial one, to the artist as well as to the businessman; he, too, should be entrusted with the task of re-educating the public so that the latter may exert an influence, and a favorable one this time, on the individuals without whose help the artists cannot express themselves in this art-industry.

The charges that can be laid against the production of dramatic films may also arise from external causes which are no less serious.

First of all, there is the practice of the double bill, which we have already mentioned in the chapter on films of life. As I recall it, this practice consists of showing two full-length films on the same program. The main effect of this is to leave little or no place on the program for films of life. But it also has serious consequences on the quality of dramatic films, resulting in overproduction, a large part of which is given over to B pictures, delightfully christened "companion features." These films are industrial products put together in a few days; they are unworthy of Hollywood, where technical care and perfection are the rule. The subjects treated are on the whole insignificant and often dangerously stupid. Such films, which belong to no genre worthy of inclusion in the general division, are harmful to the motion picture in general and to the American motion picture in particular. Why ruin Hollywood's tremendous prestige for the sake of a little extra profit and embarrass national productions in other countries? The place usurped by this unwelcome intruder could be much more happily filled with films of life and particularly with informational films. Production should be concerned with all film genres which share in the great objectives of the entertainment motion picture: poetic, fanciful, comic, or dramatic. There is nothing against creating others, such as the adventure genre, which gave us those splendid Westerns with their headlong galloping cowboys.

Finally, I should like to mention one more limitation, one that was set up with the best possible intentions of solving a real problem. I am referring to censorship.

Whoever is aware of the powerful influence exerted by the motion picture on its audience feels a natural anxiety to see that some control is exercised over its use or over the films themselves. But, even if every individual who plays a part in creating them can show a little foresight and allow his conscience to guide him, it is no less true that the state has a duty to protect law and order and public morals and that large national communities should take pains to safeguard their culture. Once these principles are laid down, there is still danger that the bodies set up to ensure that protection may become influenced by the different philosophies, habits, and customs of the individuals composing them. Since the chief attraction of the human mind lies in its diversity, we must expect to find a similar diversity of reactions in the various opinions it may express. Therefore, it would appear to be extremely difficult to find the perfect solution for a problem the known facts of which are based on so fragile and unstable a foundation.

Putting aside political censorship, which has no bearing on the present subject, we may say that numerous sincere attempts have been made, both by the state and by private groups.

In France, the motion picture has long suffered from a plethora of censorships. Indeed, every mayor had the right to mutilate or to suppress a film. If the municipal magistrate was weak-willed, he would be very apt to bow to the pressure of groups with different political, moral, or religious inclinations.

The decree that established a single censorship also placed it under the authority of the Ministry of National Education. A committee, composed of representatives from all the ministries and from a few large groups of public interest, had the responsibility of reviewing films. This censorship was a mild one and interfered only for reasons which involved law and order.

The system satisfied everybody, and, making allowances for the grumbling so necessary to Frenchmen, it seemed very close to ideal. In fact, these amiable censors functioned so benevolently that this might very well have been the reason for their blindness to the insidious propaganda carried on by the totalitarian states. On the other hand, the reassuring presence of this state organism, the official seal of approval appearing before the credit titles, had the effect of sanctioning, in the public eye, certain vulgar productions which were hardly intended for an audience of children.

To sum up, censorship in France deserved great credit for

not interfering with creative art, but it was unable to achieve its two principal aims: to protect the country against foreign propaganda and to preserve the fresh innocence of children by forbidding them to see films they cannot assimilate.

In America, the problem is particularly complicated by the considerable expanse of territory, the diversity of the people, and especially by the fact that the country consists of forty-eight states, each of which has its own domestic laws and statutes.

American producers thus found themselves in a practically impossible situation. Their films were subject to being mutilated and banned according to the whims of countless local censorships. The latter did not result solely from legal statutes but from moral and religious leagues which are especially profuse in this country. It was under these conditions that the Association of Motion Picture Producers and the Motion Picture Producers and Distributors of America entered into negotiations with the different leagues and eventually drew up a code entitled "Code to Govern the Making of Talking, Synchronized and Silent Motion Pictures."

This code was definitively adopted by the Association of Motion Picture Producers, which included all the big companies. It is still in force at this time and, from a business standpoint, is satisfactory because it ensures the fullest exploitation of films.

The spirit in which the articles of the code were drawn up is excellent; it shows that the authors were fully aware of the motion picture's objectives. Here is the preamble:

"Motion picture producers recognize the high trust and confidence which have been placed in them by the people of the world and which have made motion pictures a universal form of entertainment.

"They recognize their responsibility to the public because of this trust and because entertainment and art are important influences in the life of a nation.

"Hence, though regarding motion pictures primarily as entertainment without any explicit purpose of teaching or propaganda, they know that the motion picture within its own field of entertainment may be directly responsible for spiritual or moral progress, for higher types of social life, and for much correct thinking.

"During the rapid transition from silent to talking pictures they have realized the necessity and the opportunity of subscribing to a Code to govern the production of talking pictures and of reacknowledging this responsibility.

"On their part, they ask from the public and from public leaders a sympathetic understanding of their purposes and problems and a spirit of cooperation that will allow them the freedom and opportunity necessary to bring the motion picture to a still higher level of wholesome entertainment for all the people.

"*General Principles.*

"1. No picture shall be produced which will lower the moral standards of those who see it. Hence the sympathy of the audience shall never be thrown to the side of crime, wrong-doing, evil or sin.

"2. Correct standards of life, subject only to the requirements of drama and entertainment, shall be presented.

"3. Law, natural or human, shall not be ridiculed, nor shall sympathy be created for its violation."

Considering the impossible situation in which the American film industry had been placed by the irksome activities of these "leagues," and examining the objectives set forth above, we are compelled to admire such a display of moral conscience.

We notice that the film producers and distributors appreciate the great task and moral significance of universal entertainment. We fully understand the importance of certain articles, such as the one which forbids any detailed description of methods used in theft and other crimes. Having made ourselves clear on these points, we are nevertheless extremely sorry that the producers were compelled to state certain prohibitions which are against nature, which constitute a barrier to artistic freedom and a limitation of the imagination, the inventiveness, of film authors.

Article 3 of the general principles, for instance, is irreproachable from the moral standpoint; but in practice its effect would be to prohibit even such a figure as Punch, that forerunner of the motion picture, who represents the critical spirit, a means for the public to let off steam, but in so attractive a guise that he could scarcely be considered seditious.

In Section II, entitled Sex, Article 8, we read that *"Scenes of actual child birth, in fact or in silhouette, are never to be presented,"* and, in Article 9, that *"Children's sex organs are never to be exposed."*

Thus, a veil of silence is to be thrown around the finest and greatest acts of creation as if they were shameful and grotesque; the sublime act of childbearing is furtively to be concealed as if it were a crime, whereas in reality the transmission of life is an act of beauty. On the contrary, a dramatic film has no right to dissimulate beauty. Its most beautiful scenes should be devoted to celebrating and glorifying the sacred act of maternity. There are no greater scenes than those which show a mother nursing her child, for she is the very symbol of life.

It must be said that the public and press are not always disposed to abide by the rulings of the leagues which claim to represent them. In *Forgotten Village,* for example, which I have already mentioned in the chapter on films of life, the guardians of public morality had succeeded in having the film's finest scene suppressed. This showed a native woman in the throes of childbirth and had been filmed with perfect tact, its greatness lying entirely in the magnificent natural setting provided by the high mountains of Mexico. When the facts became known, there was such a violent outburst of public opinion in the press that the scene was put back in the film and the guardians were put in their place.

Unfortunately, the public is very rarely informed, which makes it all the more serious that the code was based on the principle of suppressing and hiding evil for fear of contagion. This rule may be justified in some cases, as in that of crime; but in its application it more often constitutes a sin against society.

In this connection, some of us may recall Oscar Wilde's charming tale about "The Happy Prince," whose royal parents wished to make him completely good and happy. They brought him up in a magnificent palace, surrounded by high walls that kept him from seeing all the ugliness and misery of life outside them. The prince became neither good nor bad: he died of boredom. A statue of him was erected outside the walls, amid the poverty, the misdeeds, and crimes of man. At last, the soul of the prince looked down on real life and sighed with sorrow; but, in doing his utmost to remedy these evils, he found the true happiness that he had never known inside the high wall guarding him from all contact with real life.

Running away from evil does not remove it. Some evils are aggravated by silence, and in that case silence becomes culpable, if not downright criminal. Article 7, Section II, of the code decrees that "*Sex hygiene* and venereal diseases are not subjects for motion pictures." I doubt whether many people will disagree with me when I say that we have no moral right to raise our children in complete ignorance of the dangers they may run and that we cannot let them go out into the world without telling them what the world is like.

Moreover, the code is terribly dated on this point. It resembles that rapidly disappearing family which, when entertaining company, looks cautiously under its Louis XVI sofa before uttering the fearful word syphilis in tones low enough so the unmarried daughter of the house will not hear it. Yet, later on, this same daughter will give herself, in a white veil and to the strains of the Wedding March, to the man who will infect her because the disease he suffered from could not be mentioned, let alone cured.

These are things that were not mentioned in the parlors of 1900, but now it is high time they were brought out and made known to the general public. Prudery, always absurd, here becomes sheer cowardice.

And so this code, which was inspired by the best of intentions and the fullest consciousness of the motion picture's great aims, in practice serves only to put fresh obstacles in the way of accomplishing these aims. It seems to me that we may find the reason to lie in the fact that the powers which forced such a code on the producers are in themselves artificial. In other words, I mean that they do not represent more than a tiny minority of the public in whose name they claim to act.

The morality leagues, the ladies who patronize works suppos-edly carried on for the protection of society, and the religious groups are guided by people with sincere convictions. But they usurp the public's rights by forcing film producers to set up these narrow bounds beyond which they dare not go for fear of incurring bans and excommunications that would make any exploitation impossible.

American producers have spent much time and effort endeav-oring to produce fine dramatic works, and they have often been successful. Though they have had to bow to the inevitable and exclude the dramatic elements contained in crime or adultery, they have done their best to put the finest and healthiest emotions into their films, for they are well aware that they will never "sell" indifferent and neutral films. People go to a dramatic film to obtain the emotion which is an indispensable supplement to the monotony of their daily existence. They bring to the screen a deep thirst for passion. If they are denied the passion contained in a crimnial act or one of adultery, then they must certainly be granted the emotion deriving from great themes such as the love of soil, a mother's sacrifice, or science working for humanity. In any event, their emotions must be aroused, and this can and always will be accomplished through films of emotion and love, films of passion in the most human and grandest sense of the word.

Such themes may be conceived and developed only where freedom of expression is complete. That is why censorship is always an empirical means, the most concrete result of which has been to set up a sort of artistic birth control.

For that matter, how can we put our trust in censors when each one of them will interpret the smallest detail of a film according to his own temperament and notions? Very often, these judges have taken the most innocent movements or words and read into them a meaning that would never have occurred either to the author or to the public. Any film is fit to be shown, provided it is treated with tact, restraint, and good taste. If we admit the need for censorship, then we must also admit that enough people can be found who are capable of passing on the æsthetics and style of film works, for ugliness and vulgarity are in truth the only grave dangers that constitute a threat to the mind of the public. But obviously this would be an extremely delicate task and it would be very easy for the censors to fall into arbitrary rulings.

In the last analysis, I believe that even the most perfect work, compelled to pass through the mill of censorship or code, would emerge from it emasculated and emptied of all intellectual content. In practice, all censorships have revealed themselves to be dangerous limitations on freedom of thought and expression in films.

The only acceptable solution appears to have been found by a Belgian law which attempts to protect the youth of the nation and at the same time to allow creative art complete freedom of expression. This law was passed by the Belgian parliament on September 1, 1920, and resulted from a profound study of the problem. It contains the following articles:

Article 1 forbids children under sixteen from entering motion picture theaters.

Article 2 makes an exception in the case of films that have been authorized by a committee and are billed as "entertainment for the family and children." A royal decree issued in 1922 outlines in detail the control of films by this committee.

Articles 3 and 4 provide for penalties, which may include even the closing down of any theater breaking the law.

This law goes as far as is humanly possible to protect children, provided we admit that at the age of sixteen the individual's mind is sufficiently developed for him to exercise his critical function. It dispels the false notion, unfortunately held by far too many people, that films are entertainment for children. The motion picture is a major art which includes, among its different genres, films comprehensible to children as well as others too complex for young minds still in the process of formation.

The Belgian law has done away with programs that are indiscriminately made up of fine and completely innocent films together with films that are too complex and at times even noxious owing to their lack of taste. As an example let me mention one program shown in Paris. The double feature included *The Ironmaster* by Georges Ahnet and *Madame Husson's Rose Bush* by Guy de Maupassant. That week, most of the people packing the huge Gaumont-Palace Theater consisted of families who had been attracted by *The Ironmaster*. This film, which Abel Gance had made with exquisite charm and taste, was ample justification for the presence of children; but the latter were also exposed to the bad taste in which the other feature had been conceived. The author of this film had at the same time ruined Maupassant and exposed, not only children, but the entire public to the dangers of a particularly crude type of vulgarity.

With the children protected, as they are in Belgium, film producers and authors are allowed the fullest freedom, provided there is no threat to law and order.

However, if they are relieved of censorship, film productions should be planned and made with discrimination, in good taste, and with a sense of responsibility that will be increased each time more freedom is gained.

At the time of writing, it is extremely difficult to foresee what the situation will be when the present world convulsion has passed. Nevertheless, we may anticipate a complete transformation of the political and economic setup in Europe. It is only by trying to envisage these new conditions that we may be lucky enough to come across a few solutions that will enable dramatic film art to overcome the obstacles now hindering it.

Every country should produce that form of art which is suitable to it. The merit of the French motion picture lies entirely in its quality of craftsmanship. The film author is an artist-craftsman. He gives concrete shape to his imagined conception with the help of a creative group which preserves the characteristics of a family of craftsmen. Only this family of craftsmen is capable of producing the personal works which are characteristic of the French dramatic film. The solution of the problem lies wholly in obtaining favorable conditions that will ensure the life of these productive cells.

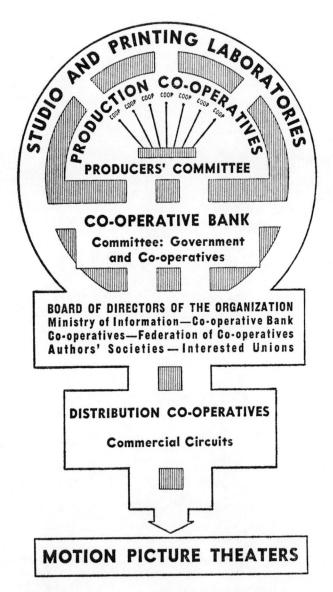

STUDIO AND PRINTING LABORATORIES

PRODUCTION CO-OPERATIVES

COOP COOP COOP COOP COOP COOP

PRODUCERS' COMMITTEE

CO-OPERATIVE BANK

Committee: Government
and Co-operatives

BOARD OF DIRECTORS OF THE ORGANIZATION
Ministry of Information—Co-operative Bank
Co-operatives—Federation of Co-operatives
Authors' Societies — Interested Unions

DISTRIBUTION CO-OPERATIVES

Commercial Circuits

MOTION PICTURE THEATERS

Chart showing co-operative organization for production and
distribution.

Since it is hard to believe that after such a cataclysm there will be a complete return to a liberal economy, we are compelled to consider a system that will take into account both the principles of a controlled economy and the imperative need of allowing dramatic films the greatest possible artistic latitude. In my opinion, the only type of organization that may be able to reconcile these two apparently contradictory conditions is the co-operative.

This is not the place to make a detailed study of how such a system would function, but the following outline will give some idea of the organization (see also Chart 3):

1. Board of Directors of the Organization.

This committee would include representatives of the Government (Ministry of Information), of the Production Co-operatives, of the Co-operative Bank, of authors' societies, and of interested unions.

2. The Co-operative Bank.

The Bank would handle the funds and regulate the economy of the system. It would work hand in glove with the Government, represented on the committee by an official of the Ministry of Finance. The Bank committee would also include representatives from the co-operatives for production and distribution.

3. Production Co-operatives.

Each of these would consist of one or more creative groups whose intellectual, artistic, and professional merit would have been passed on by a board of co-operatives. This board would be composed of representatives from the production co-operatives and would function through offices of technical studies and organization of production.

4. Studios and Printing Laboratories.

It is advisable that studios and printing laboratories belong to co-operatives so that their sets and equipment may be put to better use and production costs determined more accurately. In the meantime, the French Motion Picture Co-operative would be powerful enough to dictate a rational organization.

5. Distribution Co-operative.

This co-operative would have the task of securing the commercial circuits by a reduction in the cost of distribution, obtained through a greater concentration of resources. The Distribution Co-operative would be under the direction of specialists in distribution, subject to the control of a committee comprising representatives of the Board of Directors. An office of statistics would establish a regional scale of profits, based on actual fact. Another office would deal with matters relating to the press and publicity.

6. Foreign Productions.

Foreign companies would be free to ensure their distribution directly, provided they complied with the existing laws (dubbing, censorship, etc.), or to appeal to the good offices of the Distribution Co-operative.

7. Motion Picture Theaters.

The exploitation of theaters would remain free, subject to any antitrust laws that might be passed. The Co-operative Bank would take immediate action, either to obtain exclusive ownership of theaters in Paris and other large centers for showing films, or to make contracts with the owners of these theaters to guarantee an outlet for French productions.

This organization would ensure the economic co-ordination of the industry, guarantee artistic freedom, and ensure maximum returns to production by eliminating parasitic elements.

At one blow, all the most serious obstacles would be overthrown, particularly those deriving from the conflict between industry and authors. Indeed, each of the latter would have an opportunity to form his own co-operative society for production, either by himself with the members of his own creative group, or else with a colleague. The film author would be his own producer and would discuss the means of exploiting his film directly with the financial and commercial groups in charge of ensuring the system's economic stability.

I do not want to take the time here to elaborate any further on the plan outlined above, for I should only be dragged into a discussion of political economy; but a profound study of such an organization has already been made, while a few experiments that were carried out before 1939 have given it a solid foundation.

I consider the co-operative system to be the only one capable of putting the French motion picture on a new basis so that it may assume its rightful place in the ensemble that constitutes a universal film art.

It is equally important that the *American motion picture* continue to occupy the brilliant position it has already attained with certain genres in this ensemble. But, if dramatic film art is to express the spirit of the American people, it would seem desirable to establish conditions more favorable to it. In this connection, we have already observed that the dramatic film has to some extent been stifled and emasculated by the enormous machinery of Hollywood, that its power of expression has been weakened by artificial patterns and standards. Without wishing to make any changes in the economic principles governing the industry, which I do not feel competent to judge, I may perhaps be permitted to hazard a guess that the leaders themselves will in the natural course of events be compelled to accede to the demands of art.

All big industries need scientists who will carry out disinterested research in their laboratories or artists who will create, in their original form, the models that their machines will manufacture in mass, putting them within reach of the humblest purse. Without the contribution made by creative art, industry could not live. Therefore, it is essential for industry to protect and encourage artist-craftsmen who produce personal works so that the people will always worship the cult of Beauty.

The American motion picture industry is not in the habit of shirking its duties and obligations. For this reason, I feel it is desirable that part of its activities be devoted to helping artists who have something personal to express and to giving them favorable working conditions. I mean that in every studio a place should be set aside where one or more creative units could make what I take the liberty of calling "hand-made" products.

The film author, the writer, the composer, and the rest of the group, safely sheltered from rules and regulations, from the influence of the box office, and from the requirements of a standard make-up, would then be able to produce dramatic works worthy of the American motion picture and avoid just missing out on a "masterpiece," as a number of films have done.

Hollywood has no lack of talented film authors who are endowed with tact and taste. From time to time they manage to overcome all obstacles and produce a work of real merit. If they could be spared these fruitless struggles, their work, being conceived in freedom, would be more fertile.

Once these conditions for art creation have been met, the final step could be taken and the creative group, as a measure of justice, allowed to share in the profits.

By thus enabling film art to come into its own, the entire industry would be invigorated and the mentality of the public maintained at a certain intellectual level. Even if such productions turned out to be financial losses, the industry would amply make up for this in the new source of inspiration opened up to it. But, on the contrary, I believe that a group operating under such conditions would bring about a considerable reduction in the costs of production and at the same time produce works which, through their quality, emotional impact, and power, would make an irresistible appeal to both the intellect and the emotions of any audience.

Finally, we may be allowed to hope that the abolition of the double feature bill will enable the film of life authors to form co-operatives and that their productions will meet with a better reception in the big circuits.

Such, then, in brief, are the measures which we may anticipate will be taken so that the dramatic film can more surely achieve its aims in the art of entertainment. I have discussed them only with respect to the two countries I know best, but every nation will have to find the conditions most favorable for the marriage of art and industry to become ever more idyllic and fruitful.

14

UNIVERSAL INFLUENCES
AND OBJECTIVES OF THE
MOTION PICTURE

AT FIRST SIGHT, it may seem paradoxical to want
to consider the universal objectives of the motion picture at a
time when the world is still in the throes of an unprecedented
cataclysm. Nevertheless, I feel that there could be no better moment than now when the power of animated pictures is being
used both defensively and offensively in a struggle for the survival
of civilization. That civilization can ensure its own permanence
only if the peoples of the world come to a greater mutual understanding and if they are drawn closer together by a democratic
ideology. Today we see clearly how expedient it would have
been if we had kept that ideology alive so that it might stand
for something more in the eyes of those who benefit by it than
mere words emptied of their true significance.

Henceforth, it will be necessary for the humblest citizens of
the world to draw closer together, not only through speedy
methods of communication, but more especially through a common ideal based on certain great immutable principles such as
the Bill of Rights and the Declaration of the Rights of Man and
the Citizen, on which the American and French constitutions
are founded.

Starting now, there should be a redistribution of moral and
intellectual wealth so that everyone may benefit thereby. Every
individual should be trained to contemplate the great spectacle

of nature in its most varied aspects and to recognize the most remarkable manifestations of human genius. Whatever is ugly, vile, and false must be done away with and replaced by beauty, truth, respect for human beings, everything that goes to make up the democratic ideal, for which so many brave men have suffered and died!

Before 1939, the half-closed frontiers paralyzed trade but reacted even more unfavorably on intellectual exchanges. Peoples were thrown back on themselves and had no opportunity to know and to judge each other better, although communication facilities would have made this possible. Each country exulted in its own nationalism, its own social system, its own science, sometimes to the point of wanting to impose its own conception of civilization on other peoples. This led to new conflicts surpassing those caused by material interest, while the acceptance of a sensible ideal of internationalism in the intellectual and social sense was postponed.

Since man is a product of his environment, nothing could be more natural than the existence of a great many diverse cultures; but, instead of regarding them as competitive, we should foster among them a sincere desire to emulate one another so that the elements common to all may become apparent. Indeed, all over the world we may find the same aspirations, the same sentiments of justice and peace, the same need for art and ideals, which are like the bread of mankind.

Dominating all others, there is also a universal civilization. There is life itself, whose manifestations are so dissimilar, but which remains the same everywhere when we consider it from the human standpoint of natural motives, actions, and feelings. In all parts of the world, there are men whose everyday existence is no less poignant for being different from our own. Africa and the Orient are not merely lands rich in fantasy and abounding with peppermint candy palaces, conventional princesses, and other trinkets of the bazaar. They also contain joy and grief, the simple, real emotions to which all people are susceptible and which we should take the trouble to compare with our own so that we may realize how very similar they are. Indeed, we shall find as much humanity in a remote douar in the Atlas Mountains, where a Berber mother rocks her sick child, as in a town in central France, where François is in love with Marie, or as in a small town in America, where a mother is waiting for her son to come home from the war, as she sits at the window knitting him a pair of socks.

If we allow these universal thoughts, gestures, and ways of acting to be reflected in the mirror of the world, then man will speak to man as brother and together they will tread the path of love.

That is the tremendous aim which only the motion picture has power to accomplish, provided the thoughts that inspire its images are healthy and generous, capable of serving intelligence and promoting elevated sentiments. Let these images present life in all its reality, clothed with the illusion of dream to give it that poetry without which it would become too arid a path. Then, all the film genres—the art of life, of dream, of shining beauty—will be able to help in the creation of that great brotherhood of man for which so many people now are fighting.

The motion picture, whatever its genre, is an art which demands much tact from its devotees, for its influences are potent while their effects vary with the aims pursued and the individuals addressed. I know by experience how difficult, how often disappointing this devotion can be.

One day, the International Institute for Educational Motion Pictures undertook a wide survey to determine what results had been obtained among children by the showing of war films. I took part in this survey as general secretary for the French Committee of the Institute and as deputy delegate for MM. Louis Lumière and Henri Focillon on the general committee of the Institute.

The survey was carried out with the help of some excellent films, such as Raymond Bernard's *The Wooden Crosses.* The experiment was conducted scientifically and entrusted to people prominent all over the world.

The following results were obtained:

Those in favor of war...................86.06%
Those conscious of the horrors of war.........13.94%

Superficially, it would seem that the experiment was somewhat of a failure. This is explained by the fact that the films shown had originally been made as spectacular films, without any specific aim.

If the idea was to make an impression on the children, the experiment should have been carried out in such a way as to penetrate their understanding. Bayonet charges, the thunder of cannon, even the horror of ambulances, were to them merely a part of the natural need they all have to play soldiers. All they saw was the equivalent, in adult terms, of their own games. When we want to affect children, we should certainly take them seriously, but we should try to find images that can affect them, that bear some relation to the ideas they have formed about the world.

Instead of the sound and fury of a great battle fought by thousands of anonymous men, it would be better to tell the simple story of a family hit by the death of a son, an older brother, killed in the war. To all the members of this family, and particularly to the child, sorrow would be something tangible and constantly with them. In this way, a bond between the motion picture story and the young spectator would be created. The latter would be sharing in the horrors of war because the effects of the disaster would have been reduced to family proportions. The *drama* would thus become *his* drama.

Children and natives of primitive countries make excellent subjects for psychological experiments in determining the influence of motion pictures.

The Schleus of the Atlas range, who turned out to be splendid natural actors while I was making *Itto*, provided me with an opportunity to make the most conclusive experiments. A number of them lived in mountain douars and had never been touched by any form of modern civilization. When, after a while, they had come to look upon me as a friend, I began to show films out of doors. The programs I gave them, consisting of "documentaries" and newsreels, produced some astonishing and quite unexpected reactions. Here are some of those I recall.

A camel race brought forth general hilarity which was so contagious that we could not resist joining in ourselves. The audience found it excruciatingly funny that their most familiar domestic beasts should have been translated, by some unknown magic means, to this screen before them. They thought it even funnier to see these camels turned actors, like their storytellers and mimes who carried their art from tribe to tribe.

The opening of an exhibition by President of the Republic Lebrun left them cold until the moment when the head of the state, on departing, donned his tall silk hat. The audience chortled, shook with glee, and finally burst into a tremendous roar of laughter! They had taken the presidential headgear to be one of their kitchen utensils, a kind of queer-shaped calabash; and they were convinced the white gentleman on the screen was doing a comic skit when he put it on his head.

On the other hand, they were deeply moved by some beautifully made films showing machines in action. They maintained an attentive silence while watching those unfamiliar movements caused by *things* which seemed to have a life of their own and while listening to the sounds which seemed to issue forth from monstrous lungs. These primitive, yet intelligent and sensitive, people instinctively realized that these machines were power generators, which had been placed in the hands of the whites, by the will of Allah, to increase their authority!

While sitting under the clear, star-lit sky, in the magnificent and disturbing setting of the Atlas desert, before the clay castle of the chief and in the midst of these Schleus, draped like great noblemen in their tattered *djellabias,* I thought of all the ways in which the motion picture could be used to forward the progress of real civilization. Listening to the lugubrious barking of the famished jackals, I thought of all those human parasites, the skeptics and destroyers of work, who always stand in the path of progress, doing their best to delay it.

Actually, thanks to the efforts of far-sighted administrators such as M. Gotteland, former general director of public edu-

cation in Morocco, a successful attempt has been made to spread
the beneficial effects of motion picture and radio so that these
primitive people will have some knowledge of progress and
some contact with the outer world.

Unfortunately, the influence of motion pictures does not always manifest itself so happily. Film spectacles indiscriminately
shown, without taking into account their psychological effects,
have had particularly deplorable consequences. A film such as
Topaze, for instance, shown to a public which cannot help but
make generalizations, struck a considerable blow to the prestige
of the civil service. This work should have remained in the
theater, where it did not constitute a threat because the audiences were more restrained and, in general, gifted with a critical
sense. Transferred to the screen, it spread far and wide the
demoralizing notion that all public officials were venial. Anyone
who knows the honesty and integrity of the vast majority of
government officials, and especially to what extent those in our
colonies have devoted themselves to public service, will see
how pernicious and unjust such an influence can be. Many similar films have helped to undermine democratic government by
ridiculing it.

Other films, most numerous of all, offend the morals and
customs of natives by showing couples clasped in lengthy
embraces, women too scantily clothed, or adultery too easily for-
given! We should give thought to our splendid women, the
companions of our doctors or administrators in the North
African desert, who, by daily example, are serving the cause of
civilization, before we compromise their influence by displaying
incidents and details of western customs, the relative importance
of which cannot be fairly measured by people so different from
us in culture and habits.

It is, therefore, desirable that in this field the motion picture
spread its beneficial influence by means of films of life bearing
judicious commentaries. It might be possible for certain genres
of the entertainment film, such as filmic poetry, to achieve their
aims, but it would seem that the dramatic film might do better
to take its inspiration from local legends and folklore and create,

on the spot, among the native fauna and flora, works animated
by the marvelous natural actors of the region.

The general influence of the motion picture in our time may
be felt in the humblest images we create: our altered view is
merely the outward indication of the depths to which we have
been spiritually stirred.

The boy who tries to imitate Chaplin's walk, the young girl
who likes to dress her hair like Jeanette MacDonald will also
base their moral attitude on that of the hero or heroine whose
physical mannerisms they copy.

Is this influence good or bad? When a child jumps into the
water to save a friend, or gives some other proof of courage
or goodness, no one ever says, "That doesn't surprise me at all;
he was always going to the movies!" On the other hand, after
every crime or theft committed by an adolescent, the cry goes
up in the press: "It's the fault of the screen!"

There is a firm conviction that all American films are about
gangsters while all French films deal with adultery. Therefore,
it is understandable that a lot of good souls shudder as they
have visions of young people all over the world coming out of
the *Bijou-Cinéma* or Main Street Theater and going straight to
the guillotine or the electric chair.

To be sure, that is a ridiculous exaggeration. But, nonetheless, it is true and significant that the images we see on the screen
make a deep impression on us and imperceptibly transform our
character. The motion picture influences us in countless ways,
and, like the human tongue in Aesop's fable, it can have the
most wonderful effects as well as the most tragic consequences.

Taking everything into consideration, the motion picture,
despite the most difficult obstacles, has achieved its aims rather
well. We may say that it represents the most powerful means
for the dissemination of human thought. For that reason, it is
important that its influence be utilized to sustain the spiritual
life of the world.

The American industry itself recognized the influence of
motion pictures and felt that it should propagate a faith, an

ideal, about them. With that aim in mind, Mr. Will Hays, chairman of the Motion Picture Producers and Distributors of America, had posters made up containing general propaganda in favor of motion pictures.

It is always comforting to see propaganda rising above competition and private interests to serve the common cause of an entire corporation. What makes this publicity great is the fact that it serves not only a business and an industry but also an art and an agency for moral influence.

Here are some of the maxims it spreads:

"The lights of a motion picture theater, in the smallest village as in the largest city, are the symbol of human association and of shared delight."

"Films have the privilege of making mankind forget its thousand and one cares and of providing it with pleasure and relaxation."

"The marvel of motion pictures is that they materialize the dreams and hopes of every individual."

"The greatest tribute that can be paid the screen is to recognize that it has widened the horizon and the vision of youth, and awakened its ambition."

Like all posters, these have a commercial aim: to make as many people as possible come to the "movies." But they achieve that aim by glorifying the moral effect of motion pictures on the masses. They are all based on this great principle: Before the material power of the motion picture can be furthered, its spiritual power must be upheld, strengthened, and utilized. They illustrate the pact of friendship which has finally been made between the school, as the place of education, and the motion picture theater, as the place of diversion. For a long time these two friends were enemies, which makes their present alliance all the more impressive.

During the heroic age of the films, when neighborhood theaters began to attract schoolchildren with the shrill ringing of their bells, teachers would wax indignant over the influence of the screen, which, it must be admitted, often had nothing to show its youthful audiences but more or less harmful nonsense. Frequently, after some adolescent misdeed, numerous teachers would shake their heads and say, "He went to the movies too often."

Eventually, schools began to consider using entertainment films as a means of wholesome distraction, moral education, and general culture.

In the United States, a real alliance has been created between the universities, private groups, and the motion picture, in which the same good will is exhibited by all parties. Among the activities promoted by this alliance, the courses in visual appreciation have brought to the motion picture an enthusiastic and critical public which will contribute to the moral and artistic improvement of films.

The motion picture will thus continue to benefit more and more from this close relationship with the school, from its contact with youth, and will produce works which school and university should support. I am not speaking of teaching or educational films here but of any film which, in its invigorating role as a dispenser of ideas of justice and human feelings, gives birth to a hope, encourages an ambition, widens a horizon, brings a moment of forgetfulness, in a word, effects a transfusion of life in some way or other. In tribute to these films which transmit basic ideas and correspond to a profoundly human need, we might do well to plaster the walls in towns and villages with posters bearing this message: "Go to the movies if you want to live." For we must never forget that the motion picture is an art akin to life. And so we see that school and university have contributed their beneficial influence to the motion picture. With their help, the motion picture will be able to fulfill its true destiny by relying on the life-giving sources of Thought and of Ideal.

The motion picture, although an art-industry, cannot be compared with an ordinary industry or business. The manufactured goods do not conform to a standard pattern, while the business transactions do not consist of selling or exchanging materials or objects which differ only in their quality or appearance. The fact that, under the circumstances, industry is congenitally wedded to art presupposes a somewhat paradoxical marriage between materialism and idealism. That marriage will be more successful if the industrial partner submits to the influence of art, acknowledging that the condition for success lies in the indissolubility of its alliance with art.

The basic idea contained in a film requires that the businessman be able to diffuse it as widely as possible. On the other hand, this diffusion cannot take place unless the idea takes into account the general laws of the motion picture and the psychology of the masses, and remains in touch with the constant evolution of the world. It follows that both the moral ideal and the commercial aim of every film tend to attain universality, that is, to reach every type of audience, made up of all the strata of human society.

Film producers and authors have all coveted universal appreciation for their works; very few have obtained it because they employed artificial means. On the pretext of making necessary concessions to internationalization, they went in for a perfect orgy of expenditures. Thus, they introduced artificial luxury, confusing it with good taste. They banned all local color, thereby obtaining films which had no nationality and which no country could recognize as its own, not even the country producing it. They tried to make "universal" films, which turned out to be films belonging nowhere, for they bore no mark of origin, expressed no conviction, had no soul of their own, and were nothing but lies.

We are lying when we try to express the feelings of others as our own and ape their manners in an attempt to please them. The lie is so obvious that it covers its authors with ridicule. For instance, a few years ago a European film, in order to tempt possible American purchasers, showed all businessmen signing checks with cigars in their mouths and their feet on the desk. Certainly, more than this is needed to make a film American.

We are also lying when we try to show ourselves, not as we are, but as other people see us, out of respect for them and out of scorn for ourselves. Such a lie is worse than ridicule: it becomes a loss of dignity.

There are French films, designed for the international market, which have shown a France made up entirely of night clubs and bars in Montmartre and peopled solely by mannequins and apaches wearing caps and red scarves, a fantastic France, conforming exactly to those posters which traveling agencies stick on their doors: "Paris by night under reliable escort."

One day, a foreign buyer confided to me that the exhibitors in his own country would not dare to bill a film that did not contain at least one scene in a bar. If this were really true, the dilemma would be almost hopeless. Does the public really demand only that type of film which conceals the true face of a country under a grotesque mask? In other words, must we barter our dignity and our reputation? Must a film author be compelled to choose between love for his country and love for his occupation?

Fortunately, there is no truth in it, and we have seen countless examples proving the contrary. D. W. Griffith's *Birth of a Nation* (1915) showed the world an epic phase in a people's struggle to find a footing and how, in finding it, they created one of the greatest nations in the world. Much later, Jean Renoir's *La Marseillaise* was shown all over the world, bearing everywhere the eternal flame of the French Revolution and, at the same time, premonitory signs of the danger which once more was threatening Liberty.

Films such as Pagnol's *Harvest*, which, instead of bars and night clubs, showed the gradual resurrection of one of our ruined villages in the Lower Alps, were able to please, and consequently to "earn a living," though remaining specifically "native" products.

To please should never be a goal: he who aims only to please rarely succeeds and acquires a permanent dislike for his own work, since he does not believe in it. To please can only be the natural consequence of a sincere piece of work. All true expression has a magnetic power which exerts a spiritual attraction. Only that individual who expresses himself can be radiant and vibrant. Likewise, everything sincere is strength while everything false is weakness. The truly universal film, far from being a film which belongs nowhere, is much more likely to be one about which a country can say, in all sincerity, "That is one of our own films."

In short, a film must obey the natural law that governs all productive effort. Here again, it is the earth which furnishes us with our greatest lesson. Fruits grow and ripen according to the nourishment they receive from the natal soil, and the best of them are the ones that are exported. Only those artists who have learned this lesson in sincerity have produced great works. Every country has its own culture, its own writers; every country should have its own films.

The great vintages of Champagne and the Bordeaux country, the oranges of California, the coal of England, just like the best of Racine and Shakespeare and, among others, the fine scenes in *La Grande Illusion* and *Gone with the Wind,* are all native products.

It may be that some are more prone to laughter, others to tears, and the French, after all, to smiles, that half-ironic, half-compassionate smile, which has often been taxed with being fickle but which is merely somewhat philosophical.

French laughter is not physical laughter released by a material cause. Certainly, the masses react vociferously, in our theaters as in theaters all over the world, to slapstick comedy; but Molière's laughter, which will always be our laughter, is primarily psychological in nature.

As an example, take the hamming of the two opera stars in René Clair's *Le Million,* their smirks in front of the curtain and their quarrels behind it. Even the more inferior laughter provoked by *Le Roi des Resquilleurs* was caused by a certain study of the "gate-crashing" trait, which is a human trait.

But what do we laugh at? At human failings. We laugh at a man who might be someone we pass on the street, or our best friend, or ourselves. That is why our laughter contains a great deal of love. In literature and in the theater, we laugh at the characters of Henri Duvernois, of Tristram Bernard, but with the same sympathy we would show in laughing at ourselves.

Our film characters belong to that same human race, steeped is misery and joy. Thus, we are amused by the grownups who scurry around the imperturbably serious little hero of *Feu de Paille* like so many puppets, because we see in them our own follies. And, as all these human failings constitute a thousand little daily dramas, we may say that laughter in France is tempered by drama and will never have the hearty quality of American laughter.

For that matter, the reverse is equally true.

French drama is tempered by laughter and will never have the harshness, not without grandeur, which characterizes some foreign films.

For instance, *Jean de la Lune* is a comedy, whereas it might have been a tragedy. The complaisant brother of the libertine is an abject figure. But he makes us laugh and for that very reason draws closer to us. Once we have laughed, we cannot hate him; at a pinch, we can even see eye to eye with him on certain points; we discover a sensitive chord in him which can vibrate in tune with our own, and finally we come to forgive his abjectness for the sake of humanity.

That, people will say, is a typical example of French fickleness. Very well. But it also shows a deep understanding of human nature, which is made up of good and bad; it shows the great wisdom of taking men as they are—with a smile—so that they may return the compliment.

To be sure, the French screen has produced something besides dramatic comedies. We must not forget robust dramas such as Jean Renoir's *La Bête Humaine* and Julien Duvivier's *Poil de Carotte*, both of which have their roots in human life and suffering. These films are just as much national products as René Clair's *Sous les Toits de Paris*.

These are two clearly distinct trends in the French motion picture. But it must be observed, especially since the advent of speech on the screen, that the first trend is clearly the dominant one, its live images permeated with laughter and tears which melt into a smile of irony and pity.

In order to recreate a little of that true humanity, neither comic nor dramatic, which is reflected in our films, we are under no compulsion to spend millions. A castle may be built with a pack of cards, provided it is a dream castle and at the end tumbles down before a breath of mockery, symbolizing all the pathetic absurdity of our human illusions.

At any rate, whether we cry, or laugh, or smile, according to our temperament, the important thing is to put our soul into it, for there will always be other souls to recover it. The Marx brothers, for instance, have met with tremendous success in France, as, indeed, everywhere else. All over the world, audiences have gone into shrieks of laughter at their antics. Yet, I do not believe the French are particularly gifted with the burlesque strain, since every attempt they have made to succeed in this genre has to date fallen rather flat.

Nevertheless, it must be admitted that this exchange of souls has been made more difficult since films have begun to talk. Happy the wind, the sea, and the violin, who speak a tongue that all men understand! But, in addition to these magnificent sounds, we have wanted to enrich the screen with our own little human voice, which threatens to raise once more the barrier of language between peoples who had come to know each other so well in silence. It was not hard to understand why the great Charlie Chaplin stubbornly remained silent for so long and how reluctant he was to break that silence.

Although the most perfect dubbing will not make people understand an insincere film which is full of lies and conventions, the mere addition of a few subtitles to a really sincere film will immediately establish a contact between it and a foreign audience.

In Paris, I have seen theaters packed with audiences who, though most of them certainly could not have known more than a couple of words of English, were yet deeply stirred by the pathetic figure of Mr. Chips. The public is never mistaken. No matter what the language of the film, it knows when the latter is lying and when it is telling the truth. If we want the motion picture to remain and dramatic art to develop, we must make it more human, bring it closer to daily life.

A truly sincere film will affect people of every class, every country, and even of every period.

Often people will praise a film by saying that it is intended for an "elite" and not meant to be shown to the "general public." I wish to go on record as being entirely against this ready-made formula. I have mingled with the public in the most popular theaters and have found it to consist of good people who want to cry a little, laugh a little, and get a taste of life.

It is neither true nor even conceivable that such people will repudiate scenes which appear on the screen as a shadow cast by their own hearts. If a film is outside their comprehension, then it corresponds to nothing human. In my opinion, a so-called good film that does not make itself felt by every type of audience is a film that has failed.

The troubled and confused period we lived through before the war was characterized by an art that suffered from the same unrest. The arts were infected with the disease of the times. Art, like politics, had generally lost contact with the people and, at the same time, had also lost that stability which can be preserved only if we stick very close to nature and mankind. More so than any other art, the motion picture derives its inspiration from the people and must yield back to the latter the fruit from the seed which it provided.

Let no one conclude that I am advocating a mummified art, confined to faithful reproduction. On the contrary, I believe in a dynamic and truly creative art. I mean that if an artist seeks his inspiration in the people, he will use his imagination and sensibility to create his own interpretation. His work will have been more perfectly achieved if it has been submitted to a selective process, if it appears stripped of the cerebral waste from its conception, left in beautiful simplicity of thought and form. It is from being in touch with the people that we learn simplicity and especially sincerity. The latter quality demands intellectual honesty, for there is no question here of drawing inspiration from a cross-section of the people merely to flatter it or of laboring in the desire to please. The public has a horror of the base concessions that are made to it in order to gain its support, and this is precisely where the best safeguard against complaisance will be found.

If the primary obligation for a film author is to learn how to observe the public's reactions, if the humblest advice is rich in lessons for him, he nevertheless has the duty to express himself with sincerity, faith, and courage in the work he is creating. Thus, and only thus, will he deserve to have the people consider the ideas he lays before them. Only on these terms will motion picture art be able to fulfill its artistic and intellectual mission.

There is everything to be gained by associating with the people and studying their reactions before the screen. For my part, I am extremely grateful to that public and have a high opinion of it. At the beginning of my career, when I was making nothing but teaching films and films of life and showing them myself before the humblest audiences, I learned a· great deal from this incomparable master and I was able to judge its intelligence.

I remember vividly a certain evening in 1925, when I was attending the showing of my own film, *Pasteur*, in a little theater in Grenelle. When there appeared on the screen a close-up of two hands manipulating ordinary laboratory test tubes in which a positive reaction was obtained, the audience suddenly burst into wild applause. Obviously, no one had understood the scientific process involved, but they all felt instinctively that something wonderful had happened. In fact, it was no less than the discovery of the serum against rabies. It should be noted that this was a silent film; there was no commentary, no indication to help the audience understand. Their reaction had been motivated by intuition alone.

Obviously, such a reaction could not be produced by a scene in which a great actress would use the most dramatic expressions in her repertory in an attempt to move the audience by her own professional talent. Neither Greer Garson, in spite of her beauty and her talent as an *actress* which she uses to interpret Mme Curie, nor any other artist in the world can equal the simplicity of a scientist's gesture and the impact of two humble test tubes!

The public, our wonderful general public, has a feeling for nuance and suggestion that is peculiarly its own. I can think of nothing more thrilling for a film author than to go and see his own films, seated among the Saturday night and Sunday afternoon crowds. This public, which by daylight seems brutal and vulgar through the smoke of the men and the chatter of the women, in the darkness of the theater reveals an almost miraculous sensitivity.

The stem of a flower broken on the screen will, in an instant, conjure up for them all the drama that lies in the death of a child. It was this public that wept over *Broken Blossoms* long before the intellectual snobs decided it was fashionable to shed a few aristocratic tears over the same subject. The public will react the same way everywhere. In whatever quarter of the globe, the public reaction is the same, provided the film contains universal ideas and is imbued with humanity. People whose language and customs have nothing in common will laugh or cry over the same scenes in such films. This encourages us to believe that the oceans and mountains that separate peoples are not very important after all, since the same emotions are shared by all.

For a long time after I had returned from America, I kept receiving letters from American filmgoers. Paulette Elambert, little Marie Coeuret in *La Maternelle,* would come to show me the ones she was receiving. Surprised, she would say to me, "Why, they all understood, just as if they spoke the same language we do!" What she had not yet learned was that it is not always necessary for people to speak the same language to understand each other.

Since I have been living in America, I have also had the satisfaction of seeing the sympathy shown by the American press and public in welcoming so many French films, which are regularly repeated in theaters as classics. The reason for this certainly cannot be found in any magnificent and costly display but in the fact that the films are sincere and specifically French.

Because of their flair for display, the means at their disposal, their organization, and their technical skill, the Americans will always remain superior in the spectacular genre. The French have nothing to offer in this field. But, more than any other people, the Americans, who live so intensely, always welcome with enthusiastic generosity anything that bears the mark of broad human emotion.

My whole experience has led me to the conviction that, for a dramatic work to gain an international audience, it must above all be an essentially personal creation. Only then will it have some chance of taking a trip around the world.

A work should be stamped with its author's style. No one needs to be a specialist to recognize the work of Marcel L'Herbier, Julien Duvivier, Raymond Bernard, Jean Renoir, Jacques Feyder, René Clair, or the work of Frank Capra, William Wyler, Charlie Chaplin, D. W. Griffith, and countless others I could mention.

These films bear the imprint of the artist who created them, and the latter cheerfully accepts the imprint of his own country. An artist will do better creative work if he is on familiar ground and if he draws his inspiration from familiar sources. A film made in Paris will not become an international film merely because the author inserts a shot of Rockefeller Plaza, however fine a shot it may be; on the contrary, he must limit himself to translating his own thoughts, the natural aspirations of his own people.

A film author should take pride in saying: "Here is my country! This is what we think, this is how we live!" And the foreign spectator will say to himself: "There is France, there is Russia, there is America," or whatever country originated the film. In that case, the motion picture will have fulfilled its universal mission, for it will have introduced the people of the world to each other. It will have brought them face to face with each other's customs, cultures, daily actions and gestures, in all honesty and without deception. And for the first time, men will discover how much they resemble each other!

For instance, what notion do Europeans have about America? They think of a country where all the towns contain nothing but skyscrapers, where life goes on at a reckless, bewildering pace, where everything is electrified, like the famous Frigidaire. A country where the men are preoccupied only with making money, smoke big cigars, and sign checks all day long; where the women spend their days in the shops and turn their children over to nurses until they can be packed off to boarding school.

This false picture of a great country can be attributed to the influence of certain films which, in their desire to *please*, have created an artificial legend. The makers of these films were not aware of the motion picture's great mission, the purpose of which is to spread the beautiful and simple truth about life. By contrast, let us take a look at the true picture of the United States in connection with that of France and try to pick out the points of similarity that might suggest ideas for films designed to accomplish their universal mission.

We shall see that the life of the American people is very similar to that of the French people, even though it is also quite different. Different in its daily habits, which are so contrasting, as are its countrysides and towns, but very similar in those acts of life which are based on great universal principles, such as mother love and human fellowship.

America is full of contrasts that greet one at every step. New York is the most striking example. If one goes downtown to the business quarter, one finds enormous skyscrapers that barely allow the sunlight to penetrate. But in a sort of clearing there is a little Gothic church, standing in the midst of an old cemetery and reminding one vividly of a little country church in France. This contrast will serve well enough as a symbol of American life in general. Every big city in the United States has its skyscrapers, its little houses, and its churches similar to the one on Broadway.

In all the large cities, there are people who lead just as contrasting lives, but they all have sentiments and principles in common with us, which bring them very close to us, which link us with them. True, the athletic upbringing of the youth gives to the activities of the adults that same taste for gambling which makes them take a chance or venture where our caution would make us hesitate. But, on the other hand, every victim of an unfortunate gamble keeps the respect of his neighbors, provided he has observed the rules of fair play and is still willing to work.

By way of compensation, these men who enjoy struggling for success have the same love of family life that we do, and treat their children with the same tender care. American youth differs from ours in its physical activity, but it is very similar in its thirst for knowledge, its enthusiasm, and its filial respect and affection.

Mother's Day is almost a religious holiday in this country; mothers are honored by the nation and by their children, who would not think of letting the day go by without sending a heartfelt message to their mothers. The war has not interfered with that noble custom; soldier or sailor sons, wherever they may be—in the Pacific, in Africa, or in Italy—do not neglect some evening, in barracks or foxhole, to scribble down a few words of love or hope for their mothers. Father's Day is also marked with the most touching attentions, while the birthdays of all members of the family are an occasion to strengthen the ties which unite them.

Living in the country naturally solidifies family life and brings it even closer to our own. An American village or small town differs in appearance from one of ours, particularly in the way the houses are built mostly of wood. The white paint, carefully kept up, the green lawns, the flowers, lend these houses a surprising charm. The surrounding wall so dear to Frenchmen is absent here, which gives everyone more space and makes the little plot of land seem far bigger than it is.

But inside these houses live families which closely resemble our own. What difference does it make if they eat a larger breakfast than we do, so long as it is prepared with the same care by the mother or older sister who has come downstairs early so that everything will be ready when the father is ready to leave for work? What difference does it make if the need to make a living often requires the various members of the family to disperse, so long as Christmas brings them together again, like Noël in France, to observe the religion of their choice and to enjoy the pleasures of family life?

It is these family cells, perpetuated by the handing down of traditions and natural sentiments of love, which, in spite of all seeming contrasts, constitute the eternal foundations of the human family. When a great disaster like war affects one of these families, all the others react the same way.

When John Smith, average American, is obliged to leave his family, where life was so pleasant, and his Mary, whom he was soon to marry, he makes his painful good-bys with courage and dignity, and even a little reassuring smile; but, as he crosses Main Street, his back to the little house, he must summon up all his courage to overcome his grief and to realize that barbarians have placed him under an obligation to leave all these good things and go to defend the most precious of all: freedom.

John Smith arrives at camp, where he cheerfully submits to an intensive training program. After months of drilling, of field maneuvers, of all kinds of courses, John gets a commission as a second lieutenant. American officers know that they command a citizen army; they know how to lead men who, like themselves, have come straight from the Main Street of some American town or village, just as the officers of the French army have come from the rue de Belleville or from the main street of any town in France or her empire.

When John Smith returns home on leave, he will see a small flag with a star hanging behind the window, telling him that, although absent, he is always in the thoughts of his people. A similar little flag is hanging behind the window of every house, each bearing as many stars as the family has members serving with the armed forces.

Over the streets of towns and villages, banners are hung, showing the number of men and women from that section who are in uniform, eloquent proof of the pride and community feeling that exist in this little world of its own. Often this community feeling finds expression in a prayer inscribed on the banner: GOD BLESS OUR SONS. This prayer, repeated with equal fervor by mothers all over the world, symbolizes the great community of souls turning toward the Supreme Creator for comfort, hope, or solace.

This similarity of reactions to everyday events, the points of contact between people whose customs are apparently quite different, when high-lighted by some dramatic story, will make all people equally sensitive to imaginative creations which have materialized through contact with life. In order to simplify, I have had to cut short this parallel between the lives of two countries. I could establish the same relationship among all the people of the world, for what we are concerned with is the promotion of ideas common to all men while remaining true to ourselves and our environment.

The motion picture will remain an art because it will obey the law of diversity, which is so indispensable to the life and renewal of art in all its many forms. Composed of multiple facets reflecting national inspirations, ornamented and enriched with the folklores, customs, and traditions of all the peoples of the earth, the motion picture will appear as a magnificent panorama of world life. The peoples will impose a constant evolution upon this complete art, for it will have to adapt itself to the new forms of a perpetually changing society.

The upheaval produced by the tremendous impact of this revolutionary war will have brought about a thought transformation. People's minds will have been opened to the countless problems which were never faced by prewar audiences. The public will demand that dramatic film art offer for its consideration subjects relating to politics and economics, and keyed to its own preoccupations. At the same time, the public will need to be diverted. It will have to be taught how to laugh again, for suffering will have deprived man for too long a time of everything that makes life worth living. Information will have to answer this need for knowledge, born of a long period of exile, during which a morsel of truth would be gained at the risk of one's life. Television will add to the power of motion pictures and bring the animated newspaper into the home.

The scientific revolution, the scope of which will only be

revealed after the war, will in all probability transform social life and demand a reorganization of leisure to which the motion picture will make an important contribution.

But, however important these changes may be, the permanent values, spiritual and moral, which constitute the essential nourishment of the mind, will continue to be the fundamental and unchanging bases of filmic art. The spiritual can only achieve supremacy in a free world, where law is based on respect for the human person and for the free expression of thought which emanates from it. In order that thought may once more become free and remain free, the motion picture must be allowed to achieve its great aims, the essence of which is to preserve an ideal, to keep alive the cult of truth, of beauty, of the brotherhood of man, and to fight against that insane materialism which has brought civilization so near the brink of the abyss. The motion picture will achieve its aims only if it depends on all the moral and intellectual forces to make Thought prevail.

A few years ago, a great Czech artist, Bartosch, conceived a film in the poetic genre which was a true concrete expression of the motion picture's great mission. Somewhere on the planet, a thinker takes a piece of parchment and writes on it one basic idea: FREEDOM. The parchment flies away and travels all over the world. All the forces of oppression try to bring it down: dictators, economic and financial powers. It flies over the heroes who are being murdered and upholds them with its invisible radiance. The armies gathered to destroy it only succeed in massacring each other. No power can suppress the flying parchment, for within itself it contains a strength made invincible by the idea it bears.

Like the magic parchment, the motion picture, through the power of its shining beams, will light up the world with ideas of justice, freedom, and brotherhood, enabling man to live in a better world, one more favorable to the free development of Thought.

New York, May 1942–April 1944

15

BY WAY OF EPILOGUE

TWO LONG YEARS have passed across the world screen since I wrote what I believed to be the conclusion of my book. During that time, the film of history has recorded many tragedies, many hopes, and at long last the liberation of the enslaved peoples and the apotheosis of the long-hoped-for victory. But there is no end to this film of history, and man has no other recourse but to select an arbitrary break, a *Moment* in which to attempt to take a bearing. The *Moment* chosen by Coward-McCann, the publisher of this book, is still charged with mixed feelings of relief brought on by the end of the carnage, with disappointed hopes, and with overwhelming moral and physical misery, the frightful aftermath left by the maelstrom of brutality that engulfed the world. In view of the circumstances, I decided to read over the preceding pages, written during the most tragic period ever lived through by civilization, in order to confront them with the realities of the *Moment*. Apart from the desire to start all over again which every author experiences on seeing his completed work, I found nothing that required changing among the facts and ideas I had endeavored to bring out. This last chapter, then, will serve only to throw light on certain points and to test the ideas with the realities of the *Moment* that marks the dawn of a new world.

The Teaching Film

During the war, the teaching film continued to prove its worth and, since the end of hostilities, has given rise to great hopes. All educators are now convinced of the possibilities held by the

234

method of teaching which is taking its place among all those comprising modern pedagogy. Generally speaking, we may say that it has finally graduated from the phase of theorizing and discussion to enter directly into the phase of experimental research and practical application. Films can no longer be kept separate from the other means of audio-visual education when used for pedagogical ends. Educators are beginning to realize the advantages of creating and fostering courses in audio-visual education in universities, similar to those that exist in this country. I cannot emphasize too greatly the fact that any haphazard and unscientific use of films in teaching is calculated to bring about disastrous results.

The battle's end does not bring Peace, and the state of moral and physical ruin in which the world now finds itself should warn us not to believe that everything for which we have hoped can be accomplished in a short time. The institutions for pedagogic research which should form the foundation, the framework of the entire pedagogic system, have not yet been set up, and there are still too many official gatherings devoted exclusively to making speeches. On the other hand, there are encouraging signs everywhere, and among the most moving of these were the ones I noticed in France. In the course of the two months I spent in my country, I had an opportunity to measure the extent of the havoc. Never in the whole of her long and tragic history has France been so emptied of her substance by an invader. The latter systematically attempted the moral and physical destruction of the French people. Every means was employed, and their extent may be measured if one considers that, out of the hundreds of thousands of political or labor deportees—we may call them slaves—hardly 10 per cent ever returned to their homes. The black market, a German invention, was a weapon of moral disintegration far more than a means of obtaining economic advantages. A skillfully organized program of material destruction over a period of four years stripped factories of their equipment, took away all means of transportation, and deprived the soil of fertilizer. In spite of all this, the French people has remained miraculously alive with all its inherent virtues intact, while its intellectual elite is in full resurgence. With regard to the subject of this book, which cannot be divorced from the situation in France as a whole, it is of interest to note that genuine teaching films were made which did not come under Nazi influence. Through the efforts of the National Museum of Pedagogy, these films will be constantly circulated throughout the schools, and all indications are that there will be an increasing production of genuine teaching films. But the most important step has already been taken: the need for instruction along this line in normal school has been recognized. I at length had the great satisfaction of seeing the General Director for Cultural Relations in the Ministry of Foreign Affairs accomplish what I had been urging for so many years. Thanks to Professor Henri Laugier, five young professors from superior normal schools in St.-Cloud and Fontenay have received annual scholarships to carry on studies in the United States. At the time of writing, these young people are taking courses in audio-visual education at Teachers College in Columbia University. They were welcomed by Dean Russell as members of his family and are working under the guidance of Professor M. R. Brunstetter. They are living in an American environment among their friends and families. In this way they will not only be able to acquire knowledge indispensable to their specialty but will also return to France with friendships firmly cemented by their university life. At the end of a year, after having received their M.A., they will be the first to hold chairs of audio-visual education in normal schools and can then begin to mold the generations of teachers on whom the future of France will finally depend. This is the best concrete example of what cultural relations mean, and that is why we may rejoice at seeing the French Foreign Affairs Ministry and the State Department expand their functions. Young French professors are coming to the United States to study audio-visual education, but at the same time American students and professors will be going to France to study other problems, thereby justifying the ultimate reason for the existence of cultural relations, which for each nation consist of borrowing flowers from its neighbor's garden while leaving behind the finest of its own blooms.

In the field of practical application, I would like to point out the importance of the newly created Franco-American Center of Higher Studies. The general purpose of this center is to promote cultural understanding through activities in the field of education and to establish international teamwork in the field of learning by sending to the United States the most promising intellectuals. Already twenty young doctors, engineers, and architects have teamed up with their American colleagues. Attached to this center is an organization which is directly concerned with the utilization of teaching films: The French-American Bureau of Educational Research for the Development and Dissemination of Modern Teaching Aids (FABER).

The Bureau has a dual purpose: to provide a practical program through which educators of France and the United States may work together to improve their teaching; and through this program to establish a habit of co-operation and mutual respect which will be reflected in the minds of the hundreds of thousands of school children in the two countries.

Activities of the Bureau are based on the assumption that teaching can be enriched by the regular and considered use of teaching aids generally called audio-visual devices. The Bureau's role is, therefore, to study these devices in the light of their usefulness to certain programs of study; to improve upon existing *realia* and to develop new teaching aids with these programs in mind; and to make this audio-visual material available to schools. This is a two-way service. In France, material relating to the United States will be distributed, in co-operation with American organizations, while in this country there is a similar service regarding France. That is, from New York, the Bureau will prepare and distribute modern teaching aids, such as motion pictures, recordings, slides, photographs, dioramas, etc., to be used in connection with courses in French history, geography, language, music, art, etc.

Although for the most part prepared in France, this material is specially planned for use in American courses of study, and is in general prepared according to the specifications of the Bureau Staff in New York. An advisory council, composed of educators from all parts of the U.S.A., determines the educational policy of the Bureau. A smaller committee of teachers, the "Curriculum Committee," decides the type of material to be prepared, and will aid the Bureau Staff in designing the materials.

The Bureau, however, is not limiting itself to the distribution of its own teaching aids; with the approval of the Advisory Council or of the Curriculum Committee, it also advises on the practical details involved in this distribution to the schools. Although the headquarters of the FABER is in New York, distribution is on a national scale and is effected through existing American agencies, including state, county, or city bureaus of visual instruction.

The FABER has, ready for circulation, a certain number of French films, recordings of French music, and readings from French literature.

It is hoped that through the Bureau teachers will learn the value and uses of modern teaching aids. To this end, a permanent demonstration center for the display of audio-visual devices has been set up at the New York headquarters. The Bureau's consultant on curriculum problems is available to advise individual teachers on the integration of audio-visual material in specific school courses. On the other hand, criticism and suggestions from teachers are needed so that the Bureau can prepare material to fit their needs. By their interest and cooperation, the teachers in both countries will enable the Bureau to achieve its purpose.

Corresponding to this French-initiated project there is a tremendous amount of American good will, and the growth of audio-visual education in this country is a good omen of things to come. The universities, museums like those in New York, Worcester, and Philadelphia, are expanding their courses and their facilities. Specialized publications like *Educational Screen* and *See and Hear* are popularizing methods and establishing relations between specialists and users.

We have, therefore, every reason to be hopeful, provided this budding youngster is surrounded with attentive and delicate care. Only films specifically planned and made for that purpose should be allowed in schools, and facile solutions should be avoided. For instance, although the promotional film has its own function and importance, it should be submitted to a severe trial when intended for the classroom. Audio-visual education, of which the film is one element, and the most powerful, is a pedagogic science which should bring results only through constant research and collaboration between educator and author of specialized films.

I hope that the international organization of educational motion pictures, which should be closely tied up with the U.N.E.S.C.O., will be guided by past experience and make all its activities conform to the law of multiple genres. Without rigid adherence to this law, any action taken, whether on a national or international scale, would run the risk of adding to the confusion in the planning and making as well as in the utilization of the different genres which go to make up the motion picture.

Films in Adult Education and Information

As foreseen, the liberation of the occupied countries revealed the need, not only to guarantee a normal education for adults, but also to effect a general re-education. For over four years, the peoples of Europe were in prison, cut off from the outside world. Therefore, they need to be put back in touch with the rest of mankind. For this, regular channels of information are inadequate. Radio and the press have always been powerful media, but under the Nazis they conveyed so much false and distorted information that they have lost a good part of their prestige. As a result of certain experiences I had in France, I am convinced that the only medium of information which has any chance of succeeding is an active medium, that is, one in which the people at whom it is aimed actually participate. A few pages back, I wrote that the French people, by a miracle, is still alive. Let me add that it has lost none of its legendary common sense or critical instinct. Furthermore, those four years of isolation have imbued it with a thirst for learning and knowledge. The active information I mentioned is not concerned with political questions, which should be left up to the various parties to develop. To be precise, it should concern itself with large economic questions, with scientific advances, and more generally with human relations. From this, we may readily see that it is not a question of information in the sense generally understood but actually one of re-education. This active re-education can be effected only through the creation and growth of controlled discussion groups, like those which have so successfully spread through the United States and England.

Among the few experiments I was able to carry out during my stay in France, there is one I remember with pleasure. This occurred in a village of some thousand people in the department of Loir et Cher, where I had been asked to spend a week end. Walking down the main street after my arrival, I was astonished to see that small, hand-written notices had been put up everywhere announcing a lecture about the United States for that very evening, with my name followed by the title Professor at the New School for Social Research. Seeing this rather unattractive announcement, which seemed to me to have no drawing power, I predicted to my host that the lecture would fall somewhat short of success. As a matter of fact, knowing the curious nature of my compatriots and particularly counting on their hope of embarrassing the lecturer by their criticism, I was fairly confident. My hopes were not disappointed: at 8:30 P.M. the big hall of the inn was jammed and I was surrounded by the young sports of the community. Everyone who could manage had come from the village and neighboring hamlets. During my talk, I tried to make them understand the American people; I spoke to them of farmers very like themselves, of the miracle of production. But I particularly concentrated on giving them some notion of world solidarity, the idea of One World, on proving to them that there was no longer any important problem which could be solved on a national scale, not even in the case of big nations like the United States and

Russia. After that I opened the discussion and I would have given a lot if all the skeptics could have been there to share my feelings on hearing the questions directed at me from every point in the hall, aptly, intelligently, and spontaneously. These peasants of Loir et Cher wanted to know everything, discuss everything, just as a few days later the workers in Paris were to give me the same satisfaction at a similar gathering. Experiments of this sort may be carried out methodically and with success in every country. It will be sufficient to furnish people to guide the discussions and to train leaders who will go from town to village recruiting and instructing men and women to act as heads of community groups; the latter may easily be found in every community among the teachers, doctors, or more enthusiastic citizens.

Among all the means of education that will have to be employed, it should be understood that the motion picture will be required to play a leading role. Indeed, that is the prime function of what I have designated the lecture film. In this sense it can become the central point around which the controlled discussion will take place. I have elsewhere expressed my enthusiasm for the system of adult education followed in England and the United States. In the latter country, the various branches of diffusion are built around the libraries, museums, and large associations. In this connection, the Foreign Policy Association is to be congratulated for having successfully created an educational movement centering around the major world problems, for which this people, absorbed in its own effort and isolated by oceans, was so unprepared. The Foreign Policy Association is promoting other ventures of this nature, among which I would like to mention Dr. Brooks Emeny's Cleveland Council of World Affairs, which is doing a magnificent job in Cleveland.

The trade unions seem at last to be taking cognizance of the fact that they have an educational task to perform. In the United States, the two big federations have set up educational departments which are growing more important every day.

The C.I.O. has a central office in Washington which has the job of co-ordinating the various projects and doing research work. The Bureau is now establishing a central C.I.O. film circuit which will function through regional offices all over the country. Up till now, a few unions have made their own films and distributed them with great success. The most noteworthy advance has been made by the International Education Department of one of the most important unions affiliated with the C.I.O.—the United Automobile, Aircraft, and Agricultural Workers of America (UAW-CIO).

Jack Zeller, the head of this department, with headquarters in Detroit, has displayed ceaseless activity in all fields of education. He is helped in his task by nine regional heads, corresponding to the different unions.

Jack Zeller has written: "There is probably no technique in the field of education that exerts greater influence and effectiveness than motion pictures. As a medium for reaching people it is almost unequalled."

This statement was responsible for the creation of a film department in 1938. Since then, a number of educational films on unionism have been produced, while there has been a constant growth in the distribution of all kinds of educational films. An extensive film library contains over 600 films and serves more than 500 UAW-CIO locals in the United States and Canada. The number of spectators who have attended meetings organized by the department rose from 200,000 in 1938-39 to 4,050,000 in 1944-45. Finally, let us note that at the 1945 convention a $50,000 fund was voted for film production. One of these films, now nearing completion, has to do with racial discrimination. It would be impossible to exaggerate the importance of the recommendation which accompanied the grant of this fund and which stressed the idea of quality: "These films shall be prepared by recognized experts in the field, using latest methods and techniques so that our films will be on a par with commercial films." This commendable spirit has enabled the unions to accomplish their first task: the elimination of amateurism.

The Workers' Education Bureau of America was founded in 1921 "to serve as a clearinghouse of information and guidance in the development of workers' education in the U.S.A. During the past twenty-four years, the Bureau has become the recognized agency through which the Federation of Labor carries on a workers' educational program for its seven million members." Under the enlightened guidance of John D. Connors, the Bureau distributes its educational material to over 500 unions; it organizes lectures, summer courses, and radio broadcasts. So far as educational films are concerned, while recognizing the value of this medium, the Bureau has not yet gone beyond the planning stage. But the activities of the central bureau and the extremely interesting work done by the affiliated unions in the educational field seem full of promise.

The most important of these projects is certainly the Educational Department of the International Ladies' Garment Workers Union, which is competently and sincerely directed by Mark Starr.

Thus, taking these two big labor groups as an example, we see that the unions appear to be progressing toward the use of motion pictures to educate their members. There is no doubt but that the speed with which they are proceeding will enable the international movement to make full use of this marvelous means of communication.

Nothing strikes me as being more important or urgent than to re-educate the peoples of Europe who have suffered so from oppression, if we really want to give meaning to the word Democracy. After having given these countries the minimum material means needed for their reconstruction, it will be up to the big democracies who did not feel the oppressor's yoke to provide them with the means and methods to distribute among their peoples the intellectual wealth that is indispensable to the life of every democracy.

To this purely educational activity should be added that of information through newsreels. We must note regretfully that, although during the war and after the victory the makers of newsreels continued to produce superb documents of life, the latter have not always been given the opportunities for dissemination they deserved. In France, nearly all theater managers are refusing to pay the booking charges which they had been obliged to meet under the occupation, so that the public is deprived of this prodigious means of information. In the United States, the double feature has made it impossible to show newsreels in sufficient length.

I do not believe that a better example could be found to measure the limits within which freedom may be exercised. Certainly, freedom of expression in the newsreel, as in all other information media, must be respectéd. Yet it is hard to conceive that a government which has a proper regard for its duties would not exercise its authority in guaranteeing the right of the community to be informed. Freedom has no limits other than right, and the law should guarantee its protection. Under the circumstances, I have no hesitation in declaring that whenever those responsible for the production or distribution of newsreels fail in their task, the state has the duty to step into their place, with or without legal justification.

The editorial film has happily continued to be successful and is verging more and more toward a broader interpretation of its functions. The "reconversion" from war topics has come about quite naturally. In Canada, the series *Canada Carries On* and *The World in Action* are drawing on general culture for their subjects: *Toronto Symphony, Canadian Landscape, A City Sings,* etc.

In France, in England, in Russia, the editorial formula is gaining ground, and the need for films of this type is felt to be as great as during the war.

In the United States, the veteran *March of Time*, under Richard de Rochemont, is continuing to produce its classic masterpieces.

As the war progressed toward its close, it became increasingly difficult for a monthly release to stay abreast of military developments. Accordingly, the *March of Time* necessarily became more and more eclectic in its treatment of the solely military aspects of the closing campaigns. Consequently, *March of Time* subjects on the progress of the war with Japan emphasized over-all strategy and suggested future developments from the evidence available at the time. Among such releases were *And Then Japan,* which was made after the turning of the tide in Europe to show the three ways in which Japan could be defeated, and *Back Door to Tokyo,* which pointed out the value of reopening the Burma Road and the importance of the Asiatic mainland as a springboard for aerial attacks on Japan.

Even before V-E Day, however, the *March of Time* was concerned with the problem of the coming peace. In October 1944, some seven months before the collapse of Germany, *What to Do with Germany* was released. This film stated as clearly as possible the nature of the chronic problem of German militarism, and presented a survey of the several plans proposed at that time to prevent its recurrence after the war. Of the same general nature, but dealing with more immediate conditions, was *Report on Italy,* which showed the price paid for fascism and bluntly assayed the grim future facing Italy. Made after the war, but related to the unrest that came as the war drew to a close, was *Palestine Problem,* which sought to inquire into the conflicting interests of Jews, Arabs, and the British in the Holy Land, and to appraise the issues involved.

Although the *March of Time* has been acutely aware of its journalistic responsibility to examine and clarify the several crises that obstruct the way to world peace, it has also attempted to report with liveliness and humor such minor social phenomena of the current scene as the increasing group obviousness of adolescent girls and the intricate campaign of American women to beautify themselves. For the most part, such subjects were abandoned during the war, but with a relaxing of the pressure of world events, it has been possible for *March of Time* to do occasional pictures in which the entertainment value is of equal importance with the informational content. However, the *March of Time's* general policy continues to be to produce pictures which are serious reports on those phases of the economic, political, and social world which merit the attention of its audiences and which have more than passing significance.

In conclusion, we may say that, although the editorial film genre has got one foot inside the theater door, like the newsreel, it has not yet been accorded the place to which the importance of its mission entitles it. Nevertheless, we may take encouragement from its vitality and the welcome it is given by the public.

DOCUMENTARIES

Enough tradition has finally been built up around the various genres which comprise what we have come to call documentaries so that they have to some extent graduated from the class of poor relations. The development of these genres during the war and on the threshold of peace has been treated better than I could ever do by Iris Barry in her introduction to the superb program devoted to documentaries, covering the period from 1922 to 1945, the best of which are being shown every day by the Museum of Modern Art. Since I do not wish to turn this epilogue into the start of a new book, let me strongly advise everyone who is interested to read Iris Barry at the Museum Library, where he will find ample cause for hope in the future of the documentary.

Does this mean that we have reason to be equally satisfied with what is happening on the practical level? Certainly not, if we consider the present situation. The persistence of the double feature bill has prevented all normal distribution of documentaries and particularly of films of life belonging to the naturalist school. The documentary genre will survive only insofar as it is given the opportunity to gain its living in accordance with the law of supply and demand. This law can take effect only if the screen is made accessible to the documentary. In nontheatrical circuits, which took on such importance during the war, the organizers of local showings became accustomed to receiving films gratis from the government. They must be persuaded to adopt a more positive policy, their billings must be paid for if they do not want to lose all hope of nourishment for their starving projectors. On the other hand, the indications for the immediate future are more encouraging.

In the United States, the Film Council of America is attempting for the first time to promote concerted action on a national scale.

The Film Council of America is an outgrowth of the National Advisory Committee, which did an excellent job of distributing war films to nontheatrical audiences. The Council is made up of representatives from seven national associations:

The American Library Association (Audio-Visual Committee)

The National Association of University Extension

National Association of Visual Education Dealers

Visual Equipment Manufacturers Council

National Education Association (Dept. of Visual Instruction)

Allied Non-Theatrical Film Association

Educational Film Library Association

The purpose of the Council is to continue the great interest in information films started during the war. One of its aims is to organize visual workers into luncheon groups in about fifty cities, where the professional workers in the field may get together regularly and hear some of their leaders informally. Secondly, the Council plans to document the history of the production and use of films during the war. Thirdly, it aims to work with the users of films in *promoting the best use of films and encouraging the distribution of the outstanding independent productions.*

Among the consumer groups who have pledged co-operation are the General Federation of Women's Clubs, the National Council of Parents and Teachers, and various labor, farm, and youth groups.

The president of the Council is C. R. Reagan of Austin, Texas, to whom credit is due for organizing the distribution of films of national interest over nontheatrical circuits during the war. His methodical mind, the numerous friends he made while acting as assistant head of the Domestic Motion Picture Office in the OWI give him an authority which, we hope, will enable him to create the national organization which the United States needs so badly.

In Canada, the National Film Board remains a model organization. In the postwar period it apparently is continuing the work for which it was established, namely, the making and distribution of national films designed to help Canadians in every section of Canada understand the ways of life and the problems of Canadians in other sections; and to co-ordinate national and departmental film activities of the Government.

Nontheatrical films with which the NFB expects to be particularly concerned will present community action and organization in the fields of public health, housing, and education. Other important films will define Canada's role as a trading nation—and the relations and responsibilities involved as such (with special reference to the Food and Agriculture Organization and the United Nations Organization).

A certain change in emphasis is observable in the plans for postwar nontheatrical distribution. The National Film Board is tending to transfer distribution to film committees which are being promoted in different communities across the country. In promoting this independent community organization of visual education—including films, film strips, and graphics—the regional officers of the NFB are playing a large part. Under this plan, which is none other than an effort to decentralize nontheatrical distribution, the people who use the visual media are the ones responsible for their distribution. This, the NFB thinks, will result in a more functional relationship between production and distribution.

Starting in November 1944, the NFB sought to increase the volume and to improve the quality of its French-language productions. A new producer was assigned to this work and new personnel employed. By the end of 1945—after a year of training and apprenticeship—the new group was producing its first films, which are of considerable interest and bring a fresh viewpoint to the Canadian documentary (*Le Vent Qui Chante, Chercheurs de la Mer, Vallée des dynamos*).

The National Film Board is studying the possibility of distributing French-language films in France, in line with its policy of distribution in other foreign countries. Already, for instance, NFB films are widely shown in Mexico and other Latin American countries in Spanish and Portuguese versions; while English versions are being shown in the United States and in Great Britain.

The NFB is beginning to spread its salutary activities abroad. Mr. Ralph Foster, formerly with the NFB, has been chosen film commissioner to head the Australian National Film Board, for a period of one year, starting January 1, 1946. Also, a senior producer from the NFB, not yet designated, will go to Australia to assist in actual production.

These, among others, are carrying on in other countries and in other organizations the work started in 1939 in Canada.

John Grierson has never been the kind of man to rest on his laurels. Having created the National Film Board and watched it grow up into a sturdy adolescence, able to do without the master's constant attention, Grierson then handed in his resignation so that he could take up new activities, yet without losing track of his latest born. He regained his position as leader of the documentary movement. Abandoning oratorical and literary formulas, the coffeehouse discussions of the trade, Grierson went into action and founded "The International Film Associates," the nature and purpose of which are as follows:

1. It is a nonprofit-making organization dedicated to the public service; and in particular to the promotion of international understanding by means of films.

2. It promotes the production and the circulation of films which are concerned with themes of economic, social, and educational value; and in particular promotes the supply of films which undertake to describe technological and social progress in countries with higher standards to countries with lower standards.

3. It aids dependent or underprivileged peoples in securing the means of production and distribution for films promoting their welfare.

4. While not itself engaging in production or distribution, it secures the production and distribution of films; and in particular provides a service of research and a service of production and distribution planning for international agencies, government

bodies, and all organizations or individuals interested in films of a technological, economic, social, or educational nature and desirous of following any of the purposes outlined.

6. It serves as an intermediary for the exchange of information between production and distribution agencies which in any way further the purposes outlined, and in particular brings themes, films, and materials affecting these purposes to the attention of producers and distributors in the theatrical, newsreel, and nontheatrical fields.

7. It aids in correlating the efforts of the many documentary film groups now operating in different countries.

The Board of Directors consists of the following: John Grierson, Stuart Legg, Robert Flaherty, Walter A. Rudlin, Basil Wright, Mary Losey, and this writer.

We may be assured by the results already obtained that all these young enthusiasts in different countries will once more, thanks to John Grierson, have an opportunity to work for the glory of the documentary film.

In the Art of Entertainment

Here, the motion picture is in the throes of an evolution that will bear fruit if the leaders of the industry controlling this art prove capable of understanding their responsibilities, which, as a matter of fact, happen to coincide with their own interests. However, I am obliged to point out that, although some encouraging signs are in evidence, a complete lack of understanding of the larger problems seems yet to persist. Few people are adapting themselves to the new times; there is much talk about the atomic age but very little real awareness of the upheaval that has already occurred. Paradoxically, responsible leaders of the industry are withdrawing into a narrow shell of isolationism and at the same time are asserting a global imperialism often out of proportion to the means at their disposal. They continue to lose sight of the law of diversity, without which the motion picture cannot be an art and cannot find the economic support essential to it. The solution once more lies in a fair division of

Poster conceived and distributed by the Motion Picture Producers and Distributors of America (see page
218).

Scene from *The Southerner*. Directed by Jean Renoir. Produced by David L. Loew and Robert Hakim. Released through United Artists (see page 252).

Scene from *The Last Chance*. Produced by L. Wechsler. Directed by Leopold Lindtberg. Released through M. G. M. International Films (see page 253).

Scene from *Once There Was a Girl*. Produced by Victor Eisimart. Released by Artkino (see page 254).

standard productions. As an art-industry, the motion picture should give the finest example of intellectual and economic co-operation on an international scale. The "Big Powers" should help the economically weaker countries, stripped of their substance by the Germans, to regain their strength so that they may bring to the motion picture as a whole their national skill, the products of their soil. Then, and then only, will the harmonious blending of artistic creations give to the motion picture a new life and a fair economic balance.

In spite of these economic struggles, in spite of the sterilizing effects of censorship, the motion picture has such enormous vitality that it is now in the midst of a fortunate evolution. The film of life developed by the war is beginning to influence Hollywood. There are unmistakable signs of a return to the school of impressionism and to the motion picture as an independent means of expression. The authors of British and American films who during the war produced those superb films of life have exercised an influence over the dramatic art of their countries. The producers themselves are apparently beginning to let down the bars to films built around a theme. They are still fearful of certain words, not knowing exactly what they mean. They are afraid that films no longer contain what they call entertainment and that, as a result, the box office will suffer. The few examples we are going to discuss will, I hope, prove to them that the meaning they attach to the word may be interpreted in very different ways. If, in the comic and fanciful genres, entertainment becomes mirth, or visual satisfaction derived from the beauty of spectacle, there is nothing to prevent us finding the equivalent in the dramatic genre. Emotion, the arousal of feelings, the fact that a dramatic story presenting a great theme makes you live the joy, the despair, of another group of people, constitute entertainment in the sense that the audience forgets its own cares, its own surroundings, in a word, finds a means of escape.

The British, the Russians, the French, and gradually Hollywood, are going ahead with this evolution, signs of which may be seen in the few examples I have chosen from a wealth of others.

The Lost Weekend, winner of the New York Film Critics' Award for 1945, is the first of these examples, and I am glad that the jury rewarded the truly filmic qualities which characterized this work of Charles Brackett and Billy Wilder. Showing both talent and courage, the authors put their faith in the public, and they will retain the credit for having revived the art of Griffith. My only regret is that their amazing talents were not focused more sharply on presenting the theme and that the psychology of the character was not gone into more thoroughly. If the film had been elaborated a little more, then perhaps the publicity agent of the House of Seagram might not have had an opening for the stroke of genius he displayed in warmly congratulating the authors and declaring that the film merely confirmed their own conviction, which might be summed up in the words, "Some men should not drink." This said, *The Lost Weekend* remains a remarkable artistic and technical achievement and, in particular, a stage in the "return" to the motion picture as a "plastic art."

This movement was given a much greater impetus by Jean Renoir, who has found a way to express himself freely in Hollywood. The result is a personal work, a true Jean Renoir, that is, a film belonging to the impressionist school. I would not like to play the part of the critic in this book, which friends of the motion picture may perhaps keep in their libraries, but I believe that *The Southerner* may be considered a classic in the dramatic art of the screen. Classic because it belongs to a determined school deriving from the film of life. Classic because it truly represents a means of expression in itself and especially because of the basic theme, universal in character, which the author serves with all his talent and with an ardent faith. The theme is love for the soil, that ungrateful, harsh, and pitiless master; a love which triumphs over all temptation, stronger even than mother love. The story unfolds in a completely rural setting, which is the real star of the film. But Renoir has known how to *choose* his interpreters and make them live; every one of them is the living embodiment of the character he or she interprets. Zachary Scott and Betty Field are the central figures of the story, around whom all the dramatic elements are crystallized. The drama is heightened by the fact that it is made up of contrasts similar to those in real life. The balance between tragedy and relief gives the dramatic structure the basic outline needed for harmony of fact and image to be achieved. All the interpreters are worthy of mention, but I would like to pay special tribute to Beulah Bondi, who, in the part of the grandmother, gives a remarkable portrait. This great artist is an example of the wealth of talent that Hollywood possesses. Jean Renoir succeeded with this film because he realized that, since he was living in America, he ought to create an American work. He applied himself to gaining an understanding of the major problems confronting this people; he developed a strong affection for it; and in this way, though remaining true to himself, that is, though preserving his artistic individuality, his French affinities, and his intellectual integrity, though choosing a universal theme, he was yet able to create a specifically American film. It is only proper that we should acknowledge the credit due to the producers, David L. Loew and Robert Hakim, for having had confidence in Renoir. The enthusiastic reception by the public shows that they have proved the need for Hollywood to encourage works of this quality, and at the same time demonstrated what should be obvious, that an audience will react favorably every time its emotions are aroused by a powerful theme presented by a great artist.

Of all the hopeful signs pointing toward a better organization of international relations, there is one in particular we must note, and that is the project being undertaken by MGM to distribute European films in the United States. *The Last Chance* brings us a blast of realism, symbolizing the will for survival present in every human being. This film, made in Switzerland during the war by L. Lindtberg, after the book by R. Schweizer, and produced by Lazar Wechsler, is interpreted by *natural actors*. Most of them are reliving on the screen their own drama, the tremendous drama of refugees fleeing from the barbarians and their machine guns. The little group around which the story revolves symbolizes human solidarity in the face of danger, the will to live; but to me the basic theme that animates the film seems to be the great law stating the respect due to the human character. It is the attacks made on this law that constitute the drama. Because the author of the film was able to magnify this law, because he was able to portray the courage, the immortality of the human species, because for a long time to come criminals will persist in their efforts to abolish the rights of man, his work will never become dated and, in spite of a few weaknesses in its dramatic structure, will remain among the classics of the realistic school.

Russia has lately presented us with a kind of masterpiece which made me recall the golden age of pure motion picture in the form which gives it the rank of a major art because it constitutes a means of expression in itself. I am speaking of *Once There Was A Girl.* Victor Eisimont, the author of this film, has already made his mark as one of the authors of *Girl from Leningrad,* which merited him the Stalin Prize. A native of Leningrad, during the siege he gave up directing films to direct the building of fortifications.

"I was overwhelmed by the courage of the old people and the children of my native city," writes Eisimont; "the youngsters faced the horrors of the siege with as much fortitude as their parents and still remained charming and lovable as ever. I decided then that I would like to make a film about these children." Thus was born the idea of the film, and it took shape under the pen of Vladimir Nadobrovo, the scenario writer. Out of a simple story of children, Eisimont has created a great film. He has been able to mold in concrete form the heroic drama of the city and the human suffering of its inhabitants by showing the reactions of young children, and the struggle of the old people and women.

Without the easily achieved effects of battle scenes, shell splinters, or military parades, Victor Eisimont has made it possible to sense the plain people's share in the battle of Leningrad. The job of digging in, the building of antitank obstacles, are sufficient to express the effort of all those who tenaciously held on behind the front lines.

Bread, rare and precious, is the sacred symbol of life and is handled sparingly and with respect. The scene—so restrained in gestures and words—in which a mother cheats herself of her share of bread in order to give more to the two little girls is more eloquent than the most beautiful lines of dialogue.

Words, too, are used sparingly, for Mr. Eisimont is aware of the value of restraint—aware that nothing is more powerful than an image. He brings to the screen again the great tradition of the motion picture as an art. His characters act and speak like real people. And they speak only when they have something to say.

The children, too, are real people—a living synthesis of humanity. Nina Ivanovna and Natasha Zashipina express all the sentiments of people everywhere. They are simultaneously good, bad, tender, pitiless. These two children live through a highly dramatic chapter of modern history, unconscious of the great historical roles they are playing and never for an instant stepping out of character as children. The two little girls were placed under the proper conditions so that they could "live their parts" almost unconsciously, with the simplicity inherent in the major actions of daily life. Mr. Eisimont brought his two little girls to Leningrad for location work with the rest of the cast and the production crew a few days before the siege was finally broken. He gave the little girls an opportunity to live with Leningraders and learn what the siege was like. The fact that they had a chance to live in the surroundings which form the background of the film contributed to the realism of their performance. Like everyone who knows the powerful imagination of children, Eisimont defers to their faculty for adapting their observations to their own particular case. While he was doing his best to explain to Nina Ivanovna (aged nine) how she was to portray a little girl trying to hide her tears because there was no letter from her father at the front, Nina cut him short and said, "I know how to do that." He let her try it without any instructions and was amazed at her performance.

After the scene was over, he questioned her, for this was her first film role, and her acting had been so realistic that many of the crew and the Leningraders who watched the location shots were moved to tears. "It wasn't very hard," she said. "My daddy has been at the front for a long time, and many times when we expected a letter from him and there wasn't any, I felt just the way Nastenka does in the film. I just made believe it was real —and I didn't have to act at all." The professional actors, particularly the Mother (Nina Ivanovna), do not act: they live; and in spite of all their talent, they would not have remained so close to life if they had not been inspired by Eisimont.

The music by Benedict Pushkov is an integral part of the theme and reinforces and blends with the visual expression of the drama. It gives the background of the war, and sings the hope of deliverance. It evokes a happy normal childhood—and sharpens the vibrant humanity which animates the film.

Here, then, is a complete work, conceived and executed by an author who knows how to inspire that ideal production group which I have described in an earlier chapter. I have chosen these four examples because they are the most recent which have come to my attention, but I could as easily have found others in the French and British schools. Even the Italian motion picture appears to be rising out of the ashes of fascism, affirming the vitality of this country's artists, who will gradually be renewing their ties with the great traditions of the past.

And now it seems that, after all, I must bring this book to a close and leave to others the task of relating at some future date the evolution of an art so intimately bound up with the life of man. I would like in these concluding lines to express my faith in the destinies of the Art of the Motion Picture, provided those who serve it are ever conscious of the greatness of its mission.

April, 1946.

INDEX